The New Lighthearted Cookbook

RECIPES FOR HEART HEALTHY COOKING

Anne Lindsay

HEART AND STROKE FOUNDATION

Finding Answers. For Life.

KEY PORTER BOOKS

National Library of Canada Cataloguing in Publication

Lindsay, Anne, 1943-
    The new lighthearted cookbook : recipes for healthy heart cooking / Anne Lindsay. — 2nd ed.
Includes index.
ISBN 1-55263-533-3

    1. Heart—Diseases—Diet therapy—Recipes. I. Title.

RC684.D5L55 2003   641.5'6311   C2003-900522-4

The publisher gratefully acknowledges the support of the Canada Council for the Arts and the Ontario Arts Council for its publishing program.

We acknowledge the financial support of the Government of Canada through the Book Publishing Industry Development Program (BPIDP) for our publishing activities.

Key Porter Books Limited
70 The Esplanade
Toronto, Ontario
Canada M5E 1R2

www.keyporter.com

Project Management: Michael Mouland
Photography: Pete Patterson
Design: Peter Maher
Electronic Formatting: Jean Lightfoot Peters
Food Stylist: Olga Truchan

Printed and bound in Canada

03 04 05 06 07 5 4 3 2 1

Contents

Acknowledgments

It has been a great pleasure to have the opportunity to revise my best selling cookbook, *The Lighthearted Cookbook*. Since this book was done 15 years ago, the revision was almost like writing a new cookbook. I certainly could not have done this without assistance from many friends and co-workers. I would like to acknowledge:

- Shannon Graham, my friend, dietitian, and co-worker who once again helped with the recipe testing.
- Susan Van Hezewijk who was instrumental in making sure this book moved forward: from recipe testing to proofreading, she was terrific.
- Susan Girvan for her terrific work editing the book.
- Carol Dombrow, nutrition consultant, Heart and Stroke Foundation, for her review of the manuscript and helping to keep things on track.
- Janice Daciuk for her wonderful introduction.
- Sharyn Joliat, Info Access, for her expert nutrient analysis.
- Pete Patterson, photographer, and Olga Truchan, food stylist, for the beautiful photographs.

Everyone involved with the book at the Heart and Stroke Foundation, especially Neila Poscente, for asking me to revise this book, and for the huge amount of time they invested in this book and to the thousands of volunteers that helped to promote it.

Everyone at Key Porter, especially Anna Porter, Clare McKeon, Peter Maher, Michael Mouland, and Lyn Cadence for their commitment to this book.

And as always, a very special thanks to my family, Bob, Jeff, John, and Susie for always being there for me.

Anne Lindsay

Becel is dedicated to educating Canadians about leading a heart healthy lifestyle. Supporting the educational initiatives of the Heart and Stroke Foundation forms an integral part of this commitment.

The Heart and Stroke Foundation gratefully acknowledges the generous support of Becel in helping to make this cookbook possible. The financial support received from our sponsor does not constitute an endorsement by the Heart and Stroke Foundation or the author for the sponsor's products.

The Heart and Stroke Foundation would like to thank the following people for reviewing the introductory chapters of *The Lighthearted Cookbook*. Their expertise is invaluable in ensuring that the information is up to date and easily understood.

- Karen Lewy Fedun
- Gail Leadlay, BSc, RD
- Dr. Michele Turek, MD, FRCPC
- Sylvia Poirier, RN, MN

The Heart and Stroke Foundation would also like to acknowledge the volunteers and staff who were instrumental in making this book such a resounding success.

A special thanks goes to Dr. Anthony Graham, who was the volunteer President of the Heart and Stroke Foundation of Ontario in 1987 and was instrumental in first bringing this project to the Foundation.

Thanks also to:

- Richard Gallop, who was the CEO at the Heart and Stroke Foundation of Ontario when the initial book was developed and ensured, prior to his retirement, that this revised edition would be created.
- Neila Poscente, Vice President of Health Promotion, HSFO, for taking the leadership on this book.
- Doug MacQuarrie, Director of Health Promotion, HSFC, for his ongoing guidance.
- Carol Dombrow, RD, for helping to bring this book to fruition.
- Janice Daciuk , MS, RD, who wrote an excellent introduction.
- Susan Girvan who went above and beyond in editing this book.
- Sharyn Joliat, RD, Info Access, for the expert nutrient analysis.

The Foundation would also like to acknowledge Key Porter Books and Anne Lindsay for their important roles in bringing this book to Canadians.

Preface

Dear Friend,

It is hard to believe that *The Lighthearted Cookbook* is 15 years old. This is a book that has certainly stood the test of time, making it one of the best selling cookbooks in Canada.

The Heart and Stroke Foundation of Canada is very pleased to bring you a completely updated version of this popular resource. Since its original publication in 1988, researchers have gathered undisputed evidence that reinforces the message that a healthy diet is important for lifelong good health. While these recipes are heart-healthy, they are also great recipes for your overall health.

In the book's Introduction, you will find practical information to meet your individual needs to improve your diet. Spend some time reading through the Lighthearted Tool Kit and then move on to the Lighthearted Action Plan. As a bonus, the recipes will make it easy and delicious to follow your plan.

Anne Lindsay has certainly become a Canadian household name when it comes to preparing good, healthful food. She has a wonderful knack for making healthy and delicious recipes that are easy to prepare with ingredients that you have in the house. You will find your old favorites that have been updated with today's ingredients as well as some new recipes I'm sure you will want to try.

With the introduction of wonderful resources like this cookbook, along with many other nutrition education resources focusing on healthy food choices and managing your weight, and the addition of helpful programs like Health Check™, the Heart and Stroke Foundation is strengthening its commitment to making it easier for Canadians to make healthier choices. Health Check™ is an on-pack food information program that can help you make wise food choices at the grocery store. When you see the Health Check logo on a food package when you shop, you can be assured that the food is part of a healthy diet. And when you come home, you will have a great new resource to prepare wonderful meals.

For more information on Health Check™, visit www.healthcheck.org

For more information on making healthy food choices and managing your weight, visit www.heartandstroke.ca or call 1-888-HSF-INFO.

We know that Canadians have a high level of interest in nutrition and we are pleased to be able to provide you with some excellent resources, including this helpful one.

Carolyn Brooks

To your good health,
Carolyn Brooks, President, Heart and Stroke Foundation of Canada

Introduction

Anne Lindsay's best-selling *The Lighthearted Cookbook* was first published in 1988. Since then, it's become an invaluable guide in many Canadian kitchens. It's one of those cookbooks that is dog-eared and splattered from much use. This is because Anne confounded the skeptics and showed us that heart-healthy eating didn't have to be unappealing—it could be downright delicious.

Since the book's first publication, much has changed. Research on food and nutrition and the link between diet and health have continued. While the information has been confusing at times, steady scientific progress has equipped us to make better choices about what we eat. Many food manufacturers are taking the latest health research into account and are developing more food products that offer health benefits. Local grocery stores now stock a wide variety of healthy foods from around the world. Local farmers' markets are becoming popular sources of seasonal produce. We are learning more about organic and natural products. And coffee and chocolate are now things to be enjoyed without guilt—in moderation, of course.

Food is many things to all of us—comfort, celebration, love, sharing, and nourishment. It can also enhance health and help fight disease. We know that eating a diet that is lower in fat and includes a variety of foods is still one of the best ways to stay healthy. Eating well will also help lower the risk of developing heart disease, stroke, and other chronic health conditions such as Type 2 diabetes.

While we all want to have a healthy heart and a healthy life, most of all, we still want to enjoy delicious food. As before, *The Lighthearted Cookbook* will show you how to satisfy that desire. For a steaming hot stew on a cold winter night, try the Easy Oven Beef and Vegetable Stew on page 141. Or try Tomatoes Broiled with Goat Cheese and Basil (page 199) in summer, Asparagus and Potato Bisque (page 74) in spring, or an Apple and Raspberry Crisp (page 232) in the fall.

Anne Lindsay has been helping Canadians celebrate good health and great eating for the past two decades. Through her many wonderful cookbooks, magazine and newspaper articles, and television appearances, she has been a friend and teacher in the kitchen. With this updated version of *The Lighthearted Cookbook*, she shows us once again that to eat in heart-healthy ways means we can eat delicious food.

We've included the latest heart-health and nutrition information to help you put your "lighthearted" eating plan into action. And let's not forget Anne's fabulous recipes, updated here for us to savor, share, and enjoy. So let's dive right in and get cooking—the heart-healthy way, that is!

Janice Daciuk, MS, RD, Grimsby, Ontario

THE HEART OF THE MATTER

Heart disease develops over time. Your habits in the past affect your health and vitality today; what you do now can affect your quality of life in the future. It is a good idea to pay attention to what you eat, the amount of exercise you get, and other habits such as smoking at every age.

In the past few years, we have seen fewer deaths from heart-related disease. This is good news. However, we are also seeing a sharp rise in the occurrence of obesity among younger Canadians, and baby boomers are heading into middle age—often a time when heart disease develops. These two factors have led health-care planners to predict a big increase in heart disease in the next two decades.

But take heart—the fact that you are reading this book now means that you are probably ready to start making "lighthearted" choices.

So what exactly is cardiovascular or heart disease?

The term "cardiovascular disease" includes all diseases of the heart and of the blood vessels that lead to various parts of the body. Blood vessels include the arteries that carry blood away from your heart to other organs and the veins that bring blood back. Two of the most common conditions, heart disease and stroke, are usually caused by narrowed or blocked blood vessels.

How does heart disease happen?
When you have too much LDL or "bad" cholesterol in your blood, it can attach itself to artery walls. This sticky buildup makes it harder for the blood to pass through, and the oxygen the blood carries can't get to your brain, heart, or other important organs. When this happens, it results in heart attack or stroke, depending on where the blockage is. A heart attack occurs when there is an inadequate flow of blood to the heart muscle, while a stroke is usually caused by a lack of blood flow to the brain.

Details, Details . . . Cholesterol

Cholesterol is a soft waxy substance made by both humans and animals. Considering cholesterol's bad reputation, you may be surprised to learn that the body actually needs some to function. It is an important chemical "building block" used to make cell membranes and hormones.[1] There are different types of cholesterol. The two main types are:

- High-density lipoprotein (HDL): This is "good" cholesterol, as HDL works at taking cholesterol away from blood vessel walls.
- Low-density lipoprotein (LDL): This is better known as "bad" cholesterol because it can attach to the walls of the blood vessels and contribute to the buildup of sticky plaque.

Triglyceride is another common fat found in our bodies. While the relationship between this type of fat and heart disease isn't clear, many people who have heart disease also have high triglyceride levels. Unlike LDL cholesterol, triglycerides do not stick or attach themselves to blood vessel walls. Instead they act like a "thick cream" in the blood, making it more likely that the blood will clot and cause a blockage.

Heart disease facts:

- Heart disease, whether it takes the form of angina, heart attack, or stroke, can have a devastating impact on your life. When you're in pain, aren't physically able or comfortable, or are just feeling vulnerable and at risk, you aren't able to participate in and enjoy your usual activities.
- More Canadians die of heart disease than from any other disease. In 1999, almost 80,000 Canadians died from heart disease.
- It's not just the elderly who are affected by heart disease. Heart disease is also a major cause of death for people under the age of 75.
- Men and women are *both* at risk of developing heart disease. For women, risk increases after age 55; for men, after age 45.
- Men and women with other close family members who have had a heart attack or stroke before the age of 65 or a tendency to develop high blood cholesterol or high blood pressure are at higher risk for developing heart disease.
- Men and women of African, South Asian, and First Nations heritage are at higher risk for developing heart disease.

[1] Heart and Stroke Foundation of Canada Fact Sheet, "Risk Factors." 9/24/2001.

Recognizing Your Risk

No one wants to believe that they have or are at risk of developing heart disease or stroke. However, it is estimated that one in four Canadians has some form of heart disease or disease of the blood vessels or is at risk for stroke. And they may not know it!

The first thing you can do to protect yourself from heart disease is to be aware of what the risk factors are. Even having one risk factor means that your chances of eventually developing heart disease are greater. But once you know what you're up against, you can make positive changes to improve your heart health. It's important to manage the risk factors that you *can* influence, especially if you have other risk factors that are beyond your control.

Risk factors you can't change:[2]
- age
- gender
- family history
- race

Risk factors you *can* influence:
- smoking
- lack of exercise
- high blood pressure
- high blood cholesterol
- excess weight
- diabetes
- drinking too much alcohol
- stress

As a bonus, controlling your risk factors for heart disease will also help you maintain a healthy weight and give you energy.

The Importance of Diet in Heart Health

Fifty percent of the incidences of heart disease could be prevented by adopting a healthy lifestyle. Eating one high-fat meal isn't going to clog up your arteries or cause you to have a heart attack. However, eating

---

[2]   Heart and Stroke Foundation of Canada web site Fact Sheet, "Coronary Heart Disease Risk Factors."

high-fat foods on a regular basis *will* add up to problems. When you eat a lot of fatty meats and processed snack foods, you are getting lots of saturated and trans fats—the kinds that increase LDL (bad) blood cholesterol levels.

Lots of fat also means lots of calories. When you eat more calories than you can burn, you gain weight, and being overweight puts you at a higher risk of developing heart disease and other chronic conditions such as high blood pressure or Type 2 diabetes.

In addition, research has shown that soluble fiber, found in oats, peas, beans, and certain fruits, helps to lower artery-clogging LDL (bad) cholesterol levels in your blood. Cutting back on the fat and adding soluble fiber to your diet will help you lower your risk of developing high cholesterol levels and heart disease.

A healthy eating style will not only help lower your risk of developing heart disease, it will help you reach and maintain a healthy weight, so you'll have more energy, and will look and feel great.

So what is a healthy eating style?

A healthy eating style means you're enjoying a diet based on whole grains, vegetables, fruits, peas, beans, and lentils in combination with modest portions of leaner meats, lower-fat milk products, and unsaturated fats such as olive or canola oil. By eating this way, you are getting all of the important nutrients you need for energy for your busy days, to grow and to learn, and to help protect yourself from heart disease and stroke.

Keep in mind, though, that healthy eating is the total of the food choices you make over time. It is the *overall pattern* of foods that you eat and not any one food or meal that makes your diet healthy. This means that there are no "good" or "bad" foods. So if you've had two pieces of pie for dessert at a holiday meal (and who hasn't?), don't panic. By choosing lower-fat foods such as fruit and vegetables at another meal or on another day, you can balance out the higher-fat excesses and create an overall pattern of healthy eating.[3]

Healthy eating also means taking time out to share your table and good food with family and friends. After all, you need food for the soul as well as the body.

It's no secret that maintaining a healthy diet is one of the best things you can do to have a healthy heart. But where do you start? With the hectic pace of your life today, you likely have less time than ever to

The Bottom Line on Heart Health

What you eat has an effect on your risk of developing high blood cholesterol, high blood pressure, and obesity—all factors that increase your risk of developing heart disease and stroke. Research has consistently shown that a diet high in vegetables, fruits, and whole-grain foods helps to reduce your risk of developing heart disease and stroke. Research has also consistently shown that a diet high in fat, particularly saturated and trans fats from animal and processed foods, and low in fiber from a lack of whole grains, vegetables, and fruits puts you at a higher risk of developing heart disease.

---

[3]   Health and Welfare Canada. Food Guide Facts. Background for Educators and Communicators. 1992.

cook meals and eat together as a family. Ready-to-go meals and fast foods are convenient, but may not be very nutritious.

In the sections to come, you will find a wealth of information and tips for making better—lighthearted—food choices for you and your family. Then you'll find out how to put it all together to make your own action plan that includes enjoying delicious meals, snacks, and desserts such as Barbecued Lemon Chicken (page 117), Fettuccine with Pesto Sauce (page 164), and Blueberry Cream Flan (page 240).

THE LIGHTHEARTED TOOL KIT FOR HEALTHY EATING

Most things worth doing require some background research and take a bit of planning. Making heart-healthy changes to your diet, whether it's one small thing or a total food makeover, is easier to do when you've got lots of ideas to help you make a plan that suits your needs. This section will give you food for thought about everything from *Canada's Food Guide to Healthy Eating* to adding variety, cutting down on fat, and stocking your pantry.

Once you've had a chance to review the information, you can craft your own Lighthearted Action Plan, built on *Canada's Guidelines for Healthy Eating, Canada's Food Guide*, and *Canada's Physical Activity Guide*—a plan that will be suitable whether you are healthy or already have some health challenges.

The five key messages of *Canada's Guidelines for Healthy Eating* are:
- Enjoy a *variety* of foods. By eating many different kinds of foods, you'll be getting the particular nutrients and health benefits that each has to offer.
- *Emphasize* cereals, breads, other grain products, vegetables, and fruits. These foods contain important dietary fiber, vitamins, minerals, and other compounds such as antioxidants that help you to be healthy.
- *Choose lower-fat* dairy products, leaner meats, and foods prepared with little or no fat. Simple things such as changing from 2% to 1% milk and enjoying fresh bread without slathering on the butter help keep your fat intake in check. You can certainly eat some fat; it's how much and what kind that matters.
- Achieve and maintain a *healthy body weight* by enjoying regular physical activity and healthy eating.
- *Limit* salt, alcohol, and caffeine.

Canada's Food Guide

Canada's Food Guide to Healthy Eating takes the commonsense guidelines for healthy eating and puts them into action by showing you the key food groups and how to use them to create a healthy diet in accordance with the guidelines. Think of the *Food Guide* as your road map to better food choices. You may take some detours once in a while, but by always coming back to the road map, your overall diet will stay on course.

The *Food Guide* is designed to help you limit your consumption of total fat, especially artery-clogging saturated and trans fats, and to get enough protein, fiber, vitamins, and minerals as well as disease-fighting antioxidants, phytochemicals, and other compounds in foods.

By choosing the following more often, you will be getting all of the important nutrients you need for a healthy heart.

- whole-grain and enriched products
- dark green and orange vegetables and orange fruit
- lower-fat milk products
- leaner meats, poultry, and fish, as well as dried peas, beans, and lentils

The amount of food you need every day from the four food groups and other foods depends on your age, body size, and activity level and whether you are male or female and whether you are pregnant or breast-feeding. For example, young children can choose the lower number of servings. For active male teenagers, the higher number of servings is more appropriate. The rest of us tend to fall somewhere in the middle.

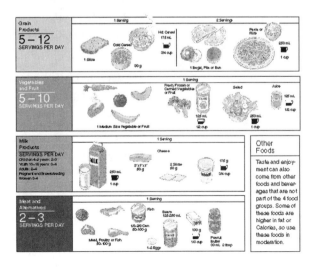

What is the right amount for you? As you make adjustments according to the *Food Guide*, your energy level and your weight will tell you if you are choosing the right number of servings.

What Are the Food Groups and How Much Is Recommended?
- Grain Products: 5 to 12 servings per day
- Vegetables and Fruits: 5 to 10 servings per day
- Milk Products: 2 to 4 servings per day for adults
- Meat and Alternatives: 2 or 3 servings per day
- Other Foods are foods and beverages that are not part of any food group. Use the following in moderation:
    - Fats and oils such as butter, margarine, cooking oils
    - Foods high in sugar such as jam, honey, syrup, and candies
    - High-fat and/or high-salt snack foods such as chips and pretzels
    - Beverages such as tea, coffee, alcohol, and soft drinks

What is a serving size?
One serving of Grain Products is:
- 1 slice of bread
- 3/4 cup/175 mL hot cereal
- 1 oz/30 g cold cereal

Two servings of Grain Products is:
- 1 bagel, pita, or bun
- 1 cup/250 mL cooked pasta or rice

One serving of Vegetables and Fruits is:
- 1 medium-size vegetable or fruit such as a banana, apple, or carrot
- 1/2 cup/125 mL fresh, frozen, or canned vegetables and fruits
- 1 cup/250 mL green salad
- 1/2 cup/125 mL juice

One serving of Milk Products is:
- 1 cup/250 mL white or chocolate milk
- 1.75 oz/50 g cheese
- 2 slices or 1.75 oz/50 g processed cheese
- 3/4 cup/175 mL yogurt

One serving of Meat and Alternatives is:
- 2–4 oz/50–100 g meat, poultry, or fish
- 1/3–2/3 can/50–100 g fish

- 1 or 2 eggs
- ¹/₂–1 cup/125–250 mL beans
- ¹/₃ cup/75 mL tofu
- 2 tbsp/25 mL peanut or other nut butter

Try these visual cues to help you remember *Food Guide* serving sizes.

One Serving of:	Amount/weight:	Visual:
Meat, fish, poultry	3 oz/90 g	Deck of cards, the palm of your hand, or cassette tape
Cheese	1.75 oz/50 g	Six dice
Nuts	1 oz/30 g	A handful
Bread	1 slice or ¹/₂ English muffin or bagel	
Potatoes, hot cereal, cooked vegetables, chopped, canned, or cooked fruit	¹/₂ cup/125 mL	A tennis ball
Raw leafy vegetables or fruits	1 cup/250 mL	The size of your fist
Oil or butter	1 tsp/5 mL	The size of the tip of your thumb

The *Food Guide* is suitable for people 4 years of age and older. Pre-schoolers can enjoy the same foods but need smaller serving sizes—use half an adult serving size as a rule of thumb. For more information about feeding children of all ages, see pages 33 to 38.

So, that's our quick tour of the *Food Guide*. Now is the time to get a copy if you don't have one already, and let it guide your food choices. You can download a copy of the *Food Guide* and a helpful booklet called *Using the Food Guide* from the office Nutrition Policy and Promotion at Health Canada's web site www.hc-sc.gc.ca. The materials are also available at your local Heart and Stroke Foundation office or you can visit their web site at www.heartandstroke.ca.

Enjoying a Variety of Foods

So why is variety so important? Isn't it okay if you eat the same meals every week as long as they are low in fat? Say, a baked, skinless chicken breast with mashed potatoes, green beans, and a glass of milk. What's wrong with that? Nothing, if you don't pile butter on the mashed potatoes, and have skim or 1% milk instead of 2%.

Despite preferences for favorite meals, if you eat the same things week after week, you will likely decide that food and cooking are boring. More important, you'll not only be passing up a lot of other delicious food choices, you will also miss out on the range of nutrients that a variety of foods can deliver. It's good that the chicken-breast meal cuts back on the fat, but why not have baked potatoes with the skins on for more fiber? And what about adding some antioxidant-rich fruit such as an orange for dessert?

Details, Details . . . the Variety of Nutrients

Current research has identified a variety of components in many foods that can potentially help lower the risk of heart disease and stroke. While it is not yet known whether the benefits come from the foods themselves or from the interaction with each other, it's still smart to eat more of these foods more often.

Food	Heart-Healthy Components	Fitting It in
Citrus fruit	Flavonoids and limonoids have strong antioxidant properties.	• Have grapefruit sections at breakfast. • Take along an orange for a mid-afternoon snack.
Garlic, types of onion	Allylic sulfides may help to lower LDL (bad) cholesterol levels.	• Use them in soups, stews, pastas, casseroles, dips, stir-fries, savory baked goods, and more. • Try different kinds of onions for variety—green, scallions, Vidalia, red, Bermuda, pearl, Spanish. • Store both garlic and onions in a cool, dry place.
Fish oils from fish such as salmon, swordfish, trout, cod, herring, mackerel, and bluefish	Omega-3 fats (eicosapentenoic acid, or epa, and docosahexanoic acid, or dha) may help reduce blood clotting.	• Have fish at least two times every week. • Cook fish without added fat by steaming, baking, or broiling.
Flaxseed Note: Flax oil does not provide the same benefits as ground flaxseed. Buy whole flaxseed and grind your own with a coffee grinder, food processor, or blender; you'll get more heart-healthy nutrients by grinding up the	• Omega-3 fat (alpha-linolenic acid) • Soluble fiber • Lignans These compounds may all help to lower LDL (bad) cholesterol levels.	• Sprinkle on hot and cold breakfast cereals and add to muffin and cookie batters, pancake mixes, and bread doughs. • Add ground flaxseed to meatballs, burgers, and casseroles. • Mix ground flaxseed into yogurt or use as topping for fruit crisps.

The New Lighthearted Cookbook

Food	Heart-Healthy Components	Fitting It in
hard outer shell. Store ground flaxseed in the refrigerator or freezer.		
Red grape juice or red wine	Flavonoids: quercetin and resveratrol have strong antioxidant properties.	• Enjoy red wine in moderation. • Try a glass of red grape juice.
Nuts, such as almonds, walnuts *Note:* Nuts are high in calories, so cut back on other added fats such as margarine or butter when adding nuts to your diet.	• Mono- and polyunsaturated fat • Fiber • The antioxidant vitamin E: alpha-linolenic acid These compounds also may help lower LDL (bad) cholesterol levels.	• Add toasted walnut or almond pieces to lower-fat yogurt. • Mix chopped walnuts or almonds into pancake or waffle batter. • Toss some walnuts or almonds into your morning cereal. • Pack a handful in your lunch or toss into salads. • Stir toasted nuts into pasta, chicken, and turkey salads. • Add chopped nuts to dips such as hummus and fruit and vegetable dips made with low-fat yogurt. • Roll toasted nuts into vegetarian lunch wraps.
Soy foods such as soy nuts, soy beverage, tofu, and soy flour (not soy sauce)	Phytoestrogens: isoflavones, saponins, and soy protein may help to lower LDL (bad) cholesterol levels. In the U.S., a daily intake of 25 g of soy protein is recommended for optimal benefits.	• Use soft silken tofu in smoothies. • Scramble firm tofu instead of eggs. • Add tofu cubes to soups and stews. • Try one of the flavored soy beverages on the market. • Snack on a handful of soy nuts or fresh/frozen soybeans (edamame).
Tomato pastes, sauces, and juice; watermelon	Lycopene is a powerful antioxidant.	• Make your own pasta sauce by cooking fresh tomatoes with a little olive oil to help the body absorb more lycopene.
Wide variety of vegetables, vegetable oils, fruit, legumes, and grains	Plant sterols can help lower LDL (bad) cholesterol levels.	• Be sure to add variety to your diet by trying new vegetables and fruits. • Experiment with different legumes and grains such as lentils, quinoa, and millet.
Tea—both black and green[4]	Polyphenols and catechins are powerful antioxidants.	• Try different kinds of tea such as Oolong, Chai, and Lapsang Souchong. Store tea in a cool, dry place.

[4]   J.M. Geleijnse, L.J. Launere, A. Hofman et al., "Tea Flavonoids May Protect against Atherosclerosis: The Rotterdam Study," *Archives of Internal Medicine* (1999) 159, 2170–2174.

Lighthearted Goals for Adding Variety

1. Follow *Canada's Food Guide to Healthy Eating.*
2. Eat foods from each food group every day.
3. Eat many different foods within each food group.

Get a couple of copies of *Canada's Food Guide to Healthy Eating* and keep them handy on the refrigerator and inside cupboard doors.

The Bottom Line on Variety

Aim for an overall diet pattern that includes a variety of foods in moderation. Try new things, and get the whole family involved.

Lighthearted Ideas for Adding Variety to Your Diet

At the grocery store:

- Make a point of picking up different fruits, vegetables, and other lower-fat items each time you shop. It's a great way to expand your food repertoire.
- Take some time to see what's new.
- Shop at local, ethnic, and farmers' markets.

At home:

- Try to have at least three of the four food groups at each meal. For example, have a bran muffin, a piece of fresh fruit, and a glass of low-fat milk, or have a piece of fish, whole-grain rice, and broccoli.
- Choose the number of servings appropriate for your age and activity level.
- Let one family member plan a different meal with new ingredients they'd like to try every week.
- Try some new recipes from this cookbook.
- Go meatless once in a while. Use dried or rinsed canned peas, beans, and lentils for protein instead.
- If some foods or cooking styles are new to you, look for cooking classes in your area that will give you some ideas.
- Pay attention to portion sizes no matter what you are eating. Too much of a good thing isn't necessarily better.

On the go:

- Try more ethnic cuisines such as Thai or Indian food.
- When eating out, don't go to the same places all the time; if you do, try different items on the menu.

A Note about DRIs (Dietary Reference Intakes)

It is important to the Heart and Stroke Foundation of Canada that they bring you the most up-to-date nutrition information and recommendations for heart health. At the time of publication, healthy eating recommendations are moving toward individualization instead of a "one-size-fits-all" approach. The goals are still to maximize health and disease prevention, including heart disease and stroke. While the numbers may be a bit different, the message is the same—carbohydrates should make up approximately half of daily calories and fat and protein about a third, depending on your individual needs—your age, gender, and activity level.

Choosing the Carbohydrate Champs

You may have heard that carbohydrates make you fat or that high-carbohydrate intake causes diabetes. These statements are not true. In fact, having carbohydrates in your diet is very important, as they supply the fuel that your brain, nervous system, and muscles rely on. Glucose, the preferred source of energy for the brain, comes from carbohydrate. If you look at *Canada's Food Guide to Healthy Eating*, it is easy to see that basing a diet on Grain Products and Vegetables and Fruits is the best way to eat for a healthy heart.

Details, Details . . . Carbohydrate

All carbohydrates are made up of a basic building block called a mono-saccharide.[5] But all carbohydrates are not alike. There are three types: starches, which are more complex arrangements of these building blocks; and simple sugars, which are made up of only one or two building blocks. The third type, dietary fiber, is discussed separately.

- Examples of foods containing starches include:
  - Brown rice
  - Legumes such as lentils, dried peas, and beans
  - Whole-grain pasta, whole-grain bread, potatoes, rice, barley, buckwheat (kasha)
  - Oats and oatmeal
  - Wheat germ and wheat bran
  - White rice, white bread, and regular pasta

- Examples of foods containing sugars include:
  - Fruits and vegetables
  - Milk Products
  - Sweet, sugary foods such as honey, candy, pastries, and regular soft drinks

Overall, the best way to have a healthy diet is to include starches and sugars that provide the most nutrition, such as whole grains, vegetables and fruits, and milk products. Variety is always important and you want to limit foods that are low in vitamins and minerals such as sweet, sugary foods. You may hesitate to increase your intake of starchy foods, as you've heard they are fattening, but it's really how much and what type

[5] Tom Brody, *Nutritional Biochemistry*, 2nd ed. Academic Press, 1999, 10.

of carbohydrate you eat that has an effect on your weight. Too much of *anything* means that you are getting more calories than you need, with the rest being stored as fat.

How you prepare your starchy foods is also important. Vegetables, bread, and other whole grains are low in calories and fat. When you add rich cheese sauces to vegetables and lots of butter to your bread, then you are increasing the calories. Processed foods such as French fries, cookies, and pastas with high-fat sauces such as Alfredo may contribute excess fat and calories. These foods should be eaten in moderation.

When it comes to heart health, choose carbohydrates that are high in fiber. Increasing your intake of starches such as legumes or whole grains will help to ensure you are getting more fiber in your diet.

THE GLYCEMIC INDEX

There is another consideration that may affect the carbohydrates some of us choose. It is called the Glycemic Index. The Glycemic Index is a measure of how quickly a food is able to raise your blood sugar levels.

Recent studies suggest that people who eat *a lot* of foods with a high value on the Glycemic Index, such as refined white bread, may increase their risk of heart disease, diabetes, and obesity.[6] For the most part, less refined or less processed whole-grain products such as barley and oats have a lower Glycemic Index rating and are carbohydrates we should choose more often. For most of us, the best thing to do is to enjoy a wide variety of carbohydrates, including whole grains, vegetables, fruits, and beans. For more information about the Glycemic Index, consult www.diabetes.ca.

Fiber focus

Fiber is a substance in food that is either not digested or only partially digested. Your grandparents called it roughage and knew it helped "keep them regular." Now there is growing evidence that fiber, particularly soluble fiber, helps to lower high levels of blood cholesterol. Fiber may also help protect the body from certain types of cancers.

Soluble fiber, meaning that it dissolves in water, is found in foods such as oats, beans, lentils, barley, apples, and cereals with psyllium. It helps reduce the level of LDL (bad) cholesterol in our blood. Insoluble fiber, on the other hand, does not dissolve in water and is found in

[6]   S. Lui et al., "A Prospective Study of Dietary Glycemic Load, Carbohydrate Intake and Risk of Coronary Heart Disease in US Women," *American Journal of Clinical Nutrition* 71 (2000), 1455–1461.

whole-wheat products, wheat bran and wheat bran cereals, corn bran, fruits, and vegetables. It's what helps to keep us regular.

Fiber supplements are not recommended, as many contain only small amounts of fiber in comparison to foods and don't supply other essential nutrients. It's important to increase your fiber intake slowly because too much too soon may result in unpleasant side effects such as gas, diarrhea, cramps, and bloating. Be sure to drink plenty of water to help the fiber to do its job.

To Increase Fiber Intake

Instead of	Choose
Orange juice	Fresh orange
White bread 100%	Whole-wheat bread
Cereals with less than 4 g fiber per serving	Cereals with 4 g of fiber or more per serving
White roll	Bran muffin
Hot dog	Chili
Noodle soup	Lentil or bean soup
Canned pasta	Canned baked beans
Iceberg lettuce salad	Spinach salad
Mashed potatoes	Potato with skin
Chips and dip	Raw veggies and dip
Puddings, pastries	Fruit desserts
Regular pasta	Whole-grain pasta

WHOLE-GRAIN KNOW-HOW

Knowing what is and what is not whole grain can be very difficult if you're not paying attention to the ingredients on the label. It can be an even bigger challenge when you're shopping in the bulk section, where there is little or no nutrition information available. A loaf of twelve-grain bread might sound as if it's a good whole-grain choice, but if the first ingredient listed is white flour, then it's not whole-grain.

When buying breads and cereals, look for the words "whole-wheat flour" or "whole-rye flour" near the top of the list of ingredients. Wheat flour and unbleached wheat flour mean the flour has been refined. When whole grains are refined, the outer bran layer that contains fiber and the nutrient-rich germ layer are both removed.

Lighthearted Goals for the Carbohydrate in Your Diet

Choose 5 to 10 servings of vegetables and fruits every day, and 5 to 12 servings of grain products every day.

Currently, the recommendations are to get 50% or more of our calories from carbohydrate. However, the trend is to recommend a range of 45 to 65% to better meet our individual needs. (Please check the Heart and Stroke web site for updates on carbohydrate and healthy eating recommendations at www.heartandstroke.ca.)

Lighthearted Ideas for Adding Carbohydrate and Dietary Fiber to Your Diet

At the grocery store:

- Choose whole-wheat foods when buying bread, pasta, English muffins, spaghetti, pita bread, hamburger buns, and crackers.
- When buying bread, pasta, rice, and other carbohydrate foods that aren't whole grain, look for those that are enriched.
- Fill your cart with fruits and vegetables. Look for ones that are dark green or orange.
- Select foods in their least prepared form. For example, look for plain frozen vegetables instead of those with sauces, cheese, butter, or breading.
- Watch for labeling that includes words such as partially hydrogenated oil, shortening, and animal fat. Choose these foods less often.
- Buy whole fruits and vegetables rather than their juices.
- Buy baked munchies (such as baked tortilla chips) instead of deep-fried brands.
- Take home breakfast cereals that have at least 4 g of fiber per serving.

At home:

- Try to have fruits and vegetables at every meal.
- Use whole-wheat flour. In most recipes, you can substitute whole-wheat flour for as much as half of the all-purpose flour. (Store whole-wheat flour in the refrigerator.)
- Get to know your legumes. Look in the Vegetables section or the index of this book for recipes that use beans such as kidney, navy, lentils, and chickpeas.
- Add bran or wheat germ to muffins, cereals (hot or cold), casseroles and toppings, meat loaf, cookies, and smoothies.
- Add chickpeas or kidney beans to soups, salads, and casseroles.
- Add dried fruits (prunes, raisins, apricots) and nuts to your cereals; use them to top fruit or ice-cream desserts.
- Choose breakfast cereals with at least 4 g of fiber per serving.
- Eat the edible skins of fruits and vegetables.
- Add extra vegetables to casseroles, soups, salads, sandwiches, and pasta and rice dishes.
- Experiment with unfamiliar whole grains: barley, buckwheat, bulgur, millet, quinoa, and wheat berries.
- Mix dried fruit—raisins, dry cranberries, and prunes—into breads, cookies, salads, cereals, and other dishes.

- If you've got a bread machine, try new recipes that use different whole grains, dried fruits, and vegetables.

On the go:
- Have your subs, sandwiches, or wraps made with whole-wheat or pumpernickel breads or buns. Skip the sauces.
- A side salad with a moderate amount of low-fat dressing will be higher in fiber and lower in calories than the fries.
- Keep fresh fruit in the fridge at work.

The Bottom Line on Carbohydrate

Increase the fruits and vegetables. Go for the whole-grain gain. Hold back on the added fat. Choose carbs that are nutrient dense.

Choosing Lower-Fat Foods

With the hubbub surrounding the importance of eating less fat, it's easy to forget that your body actually needs some fat to be at its best. An extremely low-fat diet is considered dangerous, since fat has many important functions in the body. Fat helps transport vitamins, cushions interior organs, and provides energy. While most of us have to be prudent about the amount of fat we put on our plates, for infants and young children, this isn't the case. They need a higher proportion of fat to help them grow and develop properly. For infants, breast milk or formula should provide all the necessary nutrients.

However, considering that the rates of obesity, heart disease, and Type 2 diabetes continue to rise, it's safe to say that we are getting too many calories, many of those from fats. But here's the good news—not all fats are alike. While they are all high in calories, some can actually help keep your heart healthy.

Details, Details . . . Dietary Fat
You get several different kinds of fat from your food. Each type has a different effect on your blood cholesterol levels:

Type of Fat	Heart Health Rating	What's the Potential Health Effect?	What Are the Most Common Sources?
Dietary cholesterol	Neutral	May raise LDL (bad) cholesterol levels in sensitive individuals.	Fattier meats, organ meats such as kidney and liver, butter, eggs, lard, mayonnaise, shrimp, fish roe
Monounsaturated fats (MUFA)	Positive	Lowers the LDL (bad) cholesterol levels when it replaces saturated fat; no effect on HDL (good) cholesterol levels.	Olive and canola oils; food such as non-hydrogenated (i.e., soft) margarine made from these oils, as well as nuts, seeds, avocados, olives

Type of Fat	Heart Health Rating	What's the Potential Health Effect?	What Are the Most Common Sources?
Omega-3 fatty acids	Positive	Helps to lower levels of blood triglycerides;[7] helps prevent blood from sticking and clotting.	Fatty fish such as salmon, mackerel, and trout; canola oil, walnuts, flaxseed, some soft margarine made from canola oil, Omega-3 eggs
Polyunsaturated fats (PUFA)	Positive	Lowers LDL (bad) cholesterol levels if it replaces saturated fats.	Sunflower, corn, safflower, and soybean oils; foods such as soft, non-hydrogenated margarine made from these oils, as well as nuts and seeds
Saturated fat (SFA)	Negative	Raises total and LDL (bad) cholesterol levels.	Foods that come mostly from animal sources—including higher-fat meats and dairy products such as cheese, cream, and butter; also found in palm and coconut oils
Trans fats	Negative	Raises LDL (bad) cholesterol levels and lowers HDL (good) cholesterol levels.	Processed and fast foods that contain partially hydrogenated fats or shortening, such as cookies and crackers, as well as deep-fried foods, shortening, hard margarine

From the chart above, we can see that different types of fat do have different effects on blood-cholesterol and triglyceride levels. Replacing some of the saturated fat from meat and dairy products with heart-healthy Omega-3 fatty acids and including more unsaturated fats in our diet will help lower LDL (bad) cholesterol levels.

Limiting how many trans-fat-laden processed and fast foods we eat will also help lower the risk of heart disease and stroke. In the past, it has been difficult to know how much trans fat we were getting, as it hasn't been listed in the nutrition information on food labels. As food manufacturers convert their packaging to Canada's new food-labeling requirements (see pages 29 to 31), this information will be shown. It will soon be a lot easier for us to know exactly how much trans fat, as well as other types of fat and nutrients, we're really getting. And that will help us to make better food choices for heart health.

What About Eggs?
In the past, we've heard a lot about eggs being high in cholesterol and bad for your heart's health. It's still true that eggs contain a fair amount of cholesterol, about 190 mg each, found in the egg yolk only. But for

[7]   Triglycerides are a type of fat that can also contribute to the development of heart disease.

those of us without high blood cholesterol levels or who aren't considered sensitive to dietary cholesterol, eating eggs in moderation isn't harmful.[8] The tricky part is deciding what moderation really means. Unless your doctor or dietitian tells you to restrict eggs, follow the variety message.

Eggs are an inexpensive source of protein and are rich in B vitamins, iron, and other minerals. They're also quick and easy to cook. Try soft-boiling or scrambling them or making them into an omelet or frittata chock full of delicious chopped vegetables and herbs.

What About Meat and Poultry?

Today's meat and poultry is raised to be lean. Meat and poultry are part of the Meat and Alternatives Food Group and are an important source of protein, iron, zinc, and other nutrients necessary for good health. However, foods that come from animals, including meat, poultry, and dairy products such as milk and cheese, are the major source of saturated fat in our diet, which can raise LDL (bad) cholesterol levels. But this doesn't mean we can't enjoy them as part of a heart-healthy diet.

Again, the key is to remember the variety message. For general heart health, choosing leaner meats and lower-fat dairy products helps us to keep our saturated-fat intake in check. For more information, see the lighthearted ideas for cutting back on dietary fat (pages 21–22).

Butter Versus Margarine

When it comes to what we spread on our bread, most of us have a distinct preference. For some, nothing but margarine will adorn their slices. For others, butter is the way to go.

Truth be told, both spreads have their pros and cons. Butter is an animal product, therefore it contains saturated fat that can raise LDL (bad) cholesterol levels. For flavor, however, many feel that butter can't be beat. And for special-occasion treats such as pastries, butter is often preferred.

For everyday spreading, today's soft non-hydrogenated margarine is a better choice for heart health. These products are made with vegetable oils that contain very little saturated fat, and because they are not hydrogenated, they do not contain trans fat. Hydrogenation is a process used to turn liquid oil into solid fat, which results in the formation of trans fatty acids. As we have seen in the table above, trans fatty acids are not heart healthy because they cause LDL (bad) cholesterol levels to rise.

Avoid stick margarine or margarine that is hard. This is because it

[8] F.B. Hu, M.J. Stampfer, E.B. Rimm et al., "A Prospective Study of Egg Consumption and Risk of Cardiovascular Disease in Men and Women," *JAMA* 28, no. 15 (1999), 1387–1394.

has been hydrogenated. Look for "non-hydrogenated" on the label, and check the Nutrition Facts table to be sure that the product does not contain any trans fat.

Keep in mind, however, that both butter and margarine are 80% fat. Unless you use a calorie-reduced margarine, you'll get about the same number of calories per teaspoon whichever one you choose.

Make a Switch and Reduce Fats

Choose	Instead of	g fat saved
1 glass skim milk	1 glass whole milk	8
3 tbsp/45 mL grated part-skim mozzarella	3 tbsp/45 mL grated Cheddar	5
3 tbsp/45 mL creamed cottage cheese	3 tbsp/45 mL cream cheese	13
4 oz/120 g chicken breast, no skin	4 oz/120g chicken breast, with skin	4
Bread with 1 tsp/5 mL non-hydrogenated margarine	Bread with 1 tbsp/15 mL margarine	8
Salad, 1 tbsp/15 mL light mayonnaise	Salad, 2 tbsp/30 mL regular mayonnaise	18
1 pear	1 avocado	30
½ cup/125 mL unbuttered popcorn	½ cup/125 mL peanuts	35
Apple crisp	Apple pie	8
Bran muffin	Croissant	7

Consider Meatless Meals

Even if you're not a vegetarian, meatless meals can be delicious and satisfying. Considering that one of your goals is to cut back on fat and saturated fat, having meatless meals a couple of times a week makes good sense.

LIGHTHEARTED IDEAS FOR MEATLESS MEALS

- Try tofu or tempeh instead of ground beef in your tacos, stews, and pasta dishes. Replace meat in stews, soups, chili, and casseroles with a variety of legumes such as kidney beans and chickpeas. Scramble some tofu as a replacement for scrambled eggs.
- Take a vegetarian or soy-foods cooking class for ideas and inspiration.

The New Lighthearted Cookbook

- Make the most of great grains such as millet, bulgur, couscous, quinoa, spelt, and kasha.
- Beans are fabulous for fiber. Try a variety of beans, and let your imagination be your guide. For example, make bean salads, sprinkle them in pasta or mixed green salads, put them in sandwiches and wraps, in stir-fries, spaghetti sauce, chili, casseroles, or dips or purée them to make a dip on their own.

Lighthearted Ideas for Cutting Dietary Fat

At the grocery store:

- Choose leaner cuts of meat; for beef, this means inside, outside, eye of round, rump roast, or sirloin; choose chicken or turkey without the skin; pork tenderloin.
- Buy fish more often. Choose fattier fish such as salmon, mackerel, trout, herring, and sardines because they are higher in heart-healthy Omega-3 fats.
- Avoid fatty meats such as spareribs and processed meats such as salami and regular hot dogs.
- Buy light products such as light sour cream and light mayonnaise.
- Look for cheese with 20% or less milk fat.
- Choose dairy products such as milk and yogurt with 2% or lower milk fat (m.f.) or butter fat (b.f.).
- Choose 1% or nonfat soy or rice beverages.
- Avoid high-fat snacks, prepared foods, desserts, and cookies. These products are usually made with hydrogenated fats and contain trans fat that can increase LDL (bad) cholesterol.

At home:

- Use lower-fat cooking methods such as broiling, baking, steaming, poaching, boiling, or roasting meats on a rack.
- If you fry, use a nonstick pan and a small amount of olive, canola, or other vegetable oil for frying instead of butter or margarine. Or use fruit juice, water, or wine instead.
- After browning meat, drain the fat.
- Trim visible fat from meat and remove the skin from chicken.
- Have meals with fish more often.
- Replace some of the saturated fat in your diet with nuts in moderation. A small handful is plenty. Use in salads or pasta, as a topping for soups or cereals, or in trail mixes.
- Make your own salad dressings (see pages 89 to 106) or try a low-fat version of your favorite.

Lighthearted Goals for Cutting Down Your Fat Intake

1. Limit total fat intake to 30% or less of total calories. Again, the trend is to recommend a range of 20% to 30% of calories from fat to better meet our individual needs and to encourage a higher intake of unsaturated fats. (Please check the Heart and Stroke web site for updates on fat and healthy eating recommendations at www.heartandstroke.ca.)
2. Limit the combined amount of saturated and trans fat to the lowest amount possible.
3. Increase your intake of heart-healthy unsaturated fats, including Omega-3 fatty acids.

Simple. Eat less fat. The fats you do eat should be primarily unsaturated and low in trans fat. Keep your intake of processed or fast foods to a minimum.

- Drink your coffee or tea with lower-fat milk.
- Try different kinds of non-dairy beverages until you find one you like. There are versions made from soy, tofu, rice, nuts, and grains. Read the label to make sure the one you choose is fortified with calcium and vitamin D.
- In some recipes, two egg whites can be substituted for one whole egg.
- Try adding flavor to vegetables with herbs, spices, lemon juice, soy sauce, or gingerroot.

On the go:
- Make a point of taking your lunch to work instead of eating out every day.
- Have quick and easy-to-eat nutritious foods ready to grab when you have to eat on the run: bananas, small bags of trail mix (whole-grain cereals, nuts, and raisins), juice boxes, cubes of cheese, yogurt, or raw carrots.

To Lower Saturated and Trans Fat Intake

Choose	Instead of
Non-hydrogenated soft margarine, olive oil, or canola oil	Butter
Nonfat broth or stock	Regular broth or stock
Pretzels, air-popped or light popcorn	Chips, cheesie-style snacks
Veggie dogs	Hot dogs
Nonfat or 1% evaporated milk	Cream
Arrowroot, digestive, or other plain cookies	Crème-filled cookies
Rice cakes or melba toast	Crackers
1% or skim milk	Whole or 2% milk
Sorbet or sherbet	Ice cream

Limiting Salt, Alcohol, and Caffeine

Details, Details . . . Salt

In the past, it was believed that a high salt (sodium chloride) intake caused high blood pressure, which increases the risk of stroke. We now know that salt intake has different effects on different people—for most people, their bodies just get rid of the extra if they've consumed too much. Only those who are salt-sensitive will suffer serious effects. Since most of us don't know whether we are salt-sensitive or not and there is so much salt in the North American diet, it makes sense for all of us to cut back.

Where is all the salt coming from? Processed foods account for around 50% of the sodium in the average North American diet; 25% comes from the salt shaker on the table; 24% occurs naturally in foods and water; and 1% comes from non-food items such as medications.

To complicate matters, food such as some canned soups can contain a salt mine without tasting salty.

Lighthearted Ideas for Cutting Back on Salt

At the grocery store:
- Limit your purchases of high-sodium processed foods such as salad dressings, smoked and salted meats (bacon, sausages, ham), lunch-eon meats, smoked fish, regular canned foods, pickled vegetables, salted snack foods (potato chips, pretzels, salted crackers and nuts, pickles), soy sauce, canned or dried soups, and processed cheese.
- Avoid sodium compounds as well as salt, if you can. For example, MSG, which stands for monosodium glutamate, is very high in sodium. Always read ingredient lists.
- Be cautious with commercial herb blends and salt substitutes—they often contain salt. Read the label.
- Sea salt isn't healthier than table salt. They both contain about the same amount of sodium—2,400 mg per 1 tsp/5 mL. And sea salt offers no known health advantages.
- Choose salt-reduced soups, soy sauce, pretzels, and pickles.

At home:
- Keep the saltshaker in the cabinet, not on the kitchen counter or table where it's easier to use.
- Rinse canned beans and vegetables before using.
- The taste for salt is acquired and can be un-acquired. Always taste food before you add salt, and gradually decrease the amount you add.
- Don't automatically add salt to cooking water. Add it, if necessary, after tasting, just before serving.
- Try making up some herb "shakers"—combinations of dried herbs and spices to use instead of salt. For a suggestion, see page 205.
- Cook from scratch more often. Packaged convenience foods and canned foods may contain a lot of salt. Check the labels.

Lighthearted Goal for Salt
Limit your intake of salt to 2,500–3,000 mg per day.

The Bottom Line on Salt
Put the brakes on the shaker. Eat processed and fast foods less often. Use herbs, spices, lemon, herbed vinegar, fruit juice, and other flavor boosters instead.

To Cut Down on Salt Intake

Choose	Instead of
Tomato paste	Tomato sauce
Canned whole tomatoes	Stewed tomatoes
Fresh garlic	Garlic salt
Onion	Onion salt
Salt-reduced, fat-free chicken and beef stock	Bouillon cubes
Salt-reduced or homemade soups	Regular soups
Unsalted or reduced-salt crackers	Salted crackers
Fresh and frozen vegetables	Canned vegetables
Unsalted nuts	Salted nuts
Baked tortilla chips (check the salt content)	Potato chips, corn chips
Low-salt pretzels	Pretzels
Popcorn sprinkled with herbs and spices, or unsalted popcorn	Salted popcorn
Tortilla Chips (page 65)	Potato chips, corn chips
Old-Fashioned Pickled Beets (page 206)	Olives, dill pickles
Low-Salt Bagel Thins (page 72)	Pretzels
Homemade Ketchup (page 209)	Ketchup

On the go:
- As at home, in restaurants taste your food before you take the salt-shaker to it.
- Go for freshly ground pepper on salads, pasta dishes, and vegetables.
- Ask for a wedge of lemon to squeeze on fish, vegetables, and salads to heighten flavor.
- When eating Italian, go easy on the extra Parmesan cheese—it contains a fair amount of salt.
- Recognize menu terms that may indicate a high sodium content: pickled, smoked, au jus, soy sauce, in broth.
- Request that foods be prepared without added salt.
- Ask for sauces and salad dressings on the side, because they're often high in sodium.

Details, Details . . . Alcohol

Alcohol in moderation can be a pleasure at mealtimes and is in keeping with a healthy lifestyle. However, drinking too much puts you at risk for many health problems such as high blood pressure and elevated levels of triglycerides. In addition, alcohol is high in calories and may contribute to weight gain, which could also increase your risk of developing heart disease and stroke. Overindulging can lead to liver damage and even damage to the heart muscle and increase the risk of stroke. Alcohol may also compromise the effectiveness of medications you are taking or affect other medical conditions you may have. For these reasons, you should discuss your alcohol consumption with your doctor.

There has been some positive research linking red wine and other alcoholic beverages to heart health. Compounds known as flavonoids, which are found in alcohol, can contribute to heart health by increasing the "good" HDL cholesterol, and lowering the risk of blood clotting. However, if you aren't a regular consumer of alcohol, then you shouldn't start for this reason. Lowering your total intake of fat, saturated fat, and trans fat, along with regular activity will give you far better protection from heart attack and stroke.

Lighthearted Goal for Alcohol Consumption

For healthy adults who do drink alcohol, the Heart and Stroke Foundation recommends that consumption should not exceed two drinks a day, with a weekly limit of fourteen drinks for men and nine drinks for women.

One drink is:
- 12 oz/375 mL (1 bottle) of beer (5% alcohol)
- 5 oz/160 mL wine (12% alcohol)
- 1¹/₂ oz/45 mL spirits (40% alcohol)

Lighthearted Ideas for Limiting Alcohol
- Decide before a party or holiday meal to limit drinks to one or two at the most.
- Learn to sip, not gulp, to make an alcoholic drink last longer.
- Dilute drinks with water, ice, club soda, or juice.
- Frozen drinks often take longer to sip.
- If you still feel thirsty after an alcoholic drink, drink bottled water or a soft drink instead of another alcoholic beverage.
- Order lower-alcohol or non-alcoholic beer or wine where available, or take some with you.
- Try a "virgin" cocktail. Many restaurants and bars offer fancy mocktails that don't contain any alcohol. That way, you still get to join in and enjoy a special drink.
- If you like wine, try a wine spritzer.

The Bottom Line on Alcohol

Limit drinks to one or two per day. If you don't drink alcohol, it is not recommended that you start for the sake of heart health.

Details, Details . . . Caffeine

Forget love and money, it's caffeine that makes the world go round. Or at least gives it a kick start every morning. As part of a heart-healthy eating pattern, most people can enjoy caffeine-containing beverages

Lighthearted Goals for Caffeine Intake

An intake of 400–450 mg of caffeine per day means four 6-oz/175-mL cups of regular coffee or strong tea or one espresso and 4 oz/125 mL of chocolate or two 12-oz/375-mL cans of cola.

and foods, such as coffee and chocolate, in moderation. But what is moderation? When it comes to our coffee-loving society with a coffee shop on every corner, the meaning of moderation can vary. Drinking up to four 6-oz/175-mL cups of coffee, for an intake of 400 to 450 mg of caffeine per day, does not increase the risk of heart disease or high blood pressure.[9]

Caffeine becomes a problem only when coffee, tea, and cola beverages start taking the place of more nutritious drinks such as milk and fruit juices. Be aware of just how much caffeine you normally consume during the day. Remember that the size of the drinks at coffee shops are usually far larger than a regular 8-oz/250-mL cup. You may think you're okay if you only have four cups per day—but how large are the cups? If they're 12 oz/375 mL, then it's best to cut back to just two.

For those who have trouble sleeping or who are prone to the caffeine "jitters," it is a good idea to cut back on the caffeine. Also, loading up on caffeine isn't recommended for women who are pregnant or nursing, as it can cross the placenta and appear in breast milk. You want your baby to sleep—not be raring to go! It is also a good idea for those suffering from high blood pressure, stomach problems, or ulcers to limit caffeine.

Sources	mg caffeine
Coffee per 6-oz/175-mL cup	
Automatic percolated	72–144
Filter drip	108–180
Instant regular	60–90
Instant decaffeinated	< 6.0
Espresso 3.5 oz/95 mL	212[10]
Tea per 6-oz/175-mL cup	
Weak	18–24
Strong	78–108
Soft drinks per 12-oz/375-mL can	
cola-type	28–64
Cocoa products	
Dark chocolate bar, 2 oz/60 g	40–50
Milk chocolate bar, 2 oz/60 g	3–20
Chocolate milk, 8 oz/250 mL	2–8
Hot cocoa, 6 oz/175 mL	6–30

Photo:
Chicken with Preserved Lemons, Olives, and Coriander (page 118)

[9] Health and Welfare Canada, "Food Guide Facts: Background for Educators and Communicators," 1992.
[10] USDA Nutrient Database for Standard Reference, Released 2002.

Lighthearted Ideas for Cutting Back on Caffeine
- Choose decaffeinated cola or opt for ginger ale and other clear sodas.
- Try herbal teas.
- Choose the smallest size cup available when buying beverages containing caffeine.
- Start your day with a coffee, but try fruit juice or water at coffee breaks.
- Wean yourself off a high caffeine intake by mixing regular coffee with increasing amounts of decaffeinated coffee.

The Bottom Line on Caffeine

Relax and enjoy up to four 6-oz/175-mL cups total a day of coffee, tea, or hot cocoa.

Lighthearted Choices Start in Your Cart

Your heart-healthy action plan can't begin without giving attention to some strategies for the grocery store. Take stock of what you've got on hand in your pantry, freezer, and refrigerator. Make a list—it will help keep you on track when you're faced with those cute chocolate cupcakes with squiggles of white icing on them or the artery-clogging hors d'oeuvres selection that is calling to you to take it home.

This doesn't mean you can't have some treats once in a while. Heart-healthy eating is an overall pattern, not a diet of deprivation. But if you don't have things like cakes, cookies, and chips in the house, you're less likely to indulge in them on a regular basis.

Lighthearted Ideas for Healthier Shopping Trips
- Fill your cart mostly with food from the outer aisles or perimeter of the store. That's where the produce and less processed foods are.
- Push your cart through the chip and pop aisle quickly to get your heart rate up. Don't stop. Better still, skip that aisle altogether.
- If family members tend to throw less healthy choices into the cart, leave these shoppers at home if you can. Remember—if it's not in the house, you won't be tempted to eat it.
- Try foods that are unfamiliar to you—remember to sample from the wide variety of foods available. Find a recipe in this book that uses something you don't usually cook with. Then take some home and try it out.
- Take a supermarket tour. Local public-health departments and some individual grocery stores offer these tours.
- Don't shop when you're hungry.
- Work from a list of healthy meals you've planned to serve that week. This way, you'll have the ingredients ready.

Photo:
Roasted Red Pepper, Chevre, and Arugula Salad (page 93)

- Take the time to read labels the first time you are buying a product.
- Look for the Health Check™ logo to help you make healthy choices. (See page 31 for more information.)
- As a rule, the more processed or prepared the food, the fewer the nutrients and the more fat, salt, sodium, or sugar it contains. Read the labels to find out what is in the food and how much nutrition it actually contains.

What about Organic and Natural Foods?

Today's grocery store shelves are filling up with more and more organic and natural foods and food products every year. Organic food is not new, but having a variety of organic food choices available to you is.

Many people think that the term "organic" only means "pesticide-free." While it's true that organic standards don't allow farmers to use synthetic fertilizers and pesticides, organic actually means something more. "Organic" refers to a system of producing fruits, vegetables, grains, and other foods so that the nutrients in the soil aren't destroyed. It also means that animals are treated ethically and without antibiotics and hormones. Livestock must be raised organically and be fed 100% organic feeds in order to qualify for certification.[11]

Right now in Canada, there is no national regulation of organic labeling. Instead, there are a number of groups, such as the Organic Crop Improvement Association, which decide whether or not a food or food product can be called organic. Each of these groups has its own standards that are based on the National Standard of Canada for Organic Agriculture that was approved in 1999.

To be sure that what you are paying for is really organic, look for an organic certification logo, which can be found on the product, the package, or, for fresh fruits and vegetables, on the display signs. Depending on the group that certified the food, labels may read Certified Organic, Verified Organic, or Demeter. Foods labeled "organic" must contain at least 95% organic ingredients. Foods labeled as "containing organic ingredients" must have at least 70% organic ingredients. This means, therefore, that these foods may have some non-organic ingredients.

Many people prefer to buy and eat organic foods for ethical reasons, or because they believe the food tastes better. Keep in mind, though, that just because a food is organic doesn't necessarily mean that it really is better for you—nutritionally speaking, there are no significant differences between organic and non-organically produced foods. How you store and cook foods can have a greater impact on how nutritious

[11] OMAFRA Fact Sheet, "Organic Farming in Ontario," June 2001.

they are than the methods of cultivation. For example, vegetables that have been stored too long or have been boiled in too much water will lose nutrients whether or not they're organic.

When it comes to heart health, eating lots of fruits and vegetables, whole grains, beans, and legumes is what's important—not whether they are organic or traditionally grown. Buying organic or not is a decision that you can make according to your budget, beliefs, and tastes.

Lighthearted Information for Using Organic and Natural Foods

- Look for an organic certification logo on the produce signs or on the products that you buy.
- Buy from farm stands and growers that you know. If you're not sure if something is organic, ask the grower about it.
- Wash all produce well before eating, whether it's organic or traditionally grown.
- Don't feel that you must buy organic food products—they are more expensive and may not be significantly different from the regular version as far as the nutritional value is concerned. Read labels and compare.

Details, Details . . . Nutrition Labels

In the past, finding and making sense of nutrition information labels was often a difficult and discouraging task. The information was rarely comparable from brand to brand of the same product. Sometimes, there wasn't any labeling at all! Canada is phasing in a new Nutrition Facts table that will look the same on most food products. By 2005 most products will have the new Nutrition Facts table.

The purpose of the new label is to make it easier for you to decide whether a food or food product is a healthy choice. Calories and thirteen other nutrients such as saturated fat, trans fat, fiber, sodium, and cholesterol will be listed. You will be able to compare the amount of fat and trans fat per serving in similar products and then choose the one with the lowest saturated and trans fat. The % Daily Value shows you whether there is a lot or a little of a specific nutrient such as fiber in a serving of that particular food. So if the % Daily Value for fiber on one cereal is 15% and 5% on another, you'll know that the one with the higher value is a better choice. This is all good information to have at hand when choosing heart-healthy foods.

The new labeling will also include health claims and messages about diet and your health (see Appendix C, page 256) that will help guide your choices.

Nutrition Facts	
Per 125 mL (87 g)	
Amount	**% DV***
Calories 80	
Fat 0.5 g	1 %
Saturated 0 g + Trans 0 g	0 %
Cholesterol 0 mg	
Sodium 0 mg	0 %
Carbohydrate 18 g	6 %
Fibre 2 g	8 %
Sugars 2 g	
Protein 3 g	
Vitamin A	2 %
Vitamin C	10 %
Calcium	0 %
Iron	2 %
* DV = Daily Value	

Lighthearted Ideas for Using Nutrition Labels

When you read the nutrition information on the label, you will find % Daily Value for fat, saturated fat, trans fatty acids, carbohydrate, fiber, sodium, and potassium. The Daily Values are based on the calculations you see below for a healthy 2,000-calorie diet. For such a diet, the recommended 30% of calories from fat equals 65 g of fat. The amount of fat in the food in the package will be expressed both in the number of grams and the percentage of 65 g. This helps you know whether the food has a lot or a little of the specific nutrient.

Nutrient	Daily Amount Recommended (Daily Value) for a Healthy 2,000-Calorie Diet
Total fat	65 g
Sum of saturated fat and trans fats	20 g
Carbohydrate	300 g
Dietary Fiber	25 g
Sodium	2400 mg
Potassium	3500 mg

- Check to see whether the serving size of the food is a snack or a complete meal and whether it is the amount you will be eating.
- See how the amount of the nutrient, e.g. fat, in the serving compares with your ideal daily intake (whether you are eating a 2,000-calorie diet or one smaller or larger)
- In the case of nutrients such as fat, decide whether you will still be able to have some fat in other foods and stay within your daily goal if you eat that food.
- Look for starchy foods such as breakfast cereals that have at least 4 g of fiber per serving.
- Think about where the food fits in to your Lighthearted Action Plan.

Details, Details . . . Ingredient Listing on the Label

The list of ingredients on food packages is also a useful tool for making healthy choices. Food manufacturers must list all ingredients in a product, beginning with the ingredient used the most. So if a label lists whole-wheat flour as the first ingredient, then you know that the product contains more whole-wheat flour than any other ingredient.

- Fats can be listed as fat, lard, shortening, oils (palm, coconut, vegetable, hydrogenated), monoglycerides, diglycerides, glycerol, esters, or tallow.
- Sugars can be listed as sugar, honey, molasses, anything that ends in *-ose* (dextrose, sucrose, fructose, maltose, lactose), sorbitol, mannitol, dextrin, maltodextrin, honey, molasses, sweeteners, or syrups. Foods labeled "no sugar added" or "unsweetened" may still contain large amounts of natural sugar.
- Salts can be listed as salt, MSG, sodium, sodium benzoate, disodium phosphate, baking soda, baking powder, brine, kelp, or soy sauce.

Details, Details . . . the Health Check™ Program

As well as reading labels, the Heart and Stroke Foundation of Canada's Health Check food information program makes it easy to make healthy choices. The Health Check program is based on *Canada's Food Guide to Healthy Eating,* and the logo tells you the food is part of a healthy diet. Along with the logo, there is a Nutrient Facts table and a message that explains in more detail why the product is part of a healthy diet. You will see more and more products sporting the simple Health Check logo as the program expands.

Keep in mind that foods not carrying the Health Check logo may still be healthy choices. By reading the nutrition information on the label, you'll know whether it belongs in your shopping cart. For more information on the Health Check program, visit www.healthcheck.org or contact your local Heart and Stroke Foundation office.

Look for the Health Check™ symbol.

Create a Lighthearted Pantry

A well-stocked supply means less hassle when mealtime rolls around. Having a few pantry recipes put to memory (or flagged in this book) is a timesaver.

While you'll likely have certain things on the list below—maybe you're into Thai food and can't live without your fish sauce, or maybe you love Italian and have to have fifteen different shapes of pasta—here are the basics. Use this chart as a guideline and add or remove foods to adapt it to suit your family's tastebuds.

[12] From "Healthy Eating"—Nutrition Labelling Fact Sheet, Heart and Stroke Foundation of Canada.

The Bottom Line on Healthy Shopping

Read labels and ingredient listings to make sure you know what you're really getting. Compare different foods and different brands of similar foods to find the one that fits your healthy-eating plan. Be serving-size savvy. The nutrition numbers may look great—but only if you eat the serving size listed. Buy foods in the most unprocessed state possible.

™HEART AND STROKE FOUNDATION

Food Group	Cupboard	Fridge	Freezer
Grain Products	Dried pasta (regular and whole wheat); rice (white and brown); couscous; oatmeal; pancake mix (oat bran or whole wheat); whole-grain cold cereals; assorted grains such as barley, kasha, millet; rice cakes; fig bars; dried Asian noodles; baked tortilla chips; unsalted pretzels; breadcrumbs; low-fat crackers such as melba toast	Wheat germ; whole or ground flaxseed	Pizza dough; tortillas; whole-grain bread; bagels; English muffins; pita bread
Vegetables and Fruits	Assorted dried fruit; 100% fruit and vegetable juices; pasta sauces (tomato-based); canned: corn and tomatoes; canned fruit in own juice; tomato paste; salsa; potatoes; sweet potatoes; onions; winter squash; garlic; shallots	Carrots, celery and cabbage; fresh vegetables in season such as asparagus, zucchini, peppers, green beans; baby carrots; leafy greens such as kale, mustard, and collard greens; bagged salad greens; assorted fruit such as apples, pears, and others such as peaches, strawberries in season; oranges and lemons	Unsweetened fruit juice concentrates; frozen plain fruits and vegetables and vegetable blends
Milk Products	Skim-milk powder; evaporated milk	Low-fat milk; low-fat yogurt (plain and flavored); cheese; light sour cream; calcium-fortified soy milk	Frozen yogurt, sorbet or sherbet; lower-fat ice cream
Meat and Alternatives	Canned fish (salmon, tuna, clams); dried peas, beans, lentils; variety of canned beans such as kidney, chickpeas, pinto, black and lentils; peanut and other nut butters	Eggs, tofu, nuts, lean cold cuts such as smoked turkey, pastrami, roast beef, and Black Forest ham	Frozen unbreaded fish fillets such as salmon; lean ground beef; skinless chicken and/or turkey breasts; frozen shrimp
Other Foods	Canola, olive, or other vegetable oil; canned or cubed stock; vinegars; dry herbs and spices; low-sodium soy sauce; trail mix for snacks; canned soups (preferably low-fat, low-sodium); jams and honey; meringue cookies	Soft, non-hydrogenated margarine; ketchup, mustard, and other condiments; light salad dressings; homemade salad dressings; fresh herbs; gingerroot	Angel food cake

Pantry-Friendly Meals

Here is a list of meals that can be made with ordinary pantry ingredients:

- Stir-Fry for One (page 121)
- Fettuccine with Pesto Sauce (page 164)
- Linguine with Salmon and Chives (page 166)
- Fish Fillets with Basil and Lemon (page 125)
- Fish Fillets with Herbed Crumbs (page 124)
- Barbecued Lemon Chicken (page 117)
- Herb-Breaded Chicken (page 120)
- Mexican Rice and Bean Casserole (page 176)
- Grilled Turkey Scallopini with Herbs and Garlic (page 122)
- Stir-Fried Chicken with Broccoli (page 115)

On that note, let's look at Lighthearted Action Plans to feed all ages, all the time.

CREATING YOUR LIGHTHEARTED ACTION PLAN

As you have learned, eating in a heart-healthy way is basically the same thing as healthy eating, and *Canada's Food Guide* is the best base to build on. While it's never too late to start, following heart-healthy eating habits from childhood is ideal. Besides being active, eating well is the best thing you can do to help protect yourself against disease and to enjoy a lifetime of great-tasting, good-for-you food.

Lighthearted Action Plans for All Ages

Heart-healthy eating generally means the same thing whether you're 8 or 80—namely, the *Food Guide* goals of cutting back on fat and eating more fruits, vegetables, whole grains, and legumes. But each stage of life brings with it a special set of nutritional and healthy-eating needs. These are briefly outlined below.

Nutritional Needs of Young Children (1–5)

Meeting young children's energy needs for growth, development, learning, and activity is a priority. This is also the time to introduce new and exciting tastes, textures, and colors. Helping children learn to follow a healthy eating pattern and to make nutritious food choices is important.

A smaller and often sporadic appetite is common in toddlers and preschoolers.[13] Generally speaking, children will adjust their food intake over the course of several meals or days and will meet their overall needs. Their appetites do best with small meals and nutritious snacks throughout the day. How much food children need will vary with how quickly they are growing, their body size, and their level of activity.

For children over 2, offer child-size servings around the lower end of the range for each of the food groups every day. Occasional skipped meals or food jags, when your child will eat only a few different things, are normal and shouldn't be a cause for concern. If these behaviors persist, however, you may want to talk with your family physician. He or she will be able to tell you if your child is growing at an acceptable rate.

Toddlers and preschoolers can eat foods that the family is eating, just in smaller portions or in a plainer form if necessary. Along with carbohydrate foods, small servings of higher-fat choices such as peanut butter and cheese can help young children meet their energy needs.

LIGHTHEARTED STRATEGIES FOR YOUNG CHILDREN

- Aim to make mealtimes as stress-free and pleasant as possible.[14] Provide child-size plates and cups, eating utensils with short, broad, solid handles, and forks with blunt tines. Seat your child at the table for meals and snacks—just like the older kids and grownups. Try not to rush through meals. Let your child have enough time to finish meals and snacks.
- Have a routine of planned meals and snacks. Make sure there is enough time in between for them to get hungry again.
- Start young children off with small portions. Let them know that they can have more if they want it. A rule of thumb for portions is 1 tbsp/15 mL per year of age.
- Serve foods that are easy to handle, such as meat, vegetables, bread, and cheese in strips or finger sandwiches.
- Avoid foods that may cause choking. This includes large pieces of fruits, chips, chunks of meat, round or hard candy, raw carrots and celery, nuts and seeds, raisins, marshmallows, and popcorn.
- Prepare foods that could be a choking hazard carefully. For example:
  - Cut hot dogs into lengthwise pieces instead of rounds.
  - Cut grapes or cherries into small pieces.

[13] Ball, G. et al., *Manual of Clinical Dietetics*, 6th ed. (Dietitians of Canada, American Dietetic Association co-publication, 2000).

[14] Tips adapted from information found in Chapter 4: "Toddlers and Preschool Children," in ibid.

- Spread peanut butter thinly.
- Cook or mash carrots and corn.
- Offer a variety of nutritious foods and allow your child to choose what and how much he or she eats. Let your child decide when he or she has had enough.
- Serve foods separately or plain when possible. Casseroles and sauces are not popular with this age group.
- Introduce healthy choices from an early age. Try serving new foods or a food they didn't like the first time around with a familiar food. Don't pressure them to eat the new food. Respect their preferences. It may take up to seven tries before a child decides to like a new food.
- Make water the beverage of choice between meals. Juices, fruit drinks, and even milk can fill them up. Drinking a lot of fruit juice and fruit drinks can provide a lot of extra calories and possibly unwanted pounds.
- Let the kids help decide what foods and meals to serve and participate in growing foods, food shopping, and preparation. If they are involved, they'll be more interested in eating what they've "created."
- Don't use food as a reward or punishment. Doing so may encourage an unhealthy relationship with food in your child.

Lighthearted Goals for Young Children

1. Preschoolers should have 2 cups/500 mL of vitamin D-fortified milk every day (2 or 3 servings). Serve it as a drink, on cereal or fruits, or in puddings and soups made with milk.
2. Higher-fat foods such as whole milk should *gradually* be replaced with lower-fat choices such as 2% milk after age 2.
3. Variety and enjoying many new nutritious food choices should be a focus.

Nutritional Needs of School-Age Children (6–12)

As with younger children, school-agers need different amounts of calories and fat, depending on how quickly they are growing and their activity level. Kids should understand that we need to eat some fat to be healthy but should be steered toward lower-fat food choices more often. This helps to set a life-long pattern of healthy eating.

The Heart and Stroke Foundation's Annual Report Card on Canadians' Health for 2001 found that the majority of the kids surveyed knew that eating lots of fruits and vegetables and getting exercise are good for the heart.[15] Unfortunately, the report also found that kids ages 9 to 12 are not eating nearly enough fruits and vegetables. Close to half of this group is not getting enough regular exercise, and that can lead to obesity and put them in the fast lane for developing heart disease.

As a general rule, if you let your children eat a variety of foods from each of the food groups according to their appetites, they will get the nutrients they need. That means having lots of healthy snacks on hand 24/7!

[15] Media Release, February 5, 2002, "Report Cards on Health—Tweens Could Be Headed for Trouble, Says Heart and Stroke Foundation's Annual Report Card," Heart and Stroke Foundation of Canada web site at ww2.heartandstroke.ca/.

Lighthearted Goals for School-Age Children

1. Replace some higher-fat foods with lower-fat choices. Introduce children to 1% milk, leaner meats, fish, poultry, and foods prepared with less fat to help set a life-long pattern of healthy eating.
2. Focus on helping them choose a variety of nutritious foods they like to eat.
3. Include up to three nutritious snacks a day for energy.
4. Encourage daily activity.

LIGHTHEARTED STRATEGIES FOR SCHOOL-AGE CHILDREN

- Freeze fruits such as bananas, grapes, and orange slices to make them more fun to eat. Next time your kids want a sweet snack, offer them frozen fruits instead of ice cream.
- Substitute lower-fat foods for higher-fat ones. Begin serving skim or 1% milk instead of whole milk; lean meats, chicken, and fish instead of ribs and other fattier meats; and frozen yogurt instead of ice cream.
- Mix and match lunches. Have your kids write down foods that they like to eat from each food group. Keep this list handy when you're making lunches. Choose one item from each food group, and you've got a well-balanced lunch that (hopefully) they'll eat.
- Have a loaf of fresh whole-wheat bread or buns on the kitchen counter for snacks, or choose whole-wheat pita breads or tortilla rounds for lunches and snacks.
- Make sure that the day starts with a healthy breakfast and pack healthy snacks for recess.

Nutritional Needs of Teens

As with children, not all teens need the same amount of calories and other nutrients. This will depend upon many things, including their activity level and their stage of maturation. In general, girls have higher needs for calories from food in their early teens, from ages 11 to 14, while boys need a lot of calories from about ages 15 to 18.

By the time they've reached this stage in their lives, teens of both genders should be choosing some lower-fat food options while ensuring that they are getting enough energy for growth and activity. Their diets should be in keeping with the overall lighthearted goals of choosing lower-fat food items more often, limiting their intake of foods that contain saturated and trans fat, and ensuring that they get enough fiber. Generally speaking, this means no more than 30% of calories from fat, no more than 10% of calories from saturated and trans fat combined, 25 to 30 g of fiber, and no more than 2,500 to 3,000 mg of sodium per day. However, as you saw in the Tool Kit section, researchers and health professionals are becoming more flexible by using new recommended ranges for nutrients according to the needs of the individual.

The teenage years (and up to about age 30) are also the most important years for bone growth and the deposit of calcium. According to the new RDAs, both males and females ages 9 to 18 require 1,300 mg of calcium every day.[16] By having 3 or 4 servings of Milk Products every day,

[16] National Academy of Sciences, Dietary Reference Intakes for Individuals, Vitamins, 2001.

calcium needs are covered. If your teens are vegan, lactose intolerant, or do not like milk, it will be especially important to help them find ways to meet their calcium needs (see page 58).

Iron needs are also higher for rapidly growing bodies. This is especially true for girls as they start experiencing iron loss through menstruation. The RDA for girls ages 14 to 18 years is 15 mg per day, increasing to 18 mg per day for young women ages 19 to 30 (see page 60).[17]

LIGHTHEARTED STRATEGIES FOR TEENS

- Focus on keeping your teen's total diet or overall eating pattern healthy.
- Agree on regular meals.
- Keep a variety of individually packaged nutritious meals such as Split Pea, Bean, and Barley Soup (page 85), Vegetable Lasagna (page 167), and Szechuan Orange-Ginger Chicken (page 114) in the fridge and/or freezer.
- Decide which high-fat, high-calorie snacks you will have in the house.
- Have healthier snack alternatives always available: fresh fruits, lower-fat yogurt, and pudding in single-serving cups; baked munchies such as baked tortillas or pretzels; lower-fat cheese and crackers; homemade cookies and trail mix; munch-ready veggies and low-fat dip; lower-fat milk; 100% fruit juices; air-popped or low-fat microwave popcorn; or plain nuts.
- If your teens don't like milk, try calcium-fortified soy milk, chocolate milk, puddings made with low-fat milk, yogurt, veggie dips made with yogurt cheese (yogurt drained in a sieve lined with cheesecloth for a few hours), or silken tofu.

IF YOUR TEENS ARE VEGETARIAN

Depending on which type of vegetarian diet your teens have chosen, there are five nutrients that they need to get enough of: protein, calcium, vitamin D, iron, and vitamin B12.

- Protein: Substitute vegetable sources of protein for meats. Try legumes (kidney beans, chickpeas, lentils), tempeh, soy milk, nuts, peanut butter, tahini, soy dogs, or veggie burgers.
- Calcium: Find alternative sources of calcium if they don't consume Milk Products. Try calcium-fortified soy or rice beverages, tofu made with calcium carbonate, or calcium-fortified fruit juices. Other foods

---

[17] National Academy of Sciences, Dietary Reference Intakes for Individuals, Vitamins, 2001.

Lighthearted Goals for Teens

1. Go easy on soft drinks, fried foods, and sweets.
2. Balance higher-fat choices with heart-healthy ones.
3. Be active every day.

Tell Your Teens to Hold the Guacamole!

Tacos are a favorite of many teens, and they can be a healthier choice if the toppings are chosen wisely. Instead of using bottled taco sauce, make some by adding chopped fresh hot peppers or hot pepper sauce and dried hot pepper flakes to homemade tomato sauce. Alternatively, to keep the salt at a minimum, use Tomato Salsa Sauce, page 129, and add hot chili paste to taste or a chopped jalapeño pepper.

Keep the fat in tacos down by avoiding high-fat toppings. Avocado, or guacamole, is a popular taco topping, but avocado is extremely high in fat: 1 raw avocado has about 30 g of fat, nearly half the daily requirement of a small female.

Compare	g fat	g saturated fat	mg sodium	calories
Mexican Beef Tacos [page 144] (2 tacos)	13	5	223	318
Mexican Beef Tacos or Tostadas with avocado, olives, Cheddar cheese toppings (2 tacos)	20	7	369	383

such as broccoli, kale, almonds, and sesame seeds also contain some calcium, but it isn't absorbed as well by the body. For food sources of calcium and iron, see pages 58 to 60.

- Iron: Alternative sources of iron should also be a focus. Try beans, dried fruits, fortified cereals and pastas, hot cereals such as cream of wheat, wheat germ, and eggs.
- Vitamin B12: Use fortified soy or rice beverages that have Vitamin B12 added.
- If your teens have just started a vegetarian diet or you are concerned about a dietary shortage of nutrients or variety, visit a registered dietitian, who can help plan a balanced vegetarian diet.

Nutritional Needs of Adults

By adulthood, metabolism is slowing down, and the demands of a hectic career and children to raise often coincide with a lot less energy! Maybe weight is creeping up and lunch is coming from the fast-food court too often. Or maybe cholesterol is climbing or you've already had a heart attack.

The core messages of the Lighthearted Tool Kit all apply to this population segment: eating a variety of foods, including lots of fruits and vegetables, cutting back on fat and saturated fat, increasing fiber and going easy on salt, caffeine, and alcohol will all help hearts to be healthier. If you have children, it's important to set a good example for them to follow. If you don't, it's still important to look after your health.

Compare the difference when you make healthy choices for lunch:

Healthy Lunch	g fat	g saturated fat	Calories
Spinach Salad with Sesame Seed Dressing (page 101)	7	1	89
Pasta (1 cup/250 mL) with spaghetti sauce (½ cup/125 ml) and grated Parmesan cheese (1 tbsp/15 mL)	6	2	297
Rhubarb-Strawberry Sorbet (½ cup/125 mL) (page 246)	trace	trace	113
Total (23% of calories from fat)	13	3	499
Less Healthy Lunch			
Cream of chicken soup (1 cup/250 mL)	12	5	192
Mexican beef taco (1)	20	7	383
Chocolate pudding (½ cup/125 mL)	2	1	133
Total (43% of calories from fat)	34	13	708

LIGHTHEARTED STRATEGIES FOR ADULTS

- Keep a food diary, even if it's just for a few days, to see how well you're doing on the diet front. Are you diving into the chips too many nights a week? Skipping breakfast? Eating a lot of processed baked goods such as cookies and cakes? A little low on the fruits and veggies? Writing things down will help you see where you can improve. Or if you'd prefer, make a Food Group chart and simply tick off the number of servings you have from each group every day for a couple of weeks. Either way, you'll get a good idea of what you're really eating and whether or not you're meeting your food goals.

- If you're feeling a little tight around the belt, measure out your portions for a couple of days to see if they are the size recommended by *Canada's Food Guide to Healthy Eating*. If they're not, it may be time for a readjustment.

- If your clothes still fit, but you're not sure if you're in the healthy body weight range or not, check your BMI. This is a height-to-weight ratio that will tell you if you're within a healthy weight range (see ww2.heartandstroke.ca/page.asp?pageID=1187).

- If you've become a couch potato, add more activity to your daily schedule. Use the stairs instead of the elevator. Walk to work if you

Lighthearted Goals for Adults

1. Activate a plan to achieve a healthy body weight.
2. Cut back on fat, saturated and trans fat, sodium, alcohol, and caffeine.
3. Eat a variety of fruits, vegetables, whole grains and legumes for fiber, vitamins, and antioxidants.
4. Add new foods such as soy and flaxseed to your menu.

Lighthearted Goals for Older Adults

1. Don't eat the same things every day. Go for a variety of foods from each of the four food groups.
2. Focus on whole grains, fruits, vegetables, and legumes for fiber.
3. Be fluid savvy—replace tea and coffee with milk, water, or fruit and vegetable juices.
4. Pay attention to your intake of Vitamin D, calcium, and Vitamin B12.
5. Have frequent small meals and nutritious snacks.
6. Exercise regularly and include strengthening exercises (see pages 57 to 58).

can. Park the car at the far end of the parking lot. Go for a hike with the kids. And the dog is always up for another walk. (See pages 57 to 60 to find out more.)

Nutritional Needs of Older Adults

The Heart and Stroke Foundation's nutritional recommendations are particularly important for older adults, generally those 65 and up, whose energy or calorie needs are often less, but whose nutrient needs are not. This means that the foods older people eat should be high in nutrients, or nutrient-dense. Foods such as milk products, nuts and seeds, lean meat, poultry, fish, eggs, vegetables, fruits, and whole-grain breads are good choices.

Changes in metabolism and in the body's ability to digest and absorb some foods due to aging mean that older adults are often at a greater risk of nutrient deficiency. In addition, some medical conditions and medications may require you to avoid certain foods. Pay special attention to your intake of vitamin D, calcium, and vitamin B12.

You can get vitamin D from fortified milk, margarine, and exposure to the sun. A deficiency is a real possibility if you stay indoors a great deal during the summer or in the winter in Canada. Calcium requirements remain at 1,200 mg every day. That's 2 to 4 daily servings of Milk Products in order to protect yourself from bone loss and the accompanying complications of osteoporosis. (Vitamin D is also necessary for strong bones.) Vitamin B12 from food is not absorbed as well by aging bodies. It is found in red meat, salmon, and in Milk Products and fortified beverages in small amounts. If none of the foods mentioned here are part of your usual diet, discuss alternative sources of these essential nutrients with your doctor or a dietitian.

LIGHTHEARTED STRATEGIES FOR OLDER ADULTS

- Choose a variety of foods from each food group every day to make sure you get all of the nutrients you need. Be aware that fatigue and apathy can be the result of poor nutrition, especially too little protein and iron. Not drinking enough fluids can also make you feel tired.
- Emphasize complex carbohydrates and fiber-rich foods such as fruits, vegetables, and whole-grain breads and cereals.
- Choose many different beverages throughout the day such as fruit and vegetable juices, milk, and water. Relying on tea, coffee, or cola for hydration is not a good idea, as they have a mild diuretic effect, so they make you lose some water.

The New Lighthearted Cookbook

Compare the difference when you make healthy choices for dinner:

Healthy Dinner	g fat	g saturated fat	calories
Consommé with vegetables (¾ cup/175 mL)	trace	trace	25
Fish Fillets with Basil and Lemon (page 125)	5	1	130
White long-grain rice (½ cup/125 mL)	trace	trace	134
Asparagus (6 spears) with lemon juice and non-hydrogenated margarine (1 tsp/2 mL)	4	1	56
Strawberries (1 cup/250 mL)	1	trace	45
Total (23% of calories from fat)	10	2	390
Less Healthy Dinner			
Liver Pâté (1 oz/30 g)	8	3	90
Beef sirloin, broiled with lean and fat (8 oz/250 g)	33	13	565
Potato with butter (2 tbsp/25 mL)	8	5	196
Salad (1 cup/250 mL) with 2 tbsp/25 mL Thousand Island dressing	11	1	136
Cheesecake with strawberry sauce (1 tbsp/15 mL)	16	7	279
Totals (54% of calories from fat)	76	29	1266

- Try new foods and different ethnic dishes—just because you've been cooking for years doesn't mean there isn't anything new to try.
- Keep your cupboard or pantry stocked with cans of baked beans, legumes, tuna, and salmon as well as pasta, rice, and couscous for quick salads. Have yogurt, eggs, and cheese in your refrigerator and frozen meals in your freezer.
- Bake muffins, cookies, or quick breads and freeze individual servings for a quick snack, as part of a healthy breakfast, or a spur-of-the-moment social time.
- Keep whole-grain and bran hot and cold cereals on hand. A bowl of cereal topped with a sliced banana and some lower-fat milk makes a quick and easy snack.
- Some medications, either prescription or over-the-counter drugs and laxatives, can cause vitamin and mineral deficiencies. Consult your doctor about whether you need a vitamin-mineral supplement.
- Be aware of a possible loss of sensitivity to heat. Be careful with hot foods such as soup, as you could easily burn your tongue or mouth.

Lighthearted Choices All through the Day

You've learned about the basics and a variety of nutritional needs, you've shopped, you've read labels, you've stocked your pantry—now it's time to eat!

Breakfast

Some people are conditioned to eat breakfast, while others aren't. Dietitians suggest that breakfast can be the most important meal of the day. Why? Studies have shown that children who have had breakfast perform better in school than children who haven't. In addition, without breakfast, it is much more difficult for anyone to get a day's worth of nutrients. And finally, people who maintain an ideal weight usually eat breakfast; overweight people tend to skip breakfast. If you miss breakfast and have a bran muffin, yogurt, and orange at coffee break, you are eating nutritiously; if you have a Danish and coffee, you are adding extra fat and calories without vitamins or fiber.

This doesn't mean you should be wolfing down fried eggs and bacon, but you should have some fruits or vegetables, milk, yogurt, or low-fat cheese, soft-boiled or poached eggs, and whole-grain toast, muffins, or cereal. There's no need to limit your choice of breakfast foods. Dinner leftovers, a piece of pizza, fish, or salad can be as good in the morning as at night.

LIGHTHEARTED STRATEGIES FOR BREAKFAST

- Keep your cupboards and refrigerator supplied with a selection of whole-grain cereals and breads, fresh fruits, yogurt, milk, 100% fruit juices, eggs, and lean deli meats such as smoked turkey or ham. (Say no to the sugar-shock cereals, toaster strudels, and tarts.)
- Set the breakfast dishes, cereals, and breads out the night before. Cut up some fruit so that it's ready to roll. That way, when people stumble into the kitchen, it will be easy for them to grab a bowl and start munching.
- Go all out if you have time on the weekends. Break up the cereal and toast routine by starting the day with homemade pancakes or waffles topped with berries and toasted nuts. Or create a colorful, vegetable-studded omelet or frittata.
- Have ground flaxseed available for sprinkling on top of hot or cold cereals. Or keep a supply of toasted nuts or a jar of wheat bran handy for quick fiber fill-ups.

- Make it a rule that everyone starts the day with either a glass of 100% fruit juice or a piece of fruit.
- If your family likes hot cereal such as oatmeal or a whole-grain combination to warm their mornings, the first one up should start the water boiling.
- On the weekends (or whenever you have time), bake up a few batches of your favorite fruit and fiber muffins (see pages 212–218 for recipes). Freeze them for quick warming in the microwave—just wrap them in a paper towel and heat them for 30 seconds on high (100%) power.

Compare the difference when you make healthy choices for breakfast:

	g fat	g saturated fat	calories
Healthy Breakfast			
Orange (1)	trace	trace	62
1 large Shredded Wheat biscuit	1	0	88
Skim milk (1 cup/250 mL)	trace	trace	85
Total (4% of calories from fat)	1	trace	235
Less Healthy Breakfast			
Plain croissant	12	7	231
Fried eggs (2) with 2 slices bacon on the side	23	7	292
Coffee with 2 tbsp/25 mL 10% cream	3	2	41
Total (60% of calories from fat)	38	16	564

CONSIDER THE POSSIBILITIES

- Smoothies are always a good choice when they're made with low-fat milk, fruits, and yogurt. The variety is endless, and they're portable too! Just whirl milk or yogurt or tofu and fruit in the blender or food processor. Try soy milk in your smoothie for a change of pace.
- Ready-to-eat whole-grain cereal topped with a sliced banana and yogurt
- Bran muffin with yogurt topped with berries
- Peanut butter on whole-wheat toast, with milk
- Pizza slice and a glass of orange juice
- Toasted whole-wheat waffle topped with fruit and yogurt
- Bagel topped with sliced apples and cheese with a glass of milk
- Lean ham on a toasted English muffin with a glass of vegetable juice

- Hot quick oatmeal with milk and berries
- Scrambled eggs made in the microwave, whole-wheat toast, and a melon wedge
- Oat bran pancakes with maple syrup and yogurt with a glass of orange juice
- Whole-grain hot cereal with milk and a little bit of brown sugar or a drizzle of maple syrup, and a half a grapefruit

Snacks

Having nutritious snacks on hand throughout the day is a great way to keep your energy level up and give yourself staying power. Many experts are suggesting that five or six small meals a day are now the way to go instead of our usual three squares with a big session at night. Choose foods with lots of fiber and nutrients so that you'll feel full—because when you feel full, you're less likely to make a beeline for the chips or cookies. For small children who can't eat a lot at one sitting, snacking can help ensure that they get all the nutrients they need. Just remember, *Food Guide* rules still apply!

LIGHTHEARTED STRATEGIES FOR SNACKING
- Snacks that include carbohydrate, protein, and a little bit of fat take longer to digest and will satisfy your stomach. For example, whole-grain crackers and some cheese will supply energy over a longer period of time than a cookie, which will give you an energy boost but leave you flagging in no time.
- Fatigue is often one of the first signs of dehydration. When you're rushing through the day, it's easy to confuse thirst for hunger. Remember to get enough fluids and to include beverages such as water, lower-fat milk, and fruit juices when you stop to snack.
- Make it easy for everyone to snack well. Organize your kitchen so that the healthiest choices are the easiest to grab. Put the less nutritious snack foods, such as chips or cake, at the back of the cupboard or on a high shelf.
- If you're active, you may be interested in commercial energy products—both bars and drinks. If you choose to buy these, read the labels before you buy and choose ones that are higher in fiber and have added nutrients.

CONSIDER THE POSSIBILITIES
- Fruit and vegetable juice or milk
- A bowl of fresh fruit

- Raw vegetables, washed, cut, and ready to eat
- Whole-grain cereal with dried fruits and 1% milk
- Sandwich on whole-grain bread with cheese or lean meat, lettuce, and tomato
- Hard-boiled eggs
- Rice cakes and peanut butter
- Pretzels (preferably unsalted) and nuts
- Lower-fat cookies such as animal crackers, fig bars, and ginger snaps with a glass of lower-fat milk
- Bagels and breadsticks with lower-fat cream cheese
- Cooked soybeans or edamame (usually found in the frozen-food section of the supermarket)
- Baked tortilla chips with tomato salsa
- Bran or fruit muffins with a glass of soy milk
- Low-fat yogurt in individual cups, whole-grain crackers, and cheese
- Leftover vegetable pizza
- Air-popped popcorn sprinkled with a small amount of Parmesan cheese, herbs, spices, or other flavorings
- Trail mix (in small portions—it is higher in fat than other snacks)
- Granola Energy Squares (page 218), Buttermilk Apple Cake (page 223), or Whole-Wheat Zucchini Bread (page 227)

Compare Snack Foods Before You Choose

Snack Foods	g fat	mg sodium	calories
Popcorn, plain (1 cup/250 mL)	trace	0	30
Popcorn (1 cup/250 mL, 1 tsp/5 mL oil plus salt)	3	97	55
Popcorn, sugar-coated (1 cup/250 mL)	4	72	151
Mixed nuts, dry-roasted, unsalted (1/4 cup/60 mL)	18	4	203
Mixed nuts, oil-roasted plus salt (1/4 cup/60 mL)	20	231	219
Potato chips (10 chips/20 g)	7	107	108
Pretzels, hard, plain, salted (45) 29 g	0.5	345	112
Doughnut, yeast type	14	203	239
Chocolate-chip cookies (2)	5	66	101
Milk-chocolate bar (1 oz/30 g)	9	25	154
Ice cream, 10% b.f. (1/2 cup/125 mL)	7	53	133
Frozen fruit yogurt, 6.3% b.f. (1/2 cup/125 mL)	5	58	153
Fruit yogurt, 1.4% b.f. (1/2 cup/125 mL)	2	61	123
Apple	trace	0	82
Banana	trace	1	106

- Broccoli and Mushroom Dip (page 64) with whole-wheat pita triangles
- Multigrain Date Quickbread (page 230) with a glass of skim or 1% milk
- Peanut butter and banana sandwich
- Fruit smoothie made with lots of fruit and yogurt or soy milk
- Cheese on half a bagel
- Hummus dip and whole-wheat pita triangles
- Low-fat frozen yogurt topped with berries and toasted nuts
- Tortilla wraps—fill with chicken or tuna salad, vegetables, or beans
- Homemade Oatmeal-Apricot Cookies (page 220), apple slices, and a glass of milk or soy milk

Dinners for Families on the Run

Today every family has a busy schedule. Families with both parents working full-time jobs are particularly hard-pressed to find the time and energy to make meals. With the help of the quick and easy recipes in this book, you'll find it is not difficult to make a delicious and healthy meal for four in 30 minutes if you have the ingredients in the house. Here are some tips to make mealtimes a snap.

LIGHTHEARTED STRATEGIES FOR FAMILIES

- If getting a meal on the table is a problem, make meal-planning a family activity and divide up the jobs, from shopping to putting groceries away to prepping, cooking, and cleaning up. Younger family members can help plan meals that include their favorite foods (or maybe there are new foods that they'd like to try). They can set the table, peel carrots, wash lettuce—don't worry about the mess; they eventually get tidier. Older children can help do the cooking—even taking a turn making their favorite dinner once a week. This not only divides up the tasks, it means that your children are developing important cooking skills.
- Double whatever you make on Saturday and Sunday and eat it again during the week.
- Do a little meal preparation before you go out in the morning. For example, chop up meat and maybe a vegetable for a stir-fry, or get a chicken out of the freezer to thaw in the fridge; leave a note or make arrangements for someone else to put it in the oven at a certain time.
- Use your crockpot. Soups, stews, and other dishes that require long, slow cooking are perfect. Put it on to cook when you leave in the morning, and when you come in the door, it's ready and waiting.

- Make up freezer dinners. Take them out the night before you want to use them and defrost them in the fridge.

- Many of the recipes in this book are suitable for reheating or can be eaten cold throughout the week. Easy Oven Beef and Vegetable Stew (page 141); Split Pea, Bean and Barley Soup (page 85); Chunky Vegetable-Bean Soup (page 84); Mexican Rice and Bean Casserole (page 176); Beef and Pasta Casserole for a Crowd (page 158); Pasta and Fresh Vegetable Salad (page 154) can all be made ahead.
- Cook a number of vegetables and a large roast, chicken, or turkey on the weekend, then on Monday, have it cold and reheat the vegetables. On Tuesday, use the meat in a casserole or soup.
- Make a huge batch of All-Purpose Quick Spaghetti Sauce (page 168) and freeze it in 2- or 4-cup (500-mL or 1-L) containers. It's now ready to use as a base for chili, tacos, casseroles, and lasagna, as well as spaghetti.
- Have a supply of family favorites on hand in the freezer or refrigerator. Vegetable Lasagna (page 167), Family Favorite Shepherd's Pie (page 140), and All-Purpose Quick Spaghetti Sauce (page 168) can all be put into single servings for times when the family can't sit down together for a meal.
- Use nutritious convenience products and home meal-replacement foods. Read the labels so you know whether they're good choices.
    - Use frozen vegetable mixes in stir-fries or add to soups and stews.
    - Add fresh chopped vegetables such as mushrooms and green peppers to prepared spaghetti sauces and soups.
    - Canned fruits in their own juice or frozen yogurts are perfect for a fast dessert.
    - Have plain frozen fish fillets such as salmon on hand. They are quick and chock full of heart-healthy Omega-3 fats. Spread them with hoisin sauce, and grill, broil, or microwave them for a meal in minutes.
    - Buy bags of prepared salad mixes. Look for those that include darker lettuce such as romaine. Pick up a package of baby spinach as well and mix the two for extra nutrients. Add sliced fresh tomatoes and sprinkle with extra-virgin olive oil and wine or balsamic vinegar.
    - There are some varieties of frozen and boil-in-bag dinners that are nutritious and will do in a pinch. Look for those that have

less than 30% of total calories from fat and minimal trans fat—beware of the sauces. Boost fiber by pairing them with a slice of whole-wheat bread and bagged coleslaw or raw carrots, or start with a cup of split pea, lentil, or vegetable soup.

- In the summer, barbecue frozen veggie burger patties for a change.

PLANNING SPECIAL FAMILY MEALS

A few easy choices in everyday foods can make a big difference in the amount of fat, sodium, and calories in your family's diet. Compare the difference in the table below:

Sunday Night Chicken Dinner 1	g fat	g saturated fat	mg sodium	calories
Roast Chicken (no skin)	6	2	67	180
Cranberry sauce	trace	0	10	53
Baked potato	trace	trace	11	155
with sour cream and yogurt	1	1	24	27
Baked squash	1	trace	3	38
Steamed broccoli	trace	trace	6	7
Apple and Raspberry Crisp (page 232)	7	1	81	222
Totals (19% of calories from fat)	15	4	202	682
Sunday Night Chicken Dinner 2	g fat	g saturated fat	mg sodium	calories
Roast Chicken (with skin)	10	3	67	214
Gravy	2	trace	172	24
Mashed potatoes	trace	trace	5	90
with butter and milk	4	3	47	42
Baked squash	1	trace	3	38
Steamed broccoli	trace	trace	6	7
Apple pie	17	6	418	373
Totals (38% of calories from fat)	34	12	718	788

Check the Poultry and Vegetable sections in this cookbook for more lower-fat and lower-sodium choices when you're planning a special meal.

Dinners for One

Singles, students, older adults—anyone living alone at any age—can find it hard to prepare a full, nutritious meal when they are dining solo. There's no one to challenge choices such as tea and toast or an endless supply of toaster-tarts. It's easy to open the fridge and just start eating.

Living on cheese and crackers, scrambled eggs, sandwiches, soups, raw vegetables, and fruit can get boring. And if the food doesn't make it to a plate, it's easy to overeat and gain weight. Cooking for one doesn't have to be a big deal, and the same *Food Guide* applies no matter how many are dining. Just remember that you and your health are worth it!

LIGHTHEARTED STRATEGIES FOR ONE

- Shop at a store where you can buy small portions and not everything is prepackaged.
- When possible, buy only what you will use. It's more economical to buy a small amount and use it all than to buy a larger quantity and throw half away. Freeze leftovers when you can.
- When you can't buy a small portion of a vegetable, plan to use it. For example, use broccoli (or cauliflower) in a salad, soup, omelet, stir-fry, over pasta, with cheese, or simply boiled or steamed.
- The microwave oven is not just an advantage for speed, it means you don't have to warm up a large oven to cook or reheat a small portion. A toaster oven is also great for reheating small portions.
- If you eat out often at lunch, make it your main meal of the day. Have a light meal in the evening.
- There are more and more frozen meals on the market that are nutritious. Keep a couple of single servings on hand for nights when cooking isn't an option.
- Treat yourself to special foods often. Out-of-season vegetables or a pint of strawberries in winter aren't such an extravagance when you don't have to buy a large amount.
- Many of the recipes in this book are for four servings. You can easily halve them and either freeze one portion or refrigerate the leftovers and use them the next day. Or cook it all and pop three servings into the freezer. That way, there's no need to cook every night.
- If you're a senior, many communities have Meals-on-Wheels™ programs for those who have trouble shopping and preparing food for themselves.

CONSIDER THE POSSIBILITIES

- Stir-Fry for One (page 121) served over rice or noodles, a glass of milk, and some fruit for dessert.
- Sole with Tomatoes (page 126) served with sautéed zucchini and sliced red peppers, rice, and a slice of Buttermilk Apple Cake (page 223).

- Herb-Breaded Chicken (page 120) with a baked potato, broccoli, and some Berries with Orange-Honey Yogurt (page 234) for dessert.
- Split-pea soup with a pumpernickel roll, a glass of milk, and a fig bar.
- Mushroom and cheese omelet with mixed greens drizzled with low-fat vinaigrette. Bite into a fresh pear for dessert.
- Baked potato topped with a generous amount of broccoli and a small amount of shredded Cheddar or mozzarella cheese. Put it under the broiler for a few minutes until the cheese begins to melt.
- Chili or stew (with or without meat—replace meat with kidney beans, black beans, or chickpeas), a slice of crusty bread spread with a small amount of margarine, an apple, and a plain cookie for dessert.
- Develop a repertoire of quick, nutritious meals such as:
  - scrambled eggs made with milk or a ham and cheese omelet with whole-grain toast and raw carrots, a small amount of non-hydrogenated margarine, a glass of milk or water to drink, and a pear for dessert
  - any kind of pasta tossed with leftover vegetables
  - beef barley soup with grilled cheese, applesauce, and a plain cookie for dessert
  - a baked potato topped with a sprinkle of Cheddar cheese and some cooked broccoli
  - whole-grain bagel topped with melted Swiss cheese and an apple
  - poached fish fillet with lemon, frozen mixed vegetables and a slice of whole-wheat or oat bran bread
  - green salad topped with chopped baby carrots; cubes of cheese; slices of lean deli meat or canned salmon or tuna; legumes such as chickpeas; a delicious vinaigrette; and a pumpernickel roll with non-hydrogenated margarine

Lighthearted Choices in the Fast-Food Jungle

Grabbing a quick bite at lunch or on the way home from work or order-ing in a pizza is a part of today's lifestyle. Since these foods are often high in fat and sodium but adequate in protein, the other foods or meals you eat at home should be low in fat and high in vitamins and fiber. If your dieting daughter eats lunch at fast-food chains and often has a hamburger, she can balance it out with homemade soup, raw vegetables, bread, and an apple for dinner. And remember, no matter what the meal—if there's too much, save the leftovers for later.

Many fast-food chains now have nutrition information available at their outlets or on their web sites, so there's no reason not to know the best nutritional bets on the menu. Here are some suggestions for mak-ing a fast-food meal more nutritious.

Featured Fast Food	Choose	Instead of
Asian	• dim sum and steamed dumplings • fresh spring rolls • dishes with chicken, scallops, shrimp, beef, or pork with mixed vegetables • plain or steamed rice and noodles • light soy sauce • vegetarian items that aren't breaded or deep-fried • share wonton, egg drop, or hot-and-sour soup to cut back on the sodium • soy dishes such as tofu that are grilled	• deep-fried items such as chicken balls, egg rolls, and battered, deep-fried tofu • chicken, shrimp, or other deep-fried rice • avoid using lots of sodium-heavy soy sauce
Burgers	• broiled chicken sandwiches • plain or kid-sized burgers • grilled veggie burgers, veggie wraps, or other meatless alternative • a green salad with low-fat dressing • baked potato with low-fat sour cream and chives; be sure to eat the skin for extra vitamins and fiber • chili is offered by some chains and is a good choice for adding nutrients and fiber and cutting back on some calories	• fried or deep-fried chicken sandwiches • fries and their toppings • super-sizing; you'll just be getting that much more artery-clogging saturated and trans fat • milkshakes may sound healthy, but they really provide just a load of sugar, fat, and calories • dipping sauces for fries • double and triple-decker burgers • burgers with added cheese, bacon, fried onions, mayonnaise, and other sauces
Chicken	• barbecued, baked, or broiled with skin removed • plain green salad with lower-fat dressing • chicken soup • baked potato with low-fat sour cream • chicken wraps • whole-wheat roll or bun • skim or 1% milk • fresh fruit or fruit ices for dessert	• deep-fried chicken • French fries • specialty salads such as Caesar as they can contain large amounts of fat • coleslaw if prepared with mayonnaise • macaroni and potato salads • chicken pot pie • sauces, gravies • desserts such as pie and cheesecake
Greek	• cubed lamb or pork in pita bread with tomatoes and tzatziki sauce • choose whole-wheat pita bread if available • try tzatziki or hummus as an appetizer dip • share a Greek salad and go easy on the higher-fat, higher-sodium ingredients such as anchovies, olives, and feta cheese • grilled shish-kebab or plaki (broiled fish) • tabouli salad • plain fruit desserts	• baba ghanoush • deep-fried dishes such as falafel • pan-fried dishes such as saganaki (fried cheese) • vegetable pies such as spanakopita and tyropita • baklava (or at least share it!)

Featured Fast Food	Choose	Instead of
Pizza	• all-vegetable pizzas • whole-wheat or other whole-grain crust if available • a green salad or veggies and have two slices instead of three, four, or more • ham or chicken if you must have meat on it • make your own with ready-made pizza dough or pizza shells; top with a small amount of mozzarella and lots of vegetables	• meat toppings such as bacon, sausage and pepperoni • other higher-fat topping such as olives, anchovies and extra cheese • stuffed crusts • breadsticks with dipping sauce • Caesar salad • deep-dish pizza
Mexican	• soft tortillas • black bean soup, gazpacho • jiacama • tomato salsa • refried beans (no lard)—ask your server • burritos, enchiladas, tamales, fajitas • steamed vegetables • arroz con pollo (chicken with rice) • fruit for dessert, such as guava, papaya, or mango	• crispy-type fried tortillas or taco shells • sour cream and extra cheese • taco salad • tostadas, chiles rellenos, chimichangas • refried beans (in lard) • fried ice cream
Subs and Sandwiches	• whole-wheat or other whole-grain bun or roll • layer on the vegetables • leaner meats such as roast beef, chicken, or turkey • sandwiches that are specifically offered as low-fat • a small or half-size sandwich • flavor with mustard or a couple of hot peppers	• meatballs, salami, extra cheese, and other high-fat items • extra sauces, mayonnaise, dipping sauces • extra-large sandwiches

LIGHTHEARTED STRATEGIES FOR CHOOSING FAST FOOD

Choosing wisely at take-out and fast-food restaurants isn't easy, but there are some general tips that will help. In all cases, look for menu items or foods that are baked, broiled, steamed, or grilled instead of breaded, deep-fried, or fried in oil. Where possible, choose plain salads and go easy on the dressing. The "extras" such as dipping sauces, super-sized items, and stuffed pizza crusts offered by many food chains are just that—extra fat and extra calories *without* any extra nutrients. Skip the pop and go for low-fat milk, fruit juice, or water. And remember that you don't have to eat it all. If the portions are too big, share with a friend or save the leftovers for another meal.

Lighthearted Restaurant Choices

If you travel and eat out frequently, you are much more likely to have a high-fat diet than if you eat at home regularly. If you eat out only for special occasions or once a month, enjoy your meal and order what you want. Nutritious menu choices are more of an issue only if you eat out often. In a restaurant, you usually eat more than you would at home—and it's more high-fat foods such as desserts and not enough fruits and vegetables.

LIGHTHEARTED STRATEGIES FOR EATING OUT

- Choose a restaurant where you can make nutritious choices such as salads, soups, vegetables, and fruits. Some restaurants mark low-fat dishes on the menu.
- Have a glass of water as soon as you are seated in order to control your urge to eat, as well as to ensure that you get enough fluids.
- Avoid buffets and all-you-can-eat specials if you tend to overeat.
- Order salad dressings and sauces on the side and add only a small amount, or ask for low-fat dressings.
- If you eat the breads and rolls, pass on the butter. Don't fill up on crackers and pretzels.
- Avoid gravies and sauces made with cream and butter.
- Avoid fried, sautéed, and deep-fried foods; instead, choose broiled, poached, baked, roasted, or boiled dishes.
- Trim all visible fat from meat, and skin from poultry.
- Choose chicken, fish, or lean cuts of beef; avoid duck and goose.
- Choose a baked potato over French fries. Avoid butter and go easy on the sour cream, or choose yogurt instead. Ask for extra vegetables and small portions of meat.
- Don't feel you have to eat everything on your plate just because you are paying for it. Some restaurant portions are very large and can easily be shared. Many restaurants will parcel up the leftovers and let you take them home.
- Avoid non-dairy creamer, which is high in saturated fat; for coffee or tea, choose milk instead.
- If a restaurant or hotel room-service menu doesn't offer many healthy choices, make a special request. Often they will make a special order. If enough people ask for nutritious dishes, they might change their menus.
- In Chinese restaurants, ask for dishes without MSG in order to reduce your sodium intake. Choose steamed dishes rather than ones that are deep-fried.
- Order an appetizer as your main dish.

- If you have dessert, order fresh fruits or sherbet. Avoid pastries and whipped-cream desserts.
- Share rich desserts with a friend and cut the calories in half!

Although there is no guarantee that you're getting a low-fat menu item, there are some common terms that may give you some clues.[18]

Menu Clues: Less Fat
baked, barbecued, braised, broiled, grilled, lean, poached, roasted, steamed, stir-fried.

Menu Clues: More Fat
au gratin or in cheese sauce, batter-fried, Béarnaise, beurre blanc, breaded, buttered, creamed, crispy, deep-fried, double crust, en croûte, French-fried, Hollandaise, pan-fried, pastry, prime, rich, sautéed, scalloped (escalloped), with gravy, with mayonnaise, with thick sauce.

Lighthearted Eating Made Easy

Daily Meal Plans
Here are some appealing, healthy meals ready for you to try. Each menu provides about 2,000 calories or less and will meet your food goals with a minimum of fat and saturated fat as well as plenty of fiber. Choose from four different daily plans: Menu for Busy Families, Make-Ahead Menu, Meatless Menu, and Meals-on-the-Run.

Fast and Fabulous: Menu for Busy Families

Meal	Menu	g fat	g fiber	calories
Breakfast	• Quick hot cereal with 2 tbsp raisins and 1% milk	3	4	224
	• 100% fruit juice (½ cup/125 mL)	trace	trace	54
	• Whole-grain toast with small amount of margarine, jam	5	2	121
Lunch	• Low-fat submarine sandwich with smoked turkey, tomatoes, lettuce on a whole-wheat bun + 1 tsp/5 mL reduced fat	2	4	153
	mayonnaise	2	0	15
	• Mixed bean salad	4	4	90
	• 1% milk (1 cup/250 mL)	3	0	102
	• Apple	trace	3	82
	• Easy Cranberry-Chocolate Cookie (1) (page 221)	5	1	97

[18] Roberta Larson Duyff, *The American Dietetic Association's Complete Food and Nutrition Guide,* (American Dietetic Association, 1996).

The New Lighthearted Cookbook

Fast and Fabulous: Menu for Busy Families (*continued*)

Meal	Menu	g fat	g fiber	calories
Dinner	• Take-out chicken without the skin	2	0	135
	• Frozen vegetable medley (red peppers, broccoli) + 1 tsp/5 mL non-hydrogenated	0	1	17
	margarine	4	0	34
	• Brown rice	1	1	109
	• 1% milk (1 cup/250 mL)	3	0	102
	• Rhubarb Stewed with Apple and Strawberries (page 233)	1	3	91
Snack	• Air-popped or light popcorn (3 cups/750 mL)	1	4	92
	• Fruit and yogurt smoothie (1 cup/250 mL)	1	3	143
Totals	*Food Guide:* Grain Products = 7	37	30	1661
	Vegetables and Fruits = 6			(20%
	Milk Products = 4			calories
	Meat and Alternatives = 3			from fat)

Be Prepared: Make-Ahead Menu

Meal	Menu	g fat	g fiber	calories
Breakfast	• Whole-grain cereal with skim or 1% milk (2 oz/60 g cereal)	3	4	211
	• Grapefruit (½)	trace	2	38
	• Whole-wheat toast with peanut butter	9	3	164
Lunch	• Creamy Corn Chowder with Dill (page 76) thawed and reheated	3	3	152
	• Whole-wheat roll with small amount of soft non-hydrogenated margarine	5	3	127
	• Piece of fresh fruit	trace	2	62
	• Skim or 1% milk (1 cup/250 mL)	3	0	102
Dinner	• Curried Chicken and Tomato (page 110) served with steamed rice	15	4	481
	• Frozen mixed vegetables	trace	3	54
	• Applesauce-Raisin Squares (page 216)	3	2	99
	• Skim or 1% milk (1 cup/250 mL)	3	0	102
Snack	• Granola Energy Square (page 218)	6	2	104
	• Piece of fresh fruit (apple)	trace	3	82
Totals	*Food Guide:* Grain Products = 8	50	31	1778
	Vegetables and Fruit = 7			(25% of
	Milk Products = 3			calories
	Meat and Alternatives = 3			from fat)

Eating Without Meat: Meatless Menu

Meal	Menu	g fat	g fiber	calories
Breakfast	• Soy milk smoothie with yogurt, pineapple, and wheat germ	1	4	271
	• Oatmeal-Carrot Muffin (page 215)	6	3	181
Lunch	• Whole wheat pita filled with lettuce, tomatoes, hummus, or nut butter	4	8	228
	• 100% fruit juice (½ cup/125 mL)	trace	trace	54
	• Veggies and tofu-based dip	1	1	40
	• Apple	trace	3	82
Dinner	• Cabbage and Potato Pie (page 180)	11	6	315
	• Baked Parsnips and Carrots (page 182)	3	4	115
	• Whole-wheat bun with low-fat mozzarella	10	3	233
	• Fresh fruit compote	1	5	165
	• Low-fat (skim or 1%) milk or soy milk (1 cup/250 mL)	3	0	102
Snack	• Handful of walnuts	18	2	178
	• Plain popcorn	1	4	92
Totals	*Food Guide:* Grain Products = 6 Vegetables and Fruit = 7 Milk Products = 2 Meat and Alternatives = 3	58	43	2056 (25% of calories from fat)

Here We Go: Meals-on-the-Run

Meal	Menu	g fat	g fiber	calories
Breakfast	• Buttermilk, Bran, and Blueberry Muffin (page 214)	5	6	159
	• Low-fat, fruit-flavored yogurt (in individual cup for easy transport)	3	0	177
	• Banana	1	2	106
Lunch	• Classic Tuna Salad with Fresh Dill (page 91) on Whole-Wheat Oatmeal Bread (page 224)	5	4	208
	• Carrot and celery sticks	trace	1	17
	• Skim or 1% milk (1 cup/250 mL)	3	0	102
	• Pear	1	5	100
	• Buttermilk Apple Cake (page 223)	5	2	198
Dinner (Restaurant)	• Pasta with vegetables and grilled chicken slices in a tomato-based sauce	6	10	367
	• Whole-grain roll with a small amount of flavored olive oil for dipping	6	3	133
	• Mixed greens with low-fat dressing	2	1	31
	• Coffee or tea, black (1 cup/250 mL)	0	0	5
	• Microwave Oatmeal Square (page 217)	4	1	74

Note: See our Lighthearted Strategies for Fast Food and Eating Out (pages 53–54) for other meal ideas.

Here We Go: Meals-on-the-Run (*continued*)

Meal	Menu	g fat	g fiber	calories
Snack	• Unsalted pretzels (½ cup/125 mL)	1	1	86
	• Apple slices (1 apple)	1	3	82
Totals	*Food Guide* Grain Products = 8	43	39	1845
	Vegetables and Fruit = 6			(21% of
	Milk Products = 2			calories
	Meat and Alternatives = 2			from fat)

The Activity Action Plan

As has been hinted all along, whether you're 8 or 80, being physically active goes hand in hand with a healthy diet toward lowering your risk of heart disease. It helps keep your heart muscles strong, your cholesterol levels down, and your weight in check. When you're active on a regular basis, you have less chance of having a stroke or developing high blood pressure, Type 2 diabetes, and osteoporosis.

Making exercise a priority can be a challenge, but it's easier when you know the benefits of becoming more active. Here are a few reasons to get your feet (or arms) moving.

• More energy
• Able to cope better with life stress
• May improve sex life
• Improved body image
• Greater sense of well-being
• Better sleep
• Improved mood

So what does active really mean? Are you supposed to break out the spandex thong and head to the gym every day or spend months training to run marathons? Not at all. Even the simplest and smallest changes, such as taking the stairs instead of the elevator, help increase your activity level. Remember—every little bit counts, but more is better!

Canada's Physical Activity Guide to Healthy Active Living tells us that there are three important types of physical activity for health:

• *Endurance* activities that strengthen your heart and lungs
• *Flexibility* activities that encourage you to bend, stretch, and reach
• *Strength-building* activities that build strong muscles and bones

Lighthearted Goals for Physical Activity

1. In the beginning, just get yourself and your family on the move—even if it's just around the block.

2. When increasing activity levels, do it by adding activities that you enjoy.

3. Sixty minutes of light activity every day, such as easy gardening, stretching, and easy walking will make a difference. As you progress to more strenuous activities, such as brisk walking, biking, swimming, and dancing, you can cut down to 30 minutes, four days a week.

Recommended Dietary Allowances (RDA) for calcium.

Age	RDA
1–3	500 mg
4–8	800 mg
9–18	1300 mg
19–50	1000 mg
51+	1200 mg

Calcium Tips:
- Cook green vegetables to boost their calcium content.
- If you drink tea, drink it between meals instead of with meals. The tannins in the tea will inhibit calcium absorption.
- Don't take iron supplements with calcium-rich foods. The iron will compete with the calcium for absorption in the body.
- Be sure you are getting enough vitamin D as it helps calcium to be absorbed by the body. This might be a problem if you don't drink milk or eat dairy products as they are fortified with the vitamin. Consult your dietitian or doctor.

Photo, opposite:
Black Bean and Corn Salsa (page 65) with Crisp Flatbread (page 228)

Photo, overleaf:
Coconut Shrimp Curry (page 134)

You should try to do a little bit of each every day.

LIGHTHEARTED STRATEGIES FOR INCREASING YOUR LEVEL OF PHYSICAL ACTIVITY
- Get a copy of *Canada's Physical Activity Guide* and read through it. You can find it at www.paguide.com or call 1-888-334-9769. Your local public health and Heart and Stroke Foundation offices or the web site at www.heartandstroke.ca also have copies.
- Visit your doctor before starting a new exercise regime to make sure it's safe for you to do. This is especially important for older adults who have health conditions such as arthritis, osteoporosis, and existing heart disease, and for those who are obese.
- Make a plan to start and a commitment to yourself to get moving. Make sure that your plan and your early goals are reasonable and achievable.
- Don't push yourself too hard: if you can't carry on a conversation while you're exercising or you're in pain, you're doing too much. Slow down or stop and find something else to do that's more suitable for your current fitness level. You can always take another crack at that marathon when you're in better shape.
- Find a friend to go walking with or join a class or group (e.g., a hiking group).
- Make a walk to the park or an evening at the bowling alley a family affair.
- Plan on a variety of activities to help you get maximum health benefits without getting bored by the same routine.

Food Sources Of...

Calcium

Calcium is essential for strong bones and teeth. The mineral helps with nerve function and is necessary for muscles to be able to contract and relax. Calcium also plays an important role in blood clotting and maintaining blood pressure.

If you don't get enough calcium, your body will take what it needs from your bones. Over time your bones will become thin and weaken, a condition known as osteoporosis that can lead to debilitating bone fractures later in life.

Our bodies do not absorb calcium from all foods uniformly well. While plant foods do provide some calcium, natural compounds in many

vegetables prevent some of the calcium from being absorbed. The calcium found in dairy products is absorbed very efficiently. If you are a vegetarian or don't drink milk or eat dairy products, talk to your dietitian or doctor about how you can meet your calcium needs.

Best Sources for Calcium

Food	Serving Size	Calcium
Dairy Foods		
Milk, evaporated, 2%, undiluted	1 cup (250mL)	739 mg
Cheese, Swiss or Gruyere	1.5 oz (45g)	480 mg
Skim milk powder	½ cup (125 mL)	452 mg
Milk (added Calcium)	1 cup (250 mL)	420 mg
Yogurt, plain, 1–2%	¾ cup (175 mL)	320 mg
Milk, skim	1 cup (250 mL)	319 mg
Milk, whole, 3.3%	1 cup (250 mL)	308 mg
Cheese, cheddar	1.5 oz (45g)	300 mg
Chocolate Milk	1 cup (250 mL)	300 mg
Milk, Lactaid	1 cup (250 mL)	300 mg
Cheese, ricotta	½ cup (125 mL)	270 mg
Cheese, mozzarella	1.5 oz (45g)	228 mg
Cheese, Parmesan, grated	1 tbsp (15 mL)	88 mg
Cheese, cottage	½ cup (125 mL)	82 mg
Nondairy Foods		
Calcium-fortified orange juice	1 cup (250 mL)	360 mg
Soy beverage, fortified	1 cup (250 mL)	330 mg
Blackstrap molasses	2 tbsp (30 mL)	288 mg
Tofu, raw, firm, w/calcium sulfate	4 oz. (120 g)	260 mg
Salmon, drained with bones	½ can	225 mg
Sardines, with bones	8 small	165 mg
Tempeh, cooked	1 cup (250 mL)	154 mg
Baked beans	1 cup (250 mL)	150 mg
Figs	5 medium	135 mg
Tofu, raw, regular, w/calcium sulfate	4 oz. (120 g)	130 mg
Black beans	1 cup (250 mL)	102 mg
Almonds	½ cup (60 mL)	100 mg
Broccoli, cooked	1 cup (250 mL)	94 mg
Fancy molasses	2 tbsp (30 mL)	70 mg
Kidney beans, cooked	1 cup (250 mL)	69 mg

Hazelnuts	¼ cup (60 mL)	65 mg
Soybeans, roasted	¼ cup (60 mL)	60 mg
Currants	½ cup (125 mL)	60 mg
Orange	1 medium	50 mg
Broccoli, raw	1 cup (250 mL)	42 mg
Chickpeas, canned	½ cup (125 mL)	40 mg

Recommended Dietary Allowances (RDA) for iron.

Age	RDA
1–3	7 mg
4–8	10 mg
9–13	8 mg
14–18 (male)	11 mg
14–18 (female)	15 mg
19+ (male)	8 mg
19–50 (female)	18 mg
50+ (female)	8 mg
Pregnant	27 mg

Iron Tips:

- Add a source of vitamin C, such as tomatoes, red pepper, orange juice, or grapefruit segments, to your meal. Vitamin C can enhance the body's absorption of non-heme iron.
- If you drink tea, do so between meals. Tea contains compounds called tannins that inhibit iron absorption.
- Cook your vegetables. Cooking helps to break down the phytates (phytic acid) found in many plant foods; they inhibit iron absorption.
- Iron supplements should only be taken if prescribed by your doctor or registered dietitian.

Iron

Iron is an essential mineral that is needed by the body to build red blood cells and to carry oxygen from the lungs to every cell. If you don't get enough iron, you may feel tired, sluggish, irritable, and out of breath.

There are two types of iron found in foods. The first type, *heme* iron is very easily absorbed by the body and can be found only in red meat, poultry, fish, and seafood. *Non-heme* iron is not absorbed as well or as easily as heme iron. *Non-Heme* iron is found in grains such as breakfast cereals, breads and pasta—both whole grain and enriched. Dried peas and beans, seeds and nuts, vegetables, and eggs also contain non-heme iron.

Best Sources for Iron

- Red meat
- Poultry
- Fish: lake trout, clams, oysters
- Ready-to-eat breakfast cereals (check labels)
- Enriched pasta (check labels—not all products are enriched)
- Legume (dried beans, peas, and lentils), nuts, seeds, and whole grains

APPETIZERS AND SNACKS

Salmon Spread with Capers

Spinach-Onion Dip

Broccoli and Mushroom Dip

Black Bean and Corn Salsa

Italian Tomato Bruschetta

Mussels on the Half Shell

Spiced Meatballs with Coriander Dipping Sauce

Seafood Lettuce Rolls

Marinated Mushrooms

Marinated Spiced Carrots

Curried Chicken Croustades

Low-Salt Bagel Thins

An appetizer or small first course makes a meal more special. Appetizers are my favorite part of restaurant meals; I will often pass on dessert in favor of an interesting salad or soup and will sometimes order two appetizers rather than a main course.

Some appetizers or hors d'oeuvres, such as meat or chicken liver pâtés and creamy cheeses, can be terribly high in fat, cholesterol, sodium, and calories and can quickly add to our daily calories. On the other hand, there are many terrific-tasting appetizers that aren't too heavy in calories or other elements we should keep to a minimum. Try the Black Bean and Corn Salsa or Spiced Meatballs with Coriander Dipping Sauce or others in this section, or any of the soup, salad, pasta, or fish recipes for starters, which your family and guests will ask for again and again.

When planning menus, try to make sure each course has different foods and that the whole meal is a pleasing combination of colors, textures, seasonings, flavors, and temperature. If you have a filling first course such as Fettuccine and Mussel Salad, plan a light main course of perhaps a fish and a green vegetable. If you have a main course that is high in fat and calories, choose a light first course such as a soup without cream.

Salmon Spread with Capers

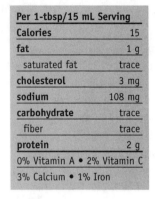

Per 1-tbsp/15 mL Serving	
Calories	15
fat	1 g
saturated fat	trace
cholesterol	3 mg
sodium	108 mg
carbohydrate	trace
fiber	trace
protein	2 g
0% Vitamin A • 2% Vitamin C	
3% Calcium • 1% Iron	

I keep a can of salmon on the shelf and a bottle of capers in the refrigerator in case someone drops in unexpectedly. Then I can make this in a few seconds to serve as a spread with crackers or pita bread, or use to stuff vegetables such as cherry tomatoes or snow peas. Green onions, chives or sweet peppers can be used instead of celery. Choose sockeye salmon for its bright red color.

1	can (7¹/₂ oz/213 g) salmon, drained and skin removed	1
¹/₃ cup	capers, drained	75 mL
¹/₃ cup	finely chopped celery	75 mL
2 tbsp	low-fat plain yogurt or light sour cream	25 mL
1 tsp	lemon juice	5 mL
	Hot pepper sauce	
2 tbsp	chopped fresh parsley or dill	25 mL

Be sure to crush salmon bones and include them; they are an excellent source of calcium.

In small bowl, flake salmon along with well-mashed bones. Add capers, celery, yogurt, and lemon juice; mix well. Add hot pepper sauce to taste. Spoon into serving bowl and sprinkle with parsley.

Makes about 1¹/₄ cups/300 mL.

Compare

Many dips are made with mayonnaise or cream cheese as a base; these are much higher in fat and calories. Just as good-tasting, if not better, dips can be made using light sour cream or yogurt.

Spinach-Onion Dip* per cup/250 mL	g fat	calories
Low-fat yogurt	3	155
2% cottage cheese	4	192
Light sour cream	9	245
Sour cream	25	303
Light mayonnaise	55	589
Mayonnaise	133	1243
Cream cheese**	61	647

*Instead of light sour cream, dip is made with 1¹/₂ cups/375 mL of ingredients listed.

**Although cream cheese is lower in total fat than mayonnaise, it is not recommended because it is higher in cholesterol and saturated fat.

Spinach-Onion Dip

This is a good, creamy yet low-fat base for many dips. Instead of spinach, you can add other vegetables, herbs or seasonings (see Variations). Serve this dip surrounded with fresh, crisp vegetables, such as carrots, celery, sweet peppers, blanched snow peas, asparagus, broccoli or cauliflower. It's best to make it at least four hours in advance so that flavors can develop.

Per 1-tbsp/15 mL Serving	
Calories	15
fat	1 g
saturated fat	trace
cholesterol	2 mg
sodium	88 mg
carbohydrate	2 g
fiber	trace
protein	1 g
7% Vitamin A • 3% Vitamin C	
3% Calcium • 3% Iron	

1	pkg (10 oz/284 g) fresh spinach (or frozen chopped, thawed)	1
1 tbsp	lemon juice	15 mL
1½ cups	light sour cream	375 mL
½ cup	chopped fresh parsley	125 mL
¼ cup	chopped green onion	50 mL
1 tsp	salt	5 mL
	Freshly ground pepper	

Trim stems and coarse leaves from spinach. Wash spinach, cook, covered, over medium heat for 3 minutes or until wilted. (If using frozen, no need to cook.) Thoroughly drain, squeezing out excess moisture; coarsely chop.

In bowl, stir together spinach, lemon juice, sour cream, parsley, onion, salt, and pepper to taste.

Cover and refrigerate for at least 4 hours or overnight to blend flavors.

Makes 2 cups/500 mL.

Variations

Parsley-Onion Dip
Instead of spinach, substitute 1 cup/250 mL coarsely chopped fresh parsley.

Fresh Basil-Onion Dip
Instead of spinach, substitute ½ cup/125 mL coarsely chopped fresh basil.

Artichoke-Onion Dip
Instead of spinach, substitute 1 cup/250 mL drained, coarsely chopped canned artichokes.

Dill Dip
Instead of spinach, substitute ¼ cup/50 mL coarsely chopped fresh parsley and ⅓ cup/75 mL chopped fresh dill (or 1 tbsp/15 mL dried dillweed).

Shrimp, Crab, or Clam Dip
Instead of spinach, add 1 cup/250 mL (or 5 oz/142 g can) drained, rinsed crab, small shrimp, or clams.

Curry Dip
Instead of spinach, heat 1 tsp/5 mL each curry powder or paste and ground cumin in skillet until fragrant; add to mixture; mix well, then season with more to taste.

Broccoli and Mushroom Dip

Chopped broccoli adds color, flavor, and fiber to this low-cal dip.

2 cups	chopped broccoli (include stalks)	500 mL
1 tbsp	canola oil	15 mL
1	clove garlic, minced	1
1/2	onion, chopped	1/2
1 1/2 cups	chopped mushrooms (about 4 oz/125 g)	375 mL
3/4 cup	low-fat cottage cheese	175 mL
1/4 cup	low-fat plain yogurt or light sour cream	50 mL
	Salt and freshly ground pepper	
	Chopped fresh parsley, chopped tomatoes	

Cucumber Canapés

Use round cucumber slices as the base for canapés. If you wish, scoop out a tiny portion of cucumber from center to form a hollow; top with a spoonful of:

• Salmon Spread with Capers (page 62)
• Classic Tuna Salad with Fresh Dill (page 91)
• Curried chicken filling (page 109)
• Best Tzatziki Sauce (page 143) or hummus
• Black Bean and Corn Salsa (page 65).

Fill hollowed-out cherry tomatoes, zucchini rounds, snow peas, or mushroom caps with any of the above spreads, or with the dip recipes in this book.

Use Belgian endive spears instead of crackers or chips for dipping.

In pot of boiling water, cook broccoli just until tender-crisp (3 minutes). Drain and refresh under cold water; drain thoroughly again and set aside.

In nonstick skillet, heat oil over medium heat; add garlic, onion, and mushrooms and cook, shaking pan to prevent sticking, for 5 minutes or until onion is tender. Set aside.

In food processor, combine cottage cheese and yogurt; process until smooth. Add mushroom mixture and broccoli; season with salt and pepper to taste. Process with on/off motion just until mixed. Cover and refrigerate for up to 2 days. Garnish with parsley and tomatoes before serving.

Makes 2 1/4 cups/550 mL.

Raw Veggies for Snacks

If you keep a supply of cut-up celery and carrots, broccoli, or cauliflower in the refrigerator, they will often be chosen for snacks over cookies and chips.

However, if you store them in a bowl of water, they will lose most of their Vitamin C; instead, store them in a plastic bag with a few drops of water.

Black Bean and Corn Salsa

Serve this popular combination as a dip with baked chips, or use as a filling for quesadillas or wraps or as a topping or filling for fajitas or tacos. (Recipe pictured opposite page 58.)

1	can (19 oz/540 mL) black beans, drained and rinsed	1
1 cup	kernel corn	250 mL
1	avocado, diced	1
1	large tomato, finely chopped	1
1/3 cup	finely chopped red onion	75 mL
1/3 cup	chopped fresh coriander	75 mL
1/4 cup	fresh lime or lemon juice	50 mL
1 tbsp	olive oil	15 mL
1 tbsp	seeded, minced jalapeño pepper	15 mL
1/2 tsp	salt	2 mL

Per 1/4-cup/50 mL Serving	
Calories	66
fat	3 g
saturated fat	trace
cholesterol	0 mg
sodium	164 mg
carbohydrate	9 g
fiber	3 g
protein	2 g
2% Vitamin A • 12% Vitamin C	
1% Calcium • 5% Iron	

In bowl, combine beans, corn, avocado, tomato, onion, and coriander. Sprinkle with lime juice, oil, jalapeño pepper, and salt; toss lightly. Cover and refrigerate up to 4 hours.

Makes about 4 cups.

Crackers

When buying crackers, it pays to spend a few minutes reading the labels. Many crackers are high in salt and contain hydrogenated vegetable oil, which means they have saturated or trans fat, which we want to avoid.

Melba toast and crispbreads are two kinds of crackers without hydrogenated vegetable oil.

For dips and spreads, instead of crackers use raw vegetables, whole-wheat pita bread rounds (tear into smaller pieces), Low-Salt Bagel Thins (page 72) or Quick Homemade Melba Toast (page 85).

Tortilla Chips

These are a healthy alternative to store-bought tortilla chips, which are high in calories, fat, and sodium. Use soft flour tortillas (whole-wheat if you can find them) for these crisp, easy-to-make chips.

Cut into 6 wedges and place on baking sheet. Bake in 400°F (200°C) oven for 3 to 5 minutes or until crisp. Let cool and store in airtight container for up to 2 weeks. (1 oz/28 g of chips has about 1 g fat, 62 calories.)

For seasoned chips: before baking, brush very lightly with olive oil and sprinkle with oregano, sesame seeds, Parmesan cheese and/or salt.

Italian Tomato Bruschetta

Per Serving	
Calories	99
fat	2 g
saturated fat	trace
cholesterol	0 mg
sodium	174 mg
carbohydrate	17 g
fiber	2 g
protein	3 g
5% Vitamin A • 12% Vitamin C	
2% Calcium • 7% Iron	

Traditionally, this Italian-style garlic bread is made by toasting thick slices of Italian bread, then rubbing them with a cut clove of garlic and drizzling with a top-quality extra-virgin olive oil. Sometimes the toast is topped with diced tomato or cheese. Here's a low-calorie, low-fat version that is equally delicious. Serve for a first course, as a snack after bridge or tennis, as an hors d'oeuvre on tiny toasted bread rounds or as part of a soup-and-salad meal.

8	slices French or Italian bread, ¹/₂-inch/1 cm thick	8
2	cloves garlic, halved	2
1 tsp	olive oil	5 mL
2 tbsp	minced onion	25 mL
1	large tomato, diced	1
2 tbsp	chopped fresh basil	25 mL
¹/₄ tsp	dried oregano	1 mL
Pinch	freshly ground pepper	Pinch
2 tsp	freshly grated Parmesan cheese (optional)	10 mL

To prepare Italian Tomato Bruschetta for a group, use the round Italian bread. Cut in half horizontally; prepare, and then cut into wedges to serve.

Mini-Pitas

Cut small (1¹/₂-inch/4 cm) pita bread rounds in half so that you have 2 pockets. Line pocket with a soft leaf lettuce and fill with any of the dips or fillings in this section.

After-Bridge Snack

Italian Tomato Bruschetta
Blueberry Cream Flan
(page 240)

Under broiler, in toaster oven or on barbecue, toast bread until brown. Rub toasted side with cut side of garlic.

While bread is toasting, heat oil in nonstick skillet over medium-high heat; add onion and cook, stirring, until tender. Remove from heat, add tomato, basil, oregano, and pepper; stir to mix.

Spoon tomato mixture over garlic side of hot toast and serve immediately. Alternatively, sprinkle with Parmesan (if using) and broil for 1 minute.

Makes 4 servings (2 slices each).

Mussels on the Half Shell

These mussels look great on an hors d'oeuvre platter, aren't difficult to make and are inexpensive compared to crab or shrimp.

2 lb	mussels	1 kg
¼ cup	water	50 mL
2 tbsp	olive oil	25 mL
2 tbsp	lemon juice	25 mL
2	cloves garlic, minced	2
½ cup	chopped fresh coriander, basil or dill	125 mL
1	medium tomato, diced	1

Per 10-piece Serving	
Calories	85
fat	6 g
saturated fat	1 g
cholesterol	12 mg
sodium	83 mg
carbohydrate	3 g
fiber	trace
protein	6 g
4% Vitamin A • 17% Vitamin C	
1% Calcium • 11% Iron	

Scrub mussels and discard any that are cracked or chipped or do not close when tapped; cut off any hairy beards. In large heavy saucepan, bring water to boil. Add mussels, cover and cook over medium-high heat for 5 to 7 minutes or until mussels open. Discard any that do not open.

Remove from heat. When mussels are cool enough to handle, using small knife, separate mussels from shell and set aside; reserve half the shells.

In bowl, combine oil, lemon juice, garlic, coriander, and tomato; add mussels and stir gently. Cover and refrigerate for up to 3 hours.

To serve, place a mussel in each half shell; spoon tomato mixture over. Arrange on a platter and pass with drinks, or arrange on individual plates and serve as first course.

Makes about 6 first-course servings or 60 pieces.

Mussels aren't nearly as high in cholesterol as previously thought; about 3½ oz (approx. 100 g) of mussels (meat only) has 50 mg cholesterol.

Hors d'Oeuvre Dinner Party

Mussels on the Half Shell
Curried Chicken Croustades (page 72)
Spiced Meatballs with Coriander Dipping Sauce (page 68)
Mushroom-Stuffed Zucchini Cups (page 70)
Marinated Spiced Carrots (page 71)
Marinated Mushrooms and Artichokes (page 70)

Spiced Meatballs
with Coriander Dipping Sauce

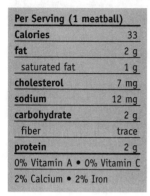

Bake rather than fry meatballs; not only is there less fat as a result, it's also much easier.

Green Bean Appetizer Salad with Fresh Tomato-Chive Dressing
Serve this as a light first course in the summer and fall when green beans and tomatoes are at their sweetest and best flavor. It's also a great way to use up any leftover cooked beans.

Line salad plates with leaf lettuce. Arrange crisp-cooked and chilled beans and sliced raw mushrooms over lettuce. Spoon Fresh Tomato-Chive Dressing (page 104) over beans, sprinkle feta cheese on top. Garnish with lemon wedges or chopped fresh herbs such as cilantro (coriander), dill or basil.

Middle Eastern seasonings cinnamon, allspice, and garlic, plus crunchy water chestnuts and juicy raisins, make these meatballs the best I've tasted; salt will never be missed. Fresh coriander, also called cilantro, is a perfect flavor match in the sauce. Don't substitute the dried coriander; instead, add curry powder to taste.

MEATBALLS

1/4 cup	raisins	50 mL
1/2 lb	lean ground lamb	250 g
1/3 cup	minced water chestnuts	75 mL
2 tbsp	minced green onions	25 mL
1	clove garlic, minced	1
1/2 tsp	ground allspice	2 mL
1/2 tsp	cinnamon	2 mL
	Freshly ground pepper	

CORIANDER DIPPING SAUCE

3/4 cup	plain 2% yogurt	175 mL
1/4 cup	minced fresh coriander leaves, lightly packed	50 mL
	Salt and freshly ground pepper	

Meatballs: Soak raisins in hot water for 15 minutes; drain and chop. In bowl, combine raisins, lamb, water chestnuts, onions, garlic, allspice, cinnamon, and pepper; mix well.

Shape into 24 balls of 1 tbsp/15 mL each. Arrange in single layer in ungreased baking dish. Bake, uncovered, in 400°F/200°C oven for 20 minutes or until no longer pink inside.

Coriander Dipping Sauce: Meanwhile, in small bowl, combine yogurt, coriander, salt, and pepper to taste; cover and refrigerate for at least 30 minutes for flavors to develop. Serve hot meatballs with toothpicks for dipping into sauce.

Makes 1 cup/250 mL sauce, 24 meatballs.

Seafood Lettuce Rolls

These surprise packages are an intriguing and delicious first course. Serve with Coriander Dipping Sauce (page 68) or Nuoc Cham Dipping Sauce (see sidebar).

1	head Boston or leaf lettuce	1
1	can (7½ oz/213 g) salmon	1
Pinch	dried red chili pepper flakes or 1 fresh jalapeño, chopped	Pinch
½ cup	low-fat plain yogurt	125 mL
1 cup	small shrimp	250 mL
2 cups	bean sprouts	500 mL
	Fresh coriander leaves	

Cut large lettuce leaves in half down center vein. In bowl, flake salmon and mash with bones and juices. Add pepper flakes (if using jalapeño, cut in half lengthwise, discard seeds and vein, and finely chop); mix into yogurt.

On narrow end of each lettuce piece, place 1 tbsp/15 mL flaked salmon, top with 1 or 2 shrimp, then approximately 2 tbsp/25 mL bean sprouts, dollop of yogurt mixture, and 1 or 2 cilantro leaves (if using). Roll into cylinder shape.

Makes 5 servings of 3 rolls each.

Cocktail Party

Broccoli and Mushroom Dip (page 64) with fresh vegetables
Spiced Meatballs with Coriander Dipping Sauce (page 68)
Curried Chicken Croustades (page 72)
Salmon Spread with Capers (page 62) on melba toast rounds

Per Serving	
Calories	109
fat	4 g
saturated fat	1 g
cholesterol	67 mg
sodium	282 mg
carbohydrate	3 g
fiber	1 g
protein	15 g

7% Vitamin A • 8% Vitamin C
15% Calcium • 11% Iron

If you enjoy Vietnamese cooking, serve the lettuce rolls with Nuoc Cham Dipping Sauce and include rice vermicelli noodles in rolls. Thin strips of cooked pork can be used instead of salmon.

Nuoc Cham Dipping Sauce

Split 2 dried chili peppers in half and discard seeds and membranes; chop finely. In small dish, combine peppers, 1 clove minced garlic, 1 tbsp/15 mL granulated sugar, 1 tbsp/15 mL lime juice, 3 tbsp/45 mL water, and 2 tbsp/25 mL bottled fish sauce (available in Asian food stores).

Marinated Mushrooms

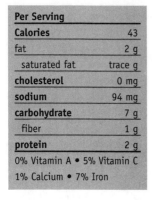

Pass these zippy mushrooms (on toothpicks) with drinks or serve as part of a relish tray or salad plate.

²/₃ cup	tarragon or wine vinegar	150 mL
¹/₃ cup	canola oil	75 mL
2 tbsp	granulated sugar	25 mL
1 tsp	each dried basil and thyme	5 mL
¹/₂ tsp	salt	2 mL
2 tbsp	water	25 mL
Dash	hot pepper sauce	Dash
¹/₄ tsp	dried hot pepper flakes (optional)	1 mL
1	clove garlic, minced	1
	Freshly ground pepper	
1	onion, thinly sliced	1
1¹/₂ lb	medium mushrooms	750 g

Marinated Mushrooms and Artichokes

Drain one can (14 oz/398 mL) artichokes. Cut in half and add to mushroom mixture before marinating.

Mushroom-Stuffed Zucchini Cups

For a light, refreshing, hot hors d'oeuvre follow recipe on page 201 using very thin zucchini cut into bite-size pieces. Serve on platter along with Spiced Meatballs with Coriander Dipping Sauce (page 68) and cherry tomatoes.

In large bowl, combine vinegar, oil, sugar, basil, thyme, salt, water, hot pepper sauce, dried hot pepper flakes (if using), garlic, and pepper to taste; stir until well mixed.

Separate onion into rings. Wash mushrooms and trim bases. Add onions and mushrooms to vinegar mixture; mix lightly. Cover and refrigerate for at least 8 hours or up to 2 days, stirring occasionally. Drain before serving.

Makes 10 appetizer servings.

Marinated Spiced Carrots

These are a favorite with the bridge club I used to play with when I lived in Ottawa. The members have been serving these along with the Marinated Mushrooms, opposite, at their year-end party for the last 30 years. A few cherry tomatoes on the platter look nice and add extra color.

1 lb	small carrots, scraped	500 g
½ cup	granulated sugar	125 mL
½ cup	white vinegar	125 mL
½ cup	water	125 mL
1 tbsp	mustard seeds	15 mL
3	whole cloves	3
1	3-inch (8 cm) stick cinnamon, broken	1

Per Serving	
Calories	42
fat	trace
saturated fat	trace
cholesterol	0 mg
sodium	14 mg
carbohydrate	10 g
fiber	1 g
protein	trace
115% Vitamin A • 7% Vitamin C	
1% Calcium • 1% Iron	

Cut carrots into 3-inch-long (8 cm), very thin sticks. Blanch in boiling water for 3 minutes; drain and cool under cold water. Drain again and place in bowl.

In saucepan, combine sugar, vinegar, water, mustard seeds, cloves, and cinnamon; bring to boil. Reduce heat and simmer for 10 minutes; pour over carrots. Let cool, then cover and refrigerate for at least 8 hours or up to 2 weeks. Drain well; discard cloves and cinnamon.

Makes about 10 appetizer servings.

Fresh Soybean Snack

Fresh or frozen soybeans in the pod, or edamame, make a wonderful snack. They are available in some supermarkets in the freezer or produce section. To serve, cook in boiling water until tender-crisp or follow package instructions. Drain and sprinkle with salt.

To eat, put whole pod in your mouth and, using your teeth, scrape out the beans, which you eat, then discard the outer shell.

Snacks and Nibbles
These can quickly add up to a great deal of fat and calories. For example, if you consume about 2,000 calories a day, you should have no more than 66 grams of fat.

High-Fat Snacks	g fat
Peanuts (½ cup/125 mL)	35
Potato chips (1 small bag/40 g)	14
Chicken liver pâté (¼ cup/50 mL)	15
Goose liver pâté (¼ cup/50 mL)	23
Cheddar cheese (1½ oz/45 g, a 2 inch/5 cm cube)	15

Lower-Fat Alternative Snacks	g fat
Popcorn (unbuttered) (1 cup/250 mL)	0
Salmon Spread with Capers (page 62) (¼ cup/50 mL)	2
Danbo cheese (1½ oz/45 g)	4
Fresh vegetables with Spinach-Onion Dip (page 63)	2

Curried Chicken Croustades

Use leftover bread trimmings to make breadcrumbs. Use in Herb-Breaded Chicken (page 120) or Fish Fillets with Herbed Crumbs (page 124) or Mushroom-Onion Stuffing (page 112).

Serve these savory tidbits at a cocktail party or make larger croustades and serve for a luncheon dish. In this recipe, tiny shells of bread are toasted and filled with curried chicken. Both parts can be made in advance, then reheated before serving. The croustades are perfect low-calorie, low-fat containers for savory fillings.

20	thin slices whole-wheat bread	20
	Curried chicken filling for crêpes (page 109)	

Using 2-inch (5 cm) cookie cutter or glass, cut out 40 rounds of bread. Press bread rounds into very small tart tins (about 1½ inches/4 cm in diameter). Bake in 300°F/150°C oven for 20 minutes or until toasted. Remove from oven and let cool. (Croustades can be prepared in advance and stored in covered container for up to 1 week or frozen for up to 2 months.)

Fill croustades with curried chicken mixture and place on baking sheet. Heat in 400°F/200°C oven for 15 minutes or until hot.

Makes 40 appetizers.

Low-Salt Bagel Thins

A non-aerosol oil pump is perfect to use in this recipe—it will create a fine spray of oil for the bagel thins.

If you love crisp, salty snacks such as potato chips, here is a healthy alternative. How crisp they are depends on how thin you can make the bagel slices.

1	large bagel	1
1 tbsp	extra-virgin olive oil	15 mL
1 tsp	dried oregano	5 mL
	Salt	

Using very sharp serrated knife, slice bagel into very thin rounds. Arrange in single layer on baking sheet; brush with oil. Sprinkle with oregano and salt to taste. Bake in 350°F/180°C oven for 12 minutes. Let cool and store in airtight container for up to 1 week.

Makes 20 pieces.

The New Lighthearted Cookbook

SOUPS

Homemade soup is such a treat and so easy to make that I wish I always had some on hand. In this section, there are elegant soups to serve as first courses at a dinner party—such as Cream of Parsnip Soup with Ginger or Fresh Beet Soup with Yogurt—or there's hearty Chunky Vegetable-Bean Soup, which is a wonderfully warming main-course dish. Main-course soups are easy to prepare, make good use of leftovers, and can be made ahead of time.

Asparagus and Potato Bisque

Per Serving	
Calories	76
fat	1 g
saturated fat	1 g
cholesterol	3 mg
sodium	46 mg
potassium	336 mg
carbohydrate	13 g
fiber	2 g
protein	5 g
6% Vitamin A • 18% Vitamin C	
10% Calcium • 5% Iron	
11% Thiamine • 13% Riboflavin	
9% Niacin • 11% Vitamin B-6	
50% Folate • 8% Vitamin B-12	
9% Zinc	

Potato helps to thicken this soup without adding the extra calories or preparation time of a butter/flour-thickened soup. It's delicious served hot or cold, but when serving hot, substitute either light cream or milk for the yogurt, since yogurt tends to curdle when boiled.

1	large potato, peeled and diced	1
1	small onion, chopped	1
1½ cups	water or chicken stock	375 mL
1 lb	fresh asparagus, ends trimmed	500 g
2 tsp	lemon juice	10 mL
1 cup	2% milk	250 mL
½ cup	low-fat plain yogurt, light cream or milk	125 mL
	Salt and freshly ground pepper	
Pinch	nutmeg	Pinch

To get the maximum flavor with the least amount of fat:
When making a vegetable soup, if you cook the vegetables first in margarine (¼ cup/50 mL margarine has 56 g fat), the margarine is absorbed into the vegetables. Instead, cook vegetables in only chicken stock. For richness of flavor, add ¼ cup/50 mL cream or milk (light cream will add 8 g fat, whipping cream 20 g fat) just before serving. You will achieve the same effect with much less fat. (The same principle applies to salt; add it at the end of cooking or just before serving.)

In saucepan, combine potato, onion, and water or chicken stock; cover and simmer until potato is nearly tender, 5 to 10 minutes.

Meanwhile, cut asparagus into about 1½-inch lengths (4 cm). Add to potato mixture; cover and simmer for 5 minutes or until asparagus is tender.

Using slotted spoon, remove asparagus tips and let cool in cold water to prevent further cooking. Drain and reserve for garnish.

In food processor or blender, purée asparagus-potato mixture; add lemon juice. Pour into bowl; cover and refrigerate until chilled; mixture can be refrigerated up to 1 day. Stir in milk and yogurt; season with salt, pepper, and nutmeg to taste. Serve cold or reheat. Garnish each serving with reserved asparagus tips.

Makes 6 servings, ¾ cup/175 mL each.

Mushroom Bisque with Tarragon

Easy to make, this creamy soup tastes so much better than anything out of a can. I usually double this recipe, as I like large servings.

8 oz	mushrooms	250 g
1 tbsp	soft non-hydrogenated margarine	15 mL
1/4 cup	minced onion	50 mL
2 tbsp	all-purpose flour	25 mL
1 cup	hot chicken stock	250 mL
1 1/2 cups	2% milk	375 mL
1 tsp	dried tarragon	5 mL
1/3 cup	minced fresh parsley	75 mL
	Salt and freshly ground pepper	
1 tbsp	dry sherry (optional)	15 mL

Per Serving	
Calories	104
fat	4 g
saturated fat	1 g
cholesterol	4 mg
sodium	282 mg
potassium	385 mg
carbohydrate	11 g
fiber	1 g
protein	6 g
11% Vitamin A • 13% Vitamin C	
12% Calcium • 10% Iron	
6% Thiamine • 20% Riboflavin	
19% Niacin • 12% Vitamin B-6	
11% Folate • 8% Vitamin B-12	
10% Zinc	

Thinly slice 4 mushroom caps and set aside; coarsely chop remaining mushrooms (if using food processor, use on-off turns).

In saucepan, melt margarine over medium-high heat; add onion and cook for 2 minutes, stirring occasionally. Add chopped mushrooms and cook for 10 minutes or until golden and no liquid remains, stirring often. Sprinkle with flour and stir until mixed. Whisk in hot chicken stock and bring to boil, whisking constantly. Reduce heat to low and add milk, tarragon, parsley, and reserved sliced mushrooms; cover and simmer for 5 minutes.

Season to taste with salt and pepper. Stir in sherry (if using).

Makes 4 servings, 3/4 cup/175 mL each.

Wild Mushroom Soup

Break 10 g (1/2 cup/125 mL) dried porcini mushrooms into 3/4-inch/2 cm pieces. Pour 1/2 cup/125 mL boiling water over mushrooms and let stand for 15 minutes.

Prepare Mushroom Bisque with Tarragon; add porcini mushrooms and soaking liquid along with milk.

Creamy Corn Chowder with Dill

Per Serving	
Calories	152
fat	3 g
saturated fat	1 g
cholesterol	5 mg
sodium	358 mg
potassium	386 mg
carbohydrate	29 g
fiber	3 g
protein	5 g
35% Vitamin A • 13% Vitamin C	
8% Calcium • 5% Iron	
8% Thiamine • 11% Riboflavin	
11% Niacin • 12% Vitamin B-6	
23% Folate • 3% Vitamin B-12	
10% Zinc	

I like to serve this soup for a casual lunch and love the flavor with fresh dill. However, fresh basil and coriander also taste great. In corn season, use any leftover cooked corn instead of frozen corn. If serving as a main course, top each serving with grated Cheddar cheese, fresh tiny salad shrimp or chopped crabmeat. Serve with Crisp Flatbread (page 228).

2 tsp	olive oil	10 mL
1	onion, chopped	1
1	carrot, chopped	1
1	stalk celery, chopped	1
1	potato, peeled and chopped	1
¼ cup	diced sweet red pepper (optional)	50 mL
½ tsp	dill seed	2 mL
1 cup	vegetable or chicken stock	250 mL
1½ cups	2% milk	375 mL
1	can (14 oz/398 mL) creamed corn	1
1 cup	frozen corn kernels	250 mL
	Salt and pepper to taste	
⅓ cup	chopped fresh dill	75 mL

Casual Lunch Party

Creamy Corn Chowder with
  Dill
Crisp Flatbread (page 228)
Italian Tomato Bruschetta
  (page 66)
Blueberry Cream Flan
  (page 240)
Fresh fruit

In nonstick saucepan, heat oil over medium heat; cook onion, stirring for 2 minutes or until onion is softened. Stir in carrot, celery, potato, red pepper (if using), dill seed, and stock; bring to a boil. Cover and simmer until vegetables are tender, about 10 minutes. Add milk, creamed corn, and frozen corn; heat until hot. Stir in salt and pepper to taste. (Can be refrigerated up to 2 days at this point.)

Stir in fresh dill. If too thick, add milk or stock to taste.

Makes 6 servings, 1 cup/250 mL each.

Cream of Parsnip Soup with Ginger

This splendid soup is the creation of Doug Andison, my friend and good cook. He microwaves parsnips and leeks separately in large amounts then freezes them in smaller portions so that he can prepare this soup easily at the last minute. He also likes to press the gingerroot through a garlic press instead of grating or chopping and might use cream instead of 2% milk.

1	onion (or whites of 2 leeks), chopped	1
4	medium parsnips, peeled and cubed (about 10 oz/280 g)	4
1 cup	water	250 mL
1 tbsp	soft non-hydrogenated margarine	15 mL
2 tbsp	all-purpose flour	25 mL
1 cup	chicken or vegetable stock	250 mL
1½ tsp	finely grated fresh gingerroot	7 mL
¾ cup	2% milk	175 mL
	Salt and pepper	
	Chopped fresh coriander or parsley	

Per Serving	
Calories	121
fat	3 g
saturated fat	2 g
cholesterol	9 mg
sodium	206 mg
potassium	396 mg
carbohydrate	20 g
fiber	3 g
protein	4 g

4% Vitamin A • 17% Vitamin C
7% Calcium • 5% Iron
8% Thiamine • 8% Riboflavin
9% Niacin • 6% Vitamin B-6
23% Folate • 5% Vitamin B-12
6% Zinc

In saucepan, combine onion, parsnips, and water; simmer, covered, for 8 to 10 minutes or until parsnips are tender. Purée in blender or food processor and set aside.

In saucepan, melt soft margarine over medium heat; stir in flour and cook for 1 minute. Stir in chicken stock and cook, stirring, until mixture comes to boil and thickens.

Add puréed parsnip mixture, gingerroot, milk, salt, and pepper to taste. Stir to mix well and heat through. Sprinkle with chopped coriander to garnish. Serve hot or cold. If too thick, thin with more milk or chicken stock. (Soup can be refrigerated for up to 3 days; reheat to serve.)

Makes 5 servings, ²/₃ cup/150 mL each.

Chicken Stock

The main nutritional advantage of homemade chicken stock (besides better flavor) is that it is low in sodium. However, if you add salt, the sodium level will be close to that of commercial soups. Anyone on a low-sodium diet should use homemade stock without adding salt. If you use stocks from a can or cube, remember that they are high in salt, so don't add any more. Doubling the ratio of water to stock powder, a stock cube or canned stock will halve the sodium content.

Chilled Cucumber-Chive Soup

This is one of my favorite summer soups. Quick to prepare, this wonderful soup is perfect for a lunch or picnic or a first course for an alfresco dinner. For packed lunches it's easy to transport in a Thermos.

½ cup	low-fat cottage cheese	125 mL
½ cup	light sour cream	125 mL
2 cups	buttermilk	500 mL
1½ cups	finely chopped, unpeeled English cucumber	375 mL
¼ cup	chopped fresh parsley	50 mL
⅓ cup	diced red radishes	75 mL
¼ cup	chopped fresh chives or green onions	50 mL
	Salt and freshly ground pepper	

Jiffy Gazpacho

Don't throw away leftover tossed green salads made with an oil-and-vinegar dressing. Instead, purée in a blender or food processor and add tomato juice to taste. Refrigerate until cold then serve in soup bowls and top with finely chopped tomato, green pepper, and garlic croutons.

In blender or food processor, process cottage cheese and sour cream until smooth; add buttermilk and process to mix.

Transfer to bowl; stir in cucumber, parsley, radishes, and chives. Season with salt and pepper to taste. Refrigerate until chilled.

Makes 6 servings, ¾ cup/175 mL each.

Carrot and Coriander Soup

Be sure to use tender young carrots when making this sweet, flavorful soup. Fresh coriander, also called cilantro, adds a special extra and fresh flavor. Coriander seeds can easily be ground in a coffee or spice grinder or bought already ground.

1	onion, chopped	1
1 lb	young carrots, scraped and sliced	500 g
1½ tsp	ground coriander	7 mL
3½ cups	chicken stock	875 mL
¼ cup	chopped fresh coriander leaves or parsley	50 mL
	Freshly ground pepper	
	Yogurt or sour cream, sunflower seeds, coriander leaves or parsley for garnish	

Per Serving	
Calories	59
fat	1 g
saturated fat	trace
cholesterol	0 mg
sodium	496 mg
potassium	302 mg
carbohydrate	9 g
fiber	2 g
protein	4 g

156% Vitamin A • 5% Vitamin C
3% Calcium • 6% Iron
3% Thiamine • 5% Riboflavin
13% Niacin • 11% Vitamin B-6
6% Folate • 7% Vitamin B-12
4% Zinc

In saucepan, combine onion, carrots, ground coriander, and chicken stock; cover and simmer until vegetables are tender, 15 to 20 minutes.

In food processor or blender, purée mixture until smooth. Stir in fresh coriander. Add pepper to taste. (At this point, soup may be refrigerated for up to 3 days.) Serve hot or cold.

Garnish each serving with spoonful of yogurt or sour cream, a sprinkling of sunflower seeds and chopped fresh coriander leaves or parsley.

Microwave Method: In microwave-safe dish, combine onion, carrots, ground coriander, and 2 tbsp/25 mL chicken stock. Cover and microwave at high (100%) power for 8 to 12 minutes or until carrots are tender. (Time will vary depending on thickness of slices and age of carrots.)

In food processor or blender, purée mixture until smooth. Stir in fresh coriander and remaining chicken stock; season with salt and pepper to taste. Reheat or refrigerate until cold.

Makes 6 servings, 3/4 cup/175 mL each.

Instead of using salt to add flavor to soups, use onion or celery, herbs (thyme, rosemary, oregano, chives, parsley, to name just a few), lemon juice, a pinch of sugar, pepper, nutmeg or garlic. Also use more of the vegetable itself; i.e., if you are making carrot soup, add extra carrots.

Harvest Pumpkin and Zucchini Soup

This is a delightful fall soup. If you don't peel the zucchini, the soup will be green in color; if peeled, it will be pumpkin-colored. You can use nearly any kind of squash instead of pumpkin. I've even made it using spaghetti squash—it always tastes terrific.

3 cups	peeled, cubed pumpkin or squash	750 mL
3 cups	cubed zucchini	750 mL
2	medium potatoes, peeled and cubed	2
1	large onion, sliced	1
2 cups	vegetable or chicken stock	500 mL
1 tbsp	olive oil	15 mL
2 tbsp	chopped fresh parsley	25 mL
2	cloves garlic, chopped	2
³/₄ cup	2% milk	175 mL
1 tsp	dried basil (or 2 tbsp/25 mL chopped fresh)	5 mL
1 tbsp	lemon juice	15 mL
	Salt and pepper to taste	
	Fresh shredded basil or mint or chopped fresh parsley	

October Dinner

Harvest Pumpkin and
   Zucchini Soup
Fish Fillets with Basil and
   Lemon (page 125)
Carrots and Leeks with
   Parsley (page 193)
New Potatoes with Herbs
   (page 181)
Streusel Plum Cake
   (page 222)

In large saucepan, combine pumpkin, zucchini, potatoes, onion, vegetable stock, oil, parsley, and garlic. Cover and simmer, stirring occasionally, for 45 minutes or until vegetables are tender. If stock simmers down, add water to reach original level.

In food processor or blender, purée mixture in batches. (At this point, soup can be refrigerated for up to 3 days.) Return to saucepan. Add milk and basil; heat until hot. Stir in lemon juice, salt, and pepper to taste and garnish each serving with shredded basil.

Makes 8 servings, ³/₄ cup/175 mL each.

Zucchini and Watercress Vichyssoise

This light, elegant, quick-to-prepare soup is perfect for the first course of a dinner party. Serve it hot in the spring when the first crop of watercress appears, or chilled in the summer for a refreshing starter.

1 lb	zucchini (about 4 small), sliced	500 g
1	large potato, peeled and diced	1
1	medium onion, chopped	1
2 cups	chicken stock	500 mL
1 tbsp	lemon juice	15 mL
½ cup	packed watercress leaves	125 mL
1 ½ cups	2% milk	375 mL
	Salt and freshly ground pepper	
	Watercress leaves for garnish	

Per Serving	
Calories	61
fat	1 g
saturated fat	trace
cholesterol	2 mg
sodium	221 mg
potassium	345 mg
carbohydrate	10 g
fiber	1 g
protein	4 g
4% Vitamin A • 10% Vitamin C	
7% Calcium • 3% Iron	
5% Thiamine • 8% Riboflavin	
9% Niacin • 7% Vitamin B-6	
7% Folate • 6% Vitamin B-12	
4% Zinc	

In saucepan, combine zucchini, potato, onion, and chicken stock; cover and simmer until vegetables are tender, 15 to 20 minutes.

In food processor or blender, purée hot mixture with lemon juice and watercress until smooth. (At this point, soup can be refrigerated for up to 3 days.) Stir in milk, salt, and pepper to taste; reheat if necessary and serve hot. Alternatively, cover and refrigerate until cold. To serve, thin with additional milk if too thick and garnish with watercress leaves.

A hand immersion blender is great to have for soups and sauces—clean-up is quick, and they are easy to use.

Microwave Method: In microwave-safe dish, combine zucchini, potato, and onion with 2 tbsp/25 mL of the chicken stock. Cover and microwave at high (100%) power until vegetables are tender, 10 to 13 minutes, rotating every few minutes and stirring after 6 minutes.

In food processor or blender, purée mixture until smooth, adding some of the remaining chicken stock if too thick to process. Return to dish and stir in remaining chicken stock, lemon juice, watercress, and milk. Add salt and pepper to taste and reheat or serve cold.

Makes 8 servings, ¾ cup/175 mL each.

Fresh Beet Soup with Yogurt

Per Serving	
Calories	84
fat	2 g
saturated fat	trace
cholesterol	1 mg
sodium	211 mg
potassium	410 mg
carbohydrate	14 g
fiber	2 g
protein	4 g
31% Vitamin A • 13% Vitamin C	
6% Calcium • 6% Iron	
4% Thiamine • 6% Riboflavin	
6% Niacin • 7% Vitamin B-6	
35% Folate • 3% Vitamin B-12	
7% Zinc	

This beautiful red soup has a wonderful fresh beet taste when made with small, tender beets. I once made the mistake of making it in the winter using large, old beets and it was not as good.

2 lb	small beets	1 kg
1 tbsp	soft non-hydrogenated margarine	15 mL
1	large onion, chopped	1
¼ cup	lemon juice	50 mL
2 tbsp	drained horseradish	25 mL
1	large carrot, grated	1
1 cup	chicken stock	250 mL
⅔ cup	low-fat plain yogurt	150 mL
	Salt and freshly ground pepper	
	Yogurt and thin strips or slices	
	lemon or orange rind for garnish	

Harvest-Dinner Party
Fresh Beet Soup with Yogurt
Roasted Red Pepper, Chèvre,
  and Arugula Salad
  (page 93)
Lamb Tenderloins with
  Rosemary and Peppercorns
  (page 146)
Mushroom-Stuffed Zucchini
  Cups (page 201)
Spaghetti Squash with
  Parsley and Garlic
  (page 186)
Peach Crêpes with Easy
  Grand Marnier Sauce
  (page 239)

Wash beets and trim, leaving 1 inch/2.5 cm of the ends attached.

In large saucepan, cover beets with water and bring to boil; reduce heat and simmer, covered, for 20 to 30 minutes or until tender. Remove beets from saucepan; reserve cooking liquid. When beets are cool enough to handle (or under cold running water), slip off skins and stems. Cut beets in half.

In large saucepan, melt margarine over medium heat; add onion and cook until tender. Add 3 cups/750 mL reserved cooking liquid, beets, lemon juice, horseradish, carrot, and chicken stock; simmer for 5 minutes.

In blender or food processor, purée mixture in batches. (At this point, soup can be refrigerated for up to 3 days). Return to saucepan; stir in yogurt. Season with salt and pepper to taste. Reheat over medium-low heat, being careful not to boil. Garnish each serving with spoonful of yogurt and strips of orange or lemon rind.

Makes 8 servings, 1 cup/250 mL each.

Fresh Tomato Soup Provençal

Fresh herbs add a delightful flavor to this soup. If the herbs called for here aren't available, use other fresh herbs, such as dill instead of basil and oregano instead of thyme. For a lighter soup, omit milk and add a little more chicken stock.

	Per Serving	
	Calories	55
	fat	1 g
	saturated fat	trace
	cholesterol	1 mg
	sodium	187 mg
	potassium	373 mg
	carbohydrate	10 g
	fiber	2 g
	protein	3 g

14% Vitamin A • 30% Vitamin C
5% Calcium • 7% Iron
6% Thiamine • 8% Riboflavin
9% Niacin • 6% Vitamin B-6
6% Folate • 4% Vitamin B-12
4% Zinc

3	large tomatoes, quartered	3
	(about 1¼ lb/625 g)	
1	medium onion, sliced	1
1	clove garlic, chopped	1
1¼ cups	chicken stock	300 mL
2 tbsp	tomato paste	25 mL
¼ cup	chopped fresh basil	50 mL
	(or 1 tsp/5 mL dried*)	
1 tbsp	chopped fresh thyme	15 mL
	(or ½ tsp/2 mL dried)	
⅔ cup	2% milk	150 mL
1 tbsp	all-purpose flour	15 mL
	Salt and freshly ground pepper	
	Fresh basil leaves or	
	thyme sprigs for garnish	

In saucepan, combine tomatoes, onion, garlic, chicken stock; cover and simmer for 15 minutes.

Transfer to blender or food processor; add tomato paste and process until smooth. Whisk flour into milk. Return soup to pot, whisk in milk and flour mixture; cook, stirring, until mixture boils. Stir in basil and thyme. Season with salt and pepper to taste. (At this point, soup may be refrigerated for up to 3 days.)

Serve hot or cold. Garnish each serving with basil leaves or thyme sprigs.

Makes 6 servings, ¾ cup/175 mL each.

*A general rule for substituting fresh for dried herbs is to use 3 times the amount of fresh. However, with Fresh Tomato Soup Provençal, I like a lot more fresh herbs than usual. The amount will also vary depending upon how tightly you pack the fresh herbs when measuring.

Chunky Vegetable-Bean Soup

Wide-mouth unbreakable Thermos containers make soups easy to pack for lunch.

Compare
1 cup/250 mL
• Canned chunky vegetable soup has 122 calories; 4 g fat; 1006 mg sodium*; 3 g protein; 1 g fiber.
• Canned vegetable soup has 72 calories; 2 g fat; 823 mg sodium; 2 g protein; 0 g fiber.
• Homemade Chunky Vegetable-Bean Soup has 108 calories; 1 g fat; 578 mg sodium; 7 g protein; 5 g fiber.

*Sodium values are based on canned chicken stock or stock made from a cube. If homemade, sodium is greatly reduced.

Onion and potato are the basis for this soup—the potato helps to thicken it, the onions add flavor. You can add any seasonal fresh vegetables—broccoli, mushrooms, zucchini, carrots, tomatoes—that you have on hand. Instead of canned kidney beans, you can add ¼ cup/50 mL uncooked noodles or rice or barley along with the potato.

1	large onion, chopped	1
1	large potato, peeled and cubed	1
4 cups	chicken stock	1 L
2 cups	water	500 mL
2	stalks celery, diced	2
1 cup	cut, green beans, (in 1-inch/2.5 cm pieces)	250 mL
¼	small cabbage, thinly sliced, and/or ½ pkg spinach, coarsely sliced	¼
1	carrot, grated or chopped	1
½ cup	chopped sweet red pepper	125 mL
1 tsp	dried dillweed (or ¼ cup/50 mL chopped fresh)	5 mL
1	can (19 oz/540 mL) kidney beans, drained and rinsed	1
	Salt, cayenne, and freshly ground pepper	
¼ cup	grated Parmesan cheese (optional)	50 mL

In large heavy saucepan, combine onion, potato, chicken stock, and water; bring to a boil. Reduce heat and simmer for 10 minutes.

Add celery, green beans, cabbage and/or spinach, carrot, sweet pepper, dillweed, and kidney beans; cover and simmer for 10 minutes or until vegetables are tender.

Season with salt, cayenne, and pepper to taste. (At this point, soup can be refrigerated for up to 3 days or frozen for 2 months.) Sprinkle each serving with Parmesan (if using).

Makes 8 servings, 1 cup/250 mL each.

Split Pea, Bean, and Barley Soup

When you want a light yet warming meal, this soup is just right.
Serve it with toast or hot French bread and a green salad.

1 tbsp	canola oil	15 mL
2	onions, chopped	2
½ cup	dried green split peas	125 mL
¼ cup	dried lima beans	50 mL
¼ cup	barley	50 mL
6 cups	water	1.5 L
1	bay leaf	1
1 tsp	celery seeds (optional)	5 mL
1	potato, diced	1
1	carrot, chopped	1
1	stalk celery (including leaves), chopped	1
1 tsp	dried basil	5 mL
1 tsp	dried oregano	5 mL
1 tsp	salt	5 mL
¼ tsp	freshly ground pepper	1 mL

Per Serving	
Calories	151
fat	2 g
saturated fat	trace
cholesterol	0 mg
sodium	349 mg
potassium	400 mg
carbohydrate	27 g
fiber	4 g
protein	6 g

26% Vitamin A • 7% Vitamin C
3% Calcium • 11% Iron
12% Thiamine • 4% Riboflavin
11% Niacin • 9% Vitamin B-6
31% Folate • 0% Vitamin B-12
11% Zinc

In large heavy saucepan, heat oil over medium heat; add onions and cook, stirring, until tender.

Rinse split peas and lima beans, discarding any shrivelled or discolored ones. Add to saucepan along with barley, water, bay leaf, and celery seeds (if using). Bring to boil; reduce heat and simmer, covered, for 1½ hours.

Add potato, carrot, celery, basil, oregano, salt, and pepper; simmer for 30 minutes or until vegetables are tender. Remove bay leaf. If too thick, add water to reach desired thickness. (Soup may be refrigerated for up to 3 days.)

Makes 7 servings, 1 cup/250 mL each.

Quick Homemade Melba Toast

Choose fine-grained bread such as whole-wheat, pumpernickel or sandwich bread. Cut into very thin slices (remove crusts if you want) and arrange in a single layer on a cookie sheet. Bake in 250°F/120°C oven for 20 to 30 minutes or until crisp. Time will vary depending on age of bread and thickness of slices.

Compare Canned and Packaged Soups

Soup Tips

The most effective way to reduce fat in soups is to cut down the amount of butter, margarine, or oil you put in them. Many recipes call for more of these than is necessary. Another way is to substitute light cream or milk for whipping cream. If you do need more fat for flavor, add it at the end of cooking—just before serving. This will give the maximum flavor for the least amount of fat.

Traditional high-fat and high-cholesterol soup thickeners are whole milk, cream, egg yolks, and high-fat cheese. Instead, thicken soups with rice, noodles, potato, legumes, puréed vegetables, low-fat cheese, 1% milk, low-fat plain yogurt.

If you add ¼ tsp/1 mL salt to 1 cup/250 mL homemade soup, you add 581 mg sodium.

Canned and packaged soups are very high in sodium. If you use only canned or packaged soups, your family will acquire a taste for heavily salted soups. To increase the nutrients and decrease the sodium of packaged or canned soup you can use them as a base and add more vegetables, such as grated carrot, grated zucchini, chopped green beans, broccoli, cubed potatoes, and/or chopped onion.

Whenever possible, add skim or 1% milk instead of water to canned soups; this way, you increase the soup's protein and calcium content.

I often add leftover cooked rice or noodles, chicken or meats, an extra mushroom, green onion or fresh herbs to soups.

Compare Homemade and Canned Soups

per cup/250 mL	g fat	mg sodium*
Asparagus and Potato Bisque (page 74)	1	61
Canned cream of asparagus (with water added)	5	1045
Mushroom Bisque with Tarragon (page 75)	6	376
Canned cream of mushroom (with water added)	11	932

Compare	mg sodium per 1 cup/250 mL*
Chicken stock diluted from can	777
Chicken stock from a cube	795
Chicken stock from powder	1483
Basic Chicken Stock (unsalted) (page 87)	32

*Sodium values in the recipes in this book are based on stock made from a cube or powder or canned. If using homemade chicken stock, sodium falls considerably.

Basic Chicken Stock

As well as its much better flavor, the main reason for recommending homemade chicken stock is its low salt content. If you're not in the habit of making chicken stock, it can seem very time-consuming. Once you start making it, you'll realize how easy it is. Any pieces of chicken can be used, even a whole chicken (giblets removed). Backs and necks are least expensive. Turkey bones or the carcass can also be used.

Per cup/250 mL	
Calories	39
fat	1 g
saturated fat	trace
cholesterol	1 mg
sodium	32 mg
potassium	200 mg
carbohydrate	1 g
fiber	0 g
protein	5 g
0% Vitamin A • 0% Vitamin C	
1% Calcium • 4% Iron	
1% Thiamine • 4% Riboflavin	
18% Niacin • 1% Vitamin B-6	
2% Folate • 2% Vitamin B-12	
2% Zinc	

4 lb	chicken, whole or pieces	2 kg
12 cups	cold water	3 L
2	carrots, chopped	2
2	onions, chopped	2
2	stalks celery, chopped	2
2	bay leaves	2
6	black peppercorns	6
2	sprigs fresh thyme (or pinch each dried thyme, basil, and marjoram)	2

In stockpot, combine chicken and water; bring to boil. Skim off any scum. Add carrots, onions, celery, bay leaves, peppercorns, and thyme; simmer, uncovered, for 4 hours.

Remove from heat and strain; cover and refrigerate stock until any fat congeals on surface. Remove fat layer. Refrigerate for up to 2 days or freeze for longer storage.

Makes about 8 cups/2 L.

Beef, Veal, or Lamb Stock:
Use beef, veal or lamb bones instead of chicken. For added flavor, roast bones before simmering in water. Spread bones in roasting pan and bake in 400°F/200°C oven for 1 hour or until browned; transfer to stockpot and continue as in Basic Chicken Stock recipe.

When Making Stock
After chicken is cooked, remove meat from bones and use in salads (see Tarragon Chicken Salad, page 90), Curried Chicken Crêpes (page 109), Curried Chicken Croustades (page 72), sandwiches, or add to soups. Freeze homemade chicken stock in ice-cube trays or 1/2-cup/125 mL containers and use in cooking whenever you want extra flavor without added salt. Use in soups, salad dressings, sauces, and stir-fries.

Turkey Noodle Soup

Per Serving	
Calories	89
fat	2 g
saturated fat	1 g
cholesterol	22 mg
sodium	58 mg
potassium	306 mg
carbohydrate	4 g
fiber	1 g
protein	12 g

23% Vitamin A • 3% Vitamin C
3% Calcium • 9% Iron
3% Thiamine • 8% Riboflavin
28% Niacin • 10% Vitamin B-6
4% Folate • 14% Vitamin B-12
12% Zinc

Whenever you roast a turkey or chicken, make this comforting soup from the leftovers. Don't be put off by the long list of ingredients; it's really quite easy to prepare. I usually start the stock simmering while I'm making dinner one night, let it simmer for a few hours that evening then finish it the next night. If you prefer, add rice instead of noodles.

STOCK

1	carcass from roast turkey (approx. 11 lbs/5 kg)	1
10–15	cups water*	2.5–3.25 L
1	bay leaf	1
1	stalk celery (including leaves), chopped	1
1	onion, quartered	1

SOUP

1/3 cup	broken noodles (1/2-inch/1 cm pieces)	75 mL
2	stalks celery (including leaves), chopped	2
1	carrot, chopped	1
3	green onions, sliced	3
1/3 cup	grated zucchini or frozen peas	75 mL
1 tsp	dried basil	5 mL
1 tsp	dried thyme	5 mL
Dash	hot pepper sauce	Dash
	Salt and freshly ground pepper	

If you don't have a leftover turkey carcass, use 6 cups/1.5 L chicken stock instead of the stock here.

For a main-course soup and to increase fiber, add 1 can (19 oz/540 mL) chick-peas or kidney beans, drained. Other additions: green peas, chopped fresh spinach, asparagus, chopped broccoli, diced potato, squash, or turnip, chopped fresh herbs such as basil or dill or pesto sauce.

Stock: In stockpot or large saucepan, combine carcass, water, bay leaf, celery, and onion. Simmer, covered, for 4 hours. Strain, reserving stock. Let bones cool, then pick out any meat and add to stock. (You should have about 6 cups/1.5 L)

Soup: In stockpot or saucepan, bring stock to boil; add noodles, celery, carrot, green onions, zucchini, basil, and thyme; simmer for 10 minutes. Stir in hot pepper sauce; season with salt and pepper to taste.

Makes 8 servings (3/4 cup/175 mL each).

*Water should cover the carcass. Use more for a larger bird.

SALADS AND DRESSINGS

My favorite salads are so simple that they hardly qualify as recipes. I love thick slices of juicy tomatoes sprinkled with fresh basil, coarsely ground pepper and a tiny drizzle of olive oil. Another favorite is fresh, tender spinach leaves, sliced mushroom, and balsamic vinegar or Boston lettuce and Walnut Oil Vinaigrette (page 104).

Salad dressings are easy to make. Homemade dressings taste much better and are less expensive and often healthier than store-bought. Commercial salad dressings tend to be high in calories and sodium, while low-calorie dressings still have a significant amount of sodium. Both are generally made of poorer-quality fats and oils.

For salad dressings, I usually use extra-virgin olive oil. For a special green salad, I love to add some walnut oil. See page 102 for more information on oils.

For pasta salads, see the pasta section on pages 152–157.

Tarragon Chicken Salad

This light and easy-to-make salad is lovely for a special lunch or dinner on a hot summer day. Serve on lettuce or with a green salad and chilled cooked asparagus or sliced tomatoes. Cook chicken in microwave or simmer in water and use liquid for stock (see Basic Chicken Stock, page 87).

3 cups	cooked cubed chicken	750 mL
1½ cups	sliced celery	375 mL
¼ cup	chopped chives or green onions	50 mL
½ cup	low-fat plain yogurt or	125 mL
	light sour cream	
¼ cup	light mayonnaise	50 mL
2 tsp	dried tarragon	10 mL
2 tbsp	toasted slivered almonds*	25 mL
	Salt and freshly ground pepper	

Chicken Salad Sandwich Deluxe

Spread Tarragon Chicken Salad on pumpernickel, a bagel or toasted Italian bread. Add any combination of arugula, watercress, leaf lettuce, basil or sliced tomato. Serve open-faced or top with bread.

In large bowl, combine chicken, celery, chives, yogurt, mayonnaise, and tarragon; mix lightly. Cover and refrigerate for 1 hour or up to 24 hours. Just before serving, add almonds; season with salt and pepper to taste.

Makes 6 servings, ¾ cup/175 mL each.

*To toast almonds, roast on pie plate in 350°F/180°C oven for 5 minutes or until golden. Or place in a nonstick skillet over medium heat for about 5 minutes, shaking pan often.

Compare (per serving)			
Tarragon Chicken Salad *made with:*	*g fat*	*mg sodium*	*calories*
Yogurt (½ cup/125 mL) *plus light mayonnaise (¼ cup/50 mL)*	*10*	*174*	*197*
Light mayonnaise (¾ cup/175 mL)	*16*	*305*	*246*
Regular mayonnaise (¾ cup/175 mL)	*29*	*229*	*355*

Classic Tuna Salad with Fresh Dill

Use this easy-to-make tuna salad as part of a summer salad plate—served, perhaps, in a hollowed-out tomato or papaya half—for sandwich fillings or as an hors d'oeuvre when stuffed in cherry tomatoes, mushrooms, or hollowed-out cucumber rounds.

1	can (6 oz/170 g) tuna, packed in water	1
1/4 cup	diced celery	50 mL
1/4 cup	chopped fresh dill	50 mL
2 tbsp	chopped fresh parsley	25 mL
2 tbsp	chopped chives or green onions	25 mL
2 tbsp	light mayonnaise	25 mL
2 tbsp	low-fat plain yogurt	25 mL
1/2 tsp	Dijon mustard	2 mL
	Salt and pepper to taste	

In bowl, mash tuna with juices.* Add celery, dill, parsley, chives, mayonnaise, yogurt, mustard, salt, and pepper; mix well.

Makes 4 servings, 1/4 cup/50 mL each.

*If you only have tuna packed in oil, drain thoroughly and add more yogurt to taste.

Alfresco Summer Supper (27% of calories are from fat)

per serving	g fat	calories
Chilled Cucumber-Chive Soup (page 78)	2	78
Pasta and Fresh Vegetable Salad (page 154)	6	161
Sliced cold chicken breast (no skin) (4 oz/125 g)	3	180
Whole-wheat roll	2	93
(1 tsp/5 mL margarine or butter)	4	34
Sliced peaches and blueberries	0	38
Milk (skim, 8 oz/250 mL)	0	85
Totals	17	669

Per Serving	
Calories	70
fat	3 g
saturated fat	1 g
cholesterol	13 mg
sodium	190 mg
carbohydrate	2 g
fiber	trace
protein	9 g
3% Vitamin A • 7% Vitamin C	
2% Calcium • 6% Iron	

Tuna Fish

When buying canned tuna fish, choose tuna packed in water rather than in oil because it is lower in fat. Both kinds have the same amount of Omega-3 fatty acids from fish oils. (The oil tuna is packed in is not usually from fish oils.)

Warm Vegetable Salad with Tomato-Shallot Dressing

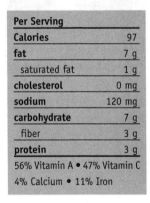
Warm vegetables over cool greens are a very pleasing combination. You can prepare the vegetables and dressing in advance, then just before serving, quickly blanch vegetables and add dressing. It's a lovely dinner-party first course or a light lunch.

5 cups	baby spinach (8 oz/250 g)	1.25 L
1	small Belgian endive	1
1 cup	green beans, cut 2 in/5 cm long	250 mL
1 cup	julienne carrots	250 mL
1 cup	small cauliflower florets	250 mL
1 cup	small broccoli florets	250 mL
3 tbsp	sunflower seeds	45 mL

Make Ahead

This salad can also be served cold. Blanch green beans, carrot, cauliflower, and broccoli, then drain and cool under cold water. Arrange vegetables over greens. Spoon dressing over salad to taste.

September Dinner Party

Warm Vegetable Salad
Brochette of Pork with
  Lemon and Herb Marinade
  (page 148)
Barley and Mushroom Pilaf
  (page 178)
Tomatoes Broiled with
  Goat Cheese and Basil
  (page 199)
Lemon Roll with Berries
  (page 244)

TOMATO-SHALLOT DRESSING

¼ cup	canola oil	50 mL
¼ cup	water	50 mL
¼ cup	lemon juice	50 mL
2	shallots, minced	2
1 tbsp	chopped fresh basil	15 mL
	(or ½ tsp/2 mL dried)	
½ tsp	Dijon mustard	2 mL
	Salt and freshly ground pepper	
3	medium tomatoes, diced	3

Wash and dry spinach. Separate endive leaves. On 8 salad plates, arrange spinach and endive leaves.

Tomato-Shallot Dressing: In food processor or mixing bowl, combine oil, water, lemon juice, shallots, basil, and mustard; mix well. Season with salt and pepper to taste.

Five minutes before serving: In large pot of boiling salted water, blanch green beans, carrots, cauliflower, and broccoli for 2 minutes; drain. Spoon warm vegetables onto greens; stir tomatoes into dressing and spoon dressing over vegetables to taste. Sprinkle with sunflower seeds. Serve immediately before vegetables cool.

Makes 8 servings.

Roasted Red Pepper, Chèvre, and Arugula Salad

In the summer and early fall, look for locally grown arugula. This oak-leaf-shaped salad green, with its nutty, peppery taste, is a delicious addition to any tossed salad. If not available, use red or green leaf lettuce and/or watercress. Buy a soft chèvre (goat cheese), or substitute feta cheese. Use bottled roasted red peppers or roast your own (see sidebar). (Recipe pictured opposite page 27.)

Per Serving	
Calories	82
fat	6 g
saturated fat	2 g
cholesterol	7 mg
sodium	72 mg
carbohydrate	4 g
fiber	1 g
protein	4 g
24% Vitamin A • 92% Vitamin C	
7% Calcium • 6% Iron	

2	roasted sweet red peppers	2
4 cups	arugula leaves, not packed	1 L
1	small head Boston lettuce, torn	1
4 oz	chèvre (goat cheese), diced	120 g
¼ cup	Mustard-Garlic Vinaigrette (page 104)	50 mL
	Salt and freshly ground pepper	

Cut peppers into thin strips about 1 in/2.5 cm long.

In salad bowl, toss together arugula, Boston lettuce, and dressing; season with salt and pepper to taste. Divide greens among 8 salad plates. Top with red peppers and chèvre.

Makes 8 servings.

My Favorite Quick Salad

I toss bagged baby arugula leaves and baby spinach leaves with a small amount of extra-virgin olive oil. Then I sprinkle on a little good balsamic or wine vinegar and salt and pepper and toss again. I top the salad with chopped fresh tomatoes and avocado slices or crumbled blue cheese and walnuts.

To roast red peppers
Place peppers on baking sheet; bake in 400°F/200°C oven for 20 to 30 minutes, turning once or twice, or until peppers are soft and skins are blackened and blistered (or barbecue until skins are blistered). Place in plastic bag; seal and let peppers steam for 10 minutes. Scrape skin from peppers; discard seeds.

White Bean, Radish, and Red Onion Salad

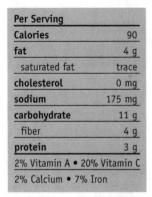
When Making Salads or Choosing from a Salad Bar

High-fat foods to avoid or choose less of: salad dressing—don't use any more than absolutely necessary; avocado; bacon bits; olives; high-fat cheese* (Cheddar, blue cheese); nuts

High-sodium foods to avoid or choose less of: anchovies; olives; salted or prepared croutons; bacon bits

High-cholesterol foods to avoid or choose less of: egg yolks*

*If salad is the main course, some protein foods, such as cheese and egg, are fine.

This looks attractive on red leaf lettuce. It goes well on a summer salad plate, a buffet dinner, or with barbecued hamburgers and lamb chops. It's also a welcome change from sandwiches in a packed lunch.

Red kidney beans or chickpeas can be used instead of white kidney beans. All are excellent sources of fiber.

1	can (19 oz/540 mL) white kidney beans, drained and rinsed	1
½ cup	red onion, chopped	125 mL
1 cup	thinly sliced or diced cucumber	250 mL
¾ cup	sliced radishes	175 mL
1	clove garlic, minced	1
½ cup	chopped fresh parsley	125 mL
3 tbsp	lemon juice or sherry vinegar	45 mL
2 tbsp	olive oil	25 mL
	Salt and freshly ground pepper	
	Red leaf lettuce	

In salad bowl, combine beans, onion, cucumber, radishes, garlic, and parsley; toss to mix. Add lemon juice, oil, salt, and pepper to taste; toss. (Salad can be prepared to this point, covered and refrigerated for up to 8 hours.)

At serving time, arrange salad on bed of red lettuce.

Makes 8 servings, ½ cup/125 mL each.

Snow Pea and Red Pepper Buffet Salad

This colorful dish is perfect for buffet meals any time of year. The salad can be prepared in advance; however, to keep the snow peas' bright green color, add the dressing just before serving. To make a larger amount, double salad ingredients but use the same amount of dressing.

Per Serving	
Calories	77
fat	5 g
saturated fat	1 g
cholesterol	0 mg
sodium	76 mg
carbohydrate	7 g
fiber	2 g
protein	3 g
6% Vitamin A • 68% Vitamin C	
2% Calcium • 9% Iron	

¾ lb	snow peas	375 g
2 tbsp	sesame seeds	25 mL
½ lb	mushrooms, sliced	250 g
1	small sweet red pepper, cut in thin strips	1

WALNUT-ORANGE DRESSING

1	clove garlic, minced	1
⅓ cup	orange juice	75 mL
3 tbsp	cider or white wine vinegar	45 mL
1 tsp	granulated sugar	5 mL
¼ tsp	salt	1 mL
2 tbsp	olive or walnut oil	25 mL
	Freshly ground pepper	

Top and string peas; blanch in boiling water for 2 minutes or until bright green and slightly pliable. Drain and rinse under cold water; dry thoroughly and set aside.

In ungreased skillet over medium heat, cook sesame seeds, shaking pan often, for 2 minutes or until lightly browned. Set aside.

Dressing: In food processor or bowl, combine garlic, orange juice, vinegar, sugar, and salt. With machine running or while mixing, gradually add oil.

In salad bowl, combine snow peas, mushrooms, and red pepper. Just before serving, add dressing and sesame seeds; toss to mix.

Makes 8 servings.

Nut oils, such as walnut oil, add a delicious flavor to salads. Use with tossed green salads or as suggested here. Store walnut oil in refrigerator and use within a few months, as it can become rancid.

Carrot and Bulgur Salad with Yogurt-Herb Dressing

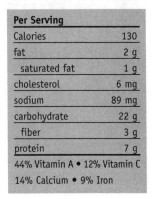
Cracked Wheat

You can substitute cracked wheat for bulgur. Instead of soaking in water, cook cracked wheat as follows: In saucepan, combine with twice as much water and simmer for 15 to 20 minutes or until tender but not mushy; drain.

To serve as a side dish, add seasonings such as salt, pepper, lemon juice, herbs, and vegetables.

To use in salads, drain well, cool and combine with dressing and chopped vegetables.

To use in stuffings, combine with onion and herbs such as sage and thyme.

For a Main-Course Salad Plate

Add slices of chicken, Classic Tuna Salad with Fresh Dill (page 91), or strips of low-fat cheese. To complete it, choose from what you have on hand—such as florets of broccoli or cauliflower.

Bulgur, made from wheat, is available at some supermarkets and most health-food stores. It is a nutty-tasting grain that is delicious in salads or as a vegetable. It's a good source of fiber. Save any leftover dressing and use as a dip with vegetables or as a sauce with fish.

½ cup	medium-grain bulgur	125 mL
½ cup	chopped green onions	125 mL
½ cup	chopped celery	125 mL
½ cup	grated carrot	125 mL
	Salt and freshly ground pepper	
½	head Boston or romaine lettuce	½
	Sliced tomatoes, cucumber, mushrooms, and radishes, chopped fresh parsley for garnish	

YOGURT-HERB DRESSING

½ cup	low-fat plain yogurt	125 mL
½ cup	light sour cream	125 mL
1 tsp	Dijon mustard	5 mL
1 tsp	each dried oregano and basil	5 mL
	(or 2 tbsp/25 mL chopped fresh)	
	Salt and freshly ground pepper	

In bowl, cover bulgur with very hot water. Let stand for 1 hour; drain well. Add green onions, celery, and carrot.

Yogurt-Herb Dressing: Combine yogurt, sour cream, mustard, oregano, basil, salt, and pepper to taste; mix well. Pour just enough dressing over bulgur mixture to moisten, reserving remaining dressing; toss to mix. Cover and refrigerate for at least 1 hour or up to 2 days.

Just before serving, toss salad again; add salt and pepper to taste. On large platter, arrange lettuce leaves. Mound bulgur salad in center. Garnish with slices of tomato, cucumber, mushrooms, and radishes; sprinkle with parsley. Pass extra dressing.

Makes 4 servings.

Italian Rice and Mozzarella Salad with Vegetables

This is a handy salad to have on hand for quick summer meals and is a great way to use up leftover cooked rice; use brown rice if you have it. It's not necessary to follow this recipe exactly; rather, use it as a guide and add whatever vegetables or cooked meats you have on hand. Chopped zucchini, cauliflower, and artichokes are nice additions.

3 cups	cooked rice	750 mL
¼ cup	diced carrots	50 mL
¼ cup	diced celery	50 mL
¼ cup	diced sweet red or green pepper	50 mL
½ cup	frozen green peas	125 mL
¼ cup	chopped red onion	50 mL
½ cup	chopped fresh parsley	125 mL
¼ cup	diced part-skim mozzarella (16% m.f.) or Danbo cheese	50 mL
2 tbsp	sliced green olives (optional)	25 mL
3 tbsp	cider vinegar	45 mL
2 tbsp	olive or canola oil	25 mL
¼ cup	orange juice	50 mL
¼ tsp	dried thyme (or 1 tsp/5 mL fresh)	1 mL
½ tsp	dried basil (or 2 tbsp/25 mL fresh)	2 mL
½ tsp	dried oregano (or 1 tbsp/15 mL fresh)	2 mL
	Salt and freshly ground pepper	

In salad bowl, combine rice, carrots, celery, sweet pepper, peas, onion, parsley, cheese, and olives (if using); set aside.

In small bowl, combine vinegar, oil, orange juice, thyme, basil, and oregano; mix well. Pour over salad and toss to mix. Season with salt and pepper to taste.

Makes 5 cups/1.25 L, 8 servings of about ⅔ cup/150 mL each.

Per Serving	
Calories	168
fat	5 g
saturated fat	1 g
cholesterol	4 mg
sodium	199 mg
carbohydrate	26 g
fiber	1 g
protein	5 g

18% Vitamin A • 32% Vitamin C
7% Calcium • 6% Iron

Curried Rice Salad

Prepare this salad, but substitute 1 tsp (5 mL) each curry powder and cumin for thyme, basil, and oregano. Add more curry to taste.

Picnic at the Beach or on the Boat

Sliced roast beef
Italian Rice and Mozzarella
  Salad with Vegetables
Old-Fashioned Pickled Beets
  (page 206)
Whole-wheat buns
Nectarines
Easy Cranberry-Chocolate
  Cookies (page 221)

Danish Potato Salad with Dill

Green peas—fresh, frozen or canned—are an excellent source of dietary fiber. Add them to soups, salads, stir-fries, and pasta dishes.

Potatoes, including skin, are a good source of fiber. Without the skin, the amount of fiber is reduced by half.

Grated Carrot and Green Pea Salad

For a quick, easy high-fiber salad, combine cooked frozen green peas, grated carrot, diced celery, chopped green onion, and fresh parsley. Mix equal parts of light sour cream and yogurt, add ¼ tsp/2 mL or more Dijon mustard and freshly ground pepper to taste; mix lightly with carrot mixture.

Sliced water chestnuts or artichoke hearts are good additions.

Dijon mustard and fresh dill add extra flavor to this summer salad. If fresh dill isn't available, use 1 tsp/5 mL dried dillweed and ½ cup/125 mL chopped fresh parsley.

2 lb	potatoes (about 5 medium)	1 kg
1 cup	low-fat plain yogurt	250 mL
3 tbsp	light mayonnaise	45 mL
½ cup	minced green onion	125 mL
1 tsp	curry powder	5 mL
1 tsp	Dijon mustard	5 mL
½ tsp	salt	2 mL
⅓ cup	chopped packed fresh dill or parsley	75 mL
	Freshly ground pepper	
	Watercress (optional) for garnish	

Wash potatoes and cook in large pot of boiling water until tender. Drain and let cool slightly; peel only if skins are tough, then cut into thin slices or chunks.

In bowl, mix together yogurt, mayonnaise, onion, curry powder, mustard, and salt. Add potatoes, dill, and pepper to taste; stir gently. Garnish each serving with watercress (if using).

Makes 6 servings.

Compare (per ¾ cup/175 mL serving)

Salad made with:	g fat	g saturated fat	mg sodium	calories
Low-fat plain yogurt (1 cup/250 mL) (plus 3 tbsp/45 mL light mayonnaise)	3	1	294	161
Light mayonnaise (1 cup plus 3 tbsp/45 mL)	15	2	556	258
Mayonnaise (1 cup plus 3 tbsp/45 mL)	35	3	435	430

Sliced Cucumbers with Chives, Yogurt, and Basil

Serve this cooling salad with curries, paella, and seafood or as part of a salad plate or buffet at any time of year. If chives aren't available, substitute green onions, and fresh chopped dill can be used instead of basil.

	Per Serving	
Calories		28
fat		1 g
saturated fat		trace
cholesterol		2 mg
sodium		184 mg
carbohydrate		4 g
fiber		1 g
protein		2 g
3% Vitamin A • 8% Vitamin C		
5% Calcium • 1% Iron		

1	English cucumber	1
½ tsp	salt	2 mL
¼ cup	light sour cream	50 mL
¼ cup	plain low-fat yogurt	50 mL
3 tbsp	chopped chives	45 mL
2 tsp	lemon juice	10 mL
3 tbsp	chopped fresh basil	45 mL
	(or ½ tsp/2 mL dried)	
¼ tsp	granulated sugar	1 mL
	Freshly ground pepper	
	Thinly sliced radishes or chive	
	flowers for garnish	

Peel cucumbers only if skin is tough or waxy. In food processor or by hand, thinly slice cucumbers. Place in colander and sprinkle with salt. Toss, then let stand for 2 hours or up to 8 hours; pat dry.

In bowl, combine sour cream, yogurt, chives, lemon juice, basil, and sugar; mix well. Stir in cucumber; season with pepper to taste.

Serve in shallow bowl or on plate, garnish with thinly sliced radishes or chive flowers.

Makes 6 servings, ½ cup/125 mL each.

You can reduce the fat in your diet considerably by using yogurt or light sour cream instead of mayonnaise in salads. If you're used to all mayonnaise, make the change gradually by using half mayonnaise and half yogurt, then gradually change to nearly all yogurt and light sour cream.

Tossed Seasonal Greens

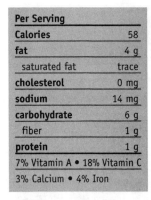

The best green salads are made up of an interesting and colorful variety of lettuces combined with a delicious dressing. Choose whatever lettuces are freshest in the market—leaf lettuce (red or green), butter (Boston or Bibb), mâche, arugula, endive, radicchio, or spinach and Belgian endive. Add watercress or a seasonal fruit or vegetable, such as the suggestions on the side of this page.

1	small head red leaf lettuce	1
1	small butter lettuce or romaine	1
1	red onion, thinly sliced	1

The darker the green in lettuce, the higher the Vitamin A and C content. Choose spinach more often than lettuce for salads; it is higher in nutrients, particularly Vitamins A and C, and fiber.

HERB VINAIGRETTE

1	clove garlic, minced	1
2 tbsp	balsamic or wine vinegar	25 mL
1 tsp	Dijon mustard	5 mL
2 tbsp	olive or walnut oil	25 mL
1 tbsp	water or orange juice	15 mL
1	green onion, minced	1
2 tbsp	chopped fresh parsley or basil	25 mL

Seasonal Salad Additions

Winter: Cherry tomatoes, sections of orange or grapefruit, sliced green apples, radish sprouts, sunflower seeds, nuts

Spring: Blanched and drained fiddleheads, blanched asparagus, chives, watercress

Summer: Radish, cucumber, tomato, green onions, fresh basil, parsley, rose or geranium petals, arugula

Fall: Red, green or yellow sweet peppers, cauliflower, broccoli, radicchio

Wash lettuce leaves; spin dry or dry in paper or tea towels. Wrap in paper towels and refrigerate until needed.

Herb Vinaigrette: In food processor, blender or bowl, combine garlic, vinegar, mustard, oil, and water; mix well. Stir in onion and parsley.

Just before serving, tear lettuce into pieces and place in salad bowl. Separate red onion into rings; add to bowl. (Add any other seasonal salad ingredients if using.) Drizzle with dressing and toss to mix.

Makes 8 servings.

Spinach Salad with Sesame Seed Dressing

Bright red strawberries are beautiful in this entertaining salad. In winter, use mandarin oranges, grapefruit sections, or sliced green apple instead of strawberries.

10 cups	baby spinach (1 lb/500 g)	2.5 L
½ cup	sliced almonds	75 mL
2 cups	firm strawberries, sliced	500 mL

SESAME SEED DRESSING

1 tbsp	sesame seeds	15 mL
¼ cup	cider vinegar	50 mL
3 tbsp	canola or walnut oil	45 mL
3 tbsp	water	45 mL
1 tbsp	granulated sugar	15 mL
1 tsp	poppy seeds	5 mL
¼ tsp	paprika	1 mL
¼ tsp	Worcestershire sauce	1 mL
1	green onion, minced	1

Wash and dry spinach; place in salad bowl and set aside.

In small skillet over medium heat, toast almonds, stirring often, until golden brown; set aside.

Sesame Seed Dressing: Place sesame seeds in small, ungreased skillet, stir over medium-high heat until lightly browned. In bowl or jar, combine sesame seeds, vinegar, oil, water, sugar, poppy seeds, paprika, Worcestershire, and green onion; mix well. (Dressing can be refrigerated for up to a week.)

Just before serving, pour dressing over spinach and toss well to coat. Top with strawberries and almonds.

Makes 10 servings.

Per Serving	
Calories	89
fat	7 g
saturated fat	1 g
cholesterol	0 mg
sodium	39 mg
carbohydrate	6 g
fiber	2 g
protein	3 g
31% Vitamin A • 50% Vitamin C	
6% Calcium • 11% Iron	

Hidden Fat in Salad Dressings

The fat content in salads comes mainly from the oil in the dressing and can be very deceptive. The amount of oil in the Tomato, Broccoli, and Pasta Salad (page 155) is at least half the amount that you would find in most salad recipes of this type. And even with a reduced amount of oil and a small amount of low-fat cheese, the fat content is higher than in some of the meat, chicken, and fish recipes in this book. A tossed green salad with 2 tbsp/25 mL of a standard oil-and-vinegar dressing per serving has 20 g of fat. This is a third of the fat most women require in a day.

Red and Green Cabbage Slaw

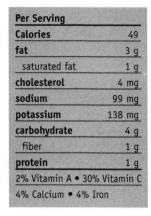
This colorful, easy-to-make salad goes well with hamburgers, toasted cheese sandwiches, and many summer barbecue menus. If red cabbage is hard to find, use only green cabbage and add 1 or 2 shredded carrots. Chopped sweet red or green pepper, celery, zucchini, onion, apple, or raisins are nice additions.

2 cups	shredded green cabbage	500 mL
1 cup	shredded red cabbage	250 mL
1/4 cup	chopped green or red onion	50 mL
1/4 cup	light mayonnaise	50 mL
1/4 cup	low-fat plain yogurt	50 mL
1/4 cup	chopped fresh parsley	50 mL
1 tsp	Dijon mustard	5 mL
1/4 tsp	celery seed	1 mL
	Salt and freshly ground pepper	

For other salad recipes, see

Curried Vermicelli Noodle
 Salad (page 157)
Shell Pasta Salad with
 Salmon and Green Beans
 (page 153)
Tortellini with Tuna Salad
 (page 152)
Pasta and Fresh Vegetable
 Salad (page 154)
Penne and Mussel Salad
 (page 156)
Beets Vinaigrette (page 106)
Old-Fashioned Pickled Beets
 (page 206)
Tomato, Broccoli, and Pasta
 Salad (page 155)

In salad bowl, combine green and red cabbage, onion, mayonnaise, yogurt, parsley, Dijon mustard, celery seed, salt, and pepper to taste. Mix well; cover and refrigerate for up to 4 hours.

Makes 6 servings.

Choosing an Oil for Salad Dressings

Oils are made up of a combination of different fats; some are much more saturated than others. The flavor should also be considered when choosing an oil.
CHOOSE:
- *safflower*
- *olive*
- *soybean*
- *walnut*
- *sunflower*
- *canola*
- *sesame*

Because walnut and olive oils are heavier, you can use a smaller amount and often combine them with another oil (such as safflower); these oils are nice for salads. Canola oil has the least amount of saturated fat. Sesame oil has a distinctive strong nutty flavor and is used sparingly, usually combined with another oil as a flavoring in a stir-fry or salad dressing. I don't find corn oil appealing for salads; it is better for cooking.
AVOID:
- *palm oil*
- *coconut oil*
- *vegetable oil (if kind of oil isn't stated on label)*

Palm oil and coconut oil are high in saturated fat. Avoid vegetable oil because when the kind of oil isn't stated on a container, it is likely to include palm, coconut or cottonseed oil.

Salad-Dressing Basics

Beware of Over-Dressing
Salads aren't always light meals when it comes to fat content. Lunch of a roll and salad can add up to more than half the amount of fat you need in a day.

- The amount of dressing (2 tbsp/25 mL) used in this chart is a conservative amount of salad dressing. If you like a lot of dressing, you could easily be using double this amount. If this is the case, you could be eating 30 g of fat just in a salad, which is about half the daily fat requirement for someone consuming 1800 calories a day.

- If you spread your bread or roll with 1 tbsp/15 mL butter or margarine, you are adding another 11 g of fat.

Next time you make a salad at home or at a salad bar, estimate how much dressing you use and compare to this:

per 2 tbsp/25 mL*	g fat	mg sodium	calories
Mustard-Garlic Vinaigrette (page 104)	9	35	86
Standard home vinaigrette	22	145**	194
Italian (store-bought)	12	229	118
Italian reduced calorie (store-bought)	1	426	13
Ranch-Style Buttermilk Dressing (page 106)	2	79	34
Ranch-style (store-bought)	15	256	141
Ranch-style reduced calorie (store-bought)	6	285	67
Blue-Cheese (page 106)	3	101	39
Blue cheese (store-bought)	15	359	146
Creamy Herb Dressing (page 105)	1	28	27
Fine herb dressing (store-bought)	11	571	103
Mayonnaise-type dressing (store-bought)	13	177	127

To Reduce Fat in Salad Dressings
Oil-based dressing: Replace half of the oil you usually use with water, fruit juice, or chicken stock.
Mayonnaise-based dressing: Use light mayonnaise and replace half of it with low-fat plain yogurt or light sour cream.

*A portion in a small ladle or a heaping dessert spoonful

**based on ½ tsp/2 mL salt per 1 cup/250 mL dressing.

Mustard-Garlic Vinaigrette

Walnut Oil Vinaigrette

Substitute walnut oil for olive oil and omit Parmesan cheese.

Compare (per tbsp/15 mL)

	g fat	calories
This recipe	5	49
Standard	11	96
vinaigrette		
(4 parts oil;		
1 part vinegar)		

By adding water to reduce the fat, and mustard and garlic to increase the flavor, we have a lower-calorie, yet flavorful, dressing.

1	clove garlic, minced	1
2 tsp	Dijon mustard	10 mL
2 tbsp	lemon juice	25 mL
1/4 cup	water	50 mL
1/2 tsp	granulated sugar	2 mL
1/4 cup	olive oil	50 mL
1 tsp	grated Parmesan cheese	5 mL
	Salt and freshly ground pepper	

In mixing bowl or jar, combine garlic, mustard, lemon juice, water, and sugar; mix well. Gradually whisk in oil. Add Parmesan; season with salt and pepper to taste.

Makes about 2/3 cup/150 mL.

Fresh Tomato-Chive Dressing

This light dressing is particularly good on appetizer salads or spooned over cold cooked vegetables. I then like to crumble feta cheese over the top. In order to get the most fiber, don't peel or seed tomatoes.

2	medium tomatoes, diced	2
2 tbsp	cider or wine vinegar	25 mL
2 tbsp	canola oil	25 mL
2 tsp	Dijon mustard	10 mL
1	clove garlic, minced (optional)	1
3 tbsp	chopped chives or green onion	50 mL
	Salt and freshly ground pepper	

In small bowl, combine tomatoes, vinegar, oil, mustard, garlic (if using), chives, salt, and pepper to taste; mix well. Cover and refrigerate for up to 3 days.

Makes 2 cups/500 mL.

Yogurt-Orange Dressing

This quick and easy dressing is delicious with a fruit salad.

²/₃ cup	low-fat plain yogurt	150 mL
1 tbsp	canola oil (optional)	15 mL
2 tbsp	frozen orange-juice concentrate	25 mL
1 tbsp	packed brown sugar	15 mL
1 tsp	grated orange rind	5 mL

Per 2-tbsp/25-mL Serving	
Calories	27
fat	trace
saturated fat	trace
cholesterol	1 mg
sodium	15 mg
carbohydrate	5 g
fiber	trace
protein	1 g
1% Vitamin A • 12% Vitamin C	
4% Calcium • 1% Iron	

In small bowl, combine yogurt, oil (if using), orange juice, sugar, and orange rind; mix thoroughly. Cover and refrigerate for up to 2 days.

Makes about 1 cup/250 mL.

Creamy Herb Dressing

Use this light yet creamy dressing on pasta salads, vegetable salads, and lettuce salads. The flavors develop upon standing, so if you want to use the dressing immediately, increase the mustard, oregano, and basil to ¹/₂ tsp/2 mL each or more to taste.

¹/₄ cup	light sour cream	50 mL
¹/₄ cup	low-fat plain yogurt	50 mL
¹/₄ tsp	Dijon mustard	1 mL
¹/₄ tsp	each dried oregano and basil	1 mL
	(or 1 tbsp/15 mL chopped fresh)	
	Salt and freshly ground pepper	

Per 2-tbsp/25-mL Serving	
Calories	27
fat	1 g
saturated fat	1 g
cholesterol	3 mg
sodium	28 mg
carbohydrate	3 g
fiber	0 g
protein	2 g
1% Vitamin A • 0% Vitamin C	
5% Calcium • 1% Iron	

In bowl, whisk together sour cream, yogurt, mustard, oregano, and basil. Add salt and pepper to taste. Cover and refrigerate for 4 hours or up to 3 days.

Makes ¹/₂ cup/125 mL.

Light sour cream has half the fat of regular sour cream and is much lower in fat than oil. One-quarter cup/50 mL dressing made with sour cream has 4 g fat; if made with light sour cream, it has 2 g fat; if made with oil, it has 28 g fat.

Ranch-Style Buttermilk Dressing

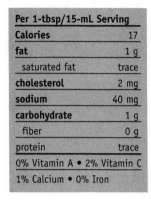

Even though this dressing contains mayonnaise, it is much lower in fat and calories than most creamy dressings. Use it with tossed green salads, coleslaw, or chilled cooked vegetables.

1 cup	buttermilk	250 mL
1/3 cup	light mayonnaise	75 mL
1	small clove garlic, minced	1
1/2 tsp	granulated sugar	2 mL
1/2 tsp	dried dillweed	2 mL
Pinch	freshly ground pepper	Pinch
2 tbsp	chopped fresh parsley	25 mL

In small bowl or jar, combine buttermilk, mayonnaise, garlic, sugar, dillweed, pepper, and parsley; mix well. Cover and refrigerate for up to 4 days.

Makes 1 1/3 cups/325 mL.

Beets Vinaigrette

Slice or julienne 1 1/2 lb/750 g cold cooked beets and toss with Mustard-Garlic Vinaigrette (page 104). (For information on cooking beets, see page 206.)

Makes 6 servings (1/2 cup/125 mL each). Add chopped onions, chives, or parsley. A beautiful addition to salad plates or appetizer salads. Use in late-summer and fall menus.

Variations

Blue-Cheese Dressing: *Add 2 tbsp/25 mL crumbled blue cheese.*
Fresh Herb: *Add 2 tbsp/25 mL chopped fresh dill, 1 tbsp/15 mL chopped fresh basil, or 2 tsp/10 mL chopped fresh tarragon.*
Watercress: *Add 1/4 cup/50 mL chopped watercress leaves.*
Onion or Chive: *Add 2 tbsp/25 mL chopped green onions or chives (or to taste).*
Celery: *Add 1 tsp/5 mL celery seed and 2 tbsp/25 mL chopped celery leaves. (Use on coleslaw.)*
Cumin: *Add 1/2 tsp/2 mL dried ground cumin.*
Curry: *Add 1 tsp/5 mL curry powder.*
Tomato: *Add 2 tbsp/25 mL tomato paste.*

For other salad dressing recipes, see:

Herb Vinaigrette (Tossed Seasonal Greens, page 100)
Tomato-Shallot Dressing (Warm Vegetable Salad with Tomato-Shallot Dressing, page 92)
Sesame Seed Dressing (Spinach Salad with Sesame Seed Dressing, page 101)
Yogurt-Herb Dressing (Carrot and Bulgur Salad with Yogurt-Herb Dressing, page 96)
Curry Dressing (Curried Vermicelli Noodle Salad, page 157)
Mustard Vinaigrette (Tomato, Broccoli, and Pasta Salad, page 155)
Italian Vinaigrette Dressing (Pasta and Fresh Vegetable Salad, page 154)
Walnut-Orange Dressing (Snow Pea and Red Pepper Buffet Salad, page 95)

POULTRY

Grilled Tandoori Chicken

Curried Chicken Crêpes

Curried Chicken and Tomato

Tarragon-Roasted Chicken ✓

Mushroom-Onion Stuffing ✓

Chicken and Shrimp Creole

Szechuan Orange-Ginger Chicken

Stir-Fried Chicken with Broccoli

Make-Ahead Paella

Barbecued Lemon Chicken ✓

Chicken with Preserved Lemons, Olives, and Coriander

Herb-Breaded Chicken

Stir-Fry for One

Grilled Turkey Scallopini with Herbs and Garlic

Selecting Poultry

Turkey, chicken, Cornish game hens, quail, and partridge are good choices. Avoid self-basting turkeys because they are injected with saturated fats. Duck and goose are very high in fat. Removing the skin from poultry significantly reduces fat content.

Grilled Tandoori Chicken

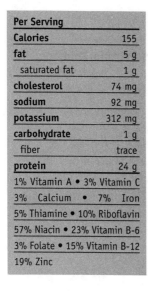

The Indian yogurt-and-spice marinade makes the chicken moist and flavorful. Serve with rice and a green vegetable such as asparagus, green beans or broccoli or see the Summer Barbecue menu on this page.

1 tbsp	Dijon mustard	15 mL
1 tbsp	canola oil	15 mL
½ cup	low-fat plain yogurt	125 mL
2 tbsp	minced fresh gingerroot	25 mL
1 tsp	ground cumin	5 mL
1 tsp	ground coriander	5 mL
½ tsp	ground turmeric	2 mL
¼ tsp	cayenne	1 mL
2 tbsp	chopped canned green chili or	25 mL
	1 jalapeño, seeded and chopped	
2 tbsp	lemon juice	25 mL
2 lb	skinless chicken pieces	1 kg

Summer Barbecue

Grilled Tandoori Chicken

New Potatoes with Herbs
  (page 181)

Sliced tomatoes with basil

Whole-Berry Blueberry Sorbet
  (page 246)

Microwave Oatmeal Squares
  (page 217)

Place mustard in mixing bowl; whisk in oil, drop by drop, until well blended. Stir in yogurt and gingerroot; set aside.

In skillet over medium heat, cook cumin, coriander, turmeric, and cayenne 1 to 2 minutes or until fragrant; stir into yogurt mixture with green chili; add lemon juice and mix well.

Using knife, make very small cuts in chicken. Arrange in shallow dish or place in plastic bag; pour yogurt-spice mixture over chicken and be sure to coat all pieces. Cover and refrigerate for at least 8 hours or up to 24 hours.

On greased grill over medium heat or under broiler, grill chicken for 15 to 20 minutes on each side (15 minutes if top is down on barbecue) or until chicken is tender and juices run clear when chicken is pierced with fork. Watch carefully and turn to prevent burning.

Makes 4 servings.

Curried Chicken Crêpes

This is a delicious dish to consider when you want a make-ahead dish for brunch, lunch, or dinner. If you keep crêpes in your freezer and have any leftover cooked chicken or turkey, this can be a quick and easy dinner. Cooked turkey, shrimp, or pork can be used instead of chicken.

Per Serving (2 crêpe)	
Calories	264
fat	11 g
saturated fat	4 g
cholesterol	60 mg
sodium	372 mg
potassium	352 mg
carbohydrate	19 g
fiber	1 g
protein	22 g
6% Vitamin A • 3% Vitamin C	
9% Calcium • 14% Iron	
13% Thiamine • 21% Riboflavin	
46% Niacin • 17% Vitamin B-6	
16% Folate • 14% Vitamin B-12	
18% Zinc	

2 tsp	canola oil	10 mL
½	medium onion, chopped	½
½ cup	diced celery	125 mL
1 tbsp	all-purpose flour	15 mL
1½ tsp	(approx.) curry powder or paste	7 mL
¼ tsp	salt	1 mL
½ cup	chicken stock	125 mL
1½ cups	diced cooked chicken (about	375 mL
	³/₄ lb/375 g boneless chicken breasts)	
¼ cup	sour cream	50 mL
¼ cup	low-fat plain yogurt	50 mL
8	Basic Crêpes (page 238)	8
	Yogurt, chutney, green grapes for garnish	

In saucepan, heat oil; over medium heat, cook onion and celery, stirring, until onion is softened. Add flour, curry powder, and salt; cook, stirring, for 1 minute.

Whisk in chicken stock and bring to simmer while whisking. Reduce heat to low and simmer, stirring, for 2 minutes. Remove from heat and stir in chicken, sour cream, and yogurt. Taste and add more curry powder if desired.

Place 2 or 3 large spoonfuls of chicken mixture across center of each crêpe. Roll up and place seam-side-down in lightly greased shallow baking dish.

Bake in 375°F/190°C oven for 20 minutes or microwave at high (100%) power for 2 minutes or until heated through. Top each serving with spoonful of yogurt and another of chutney; garnish plate with grapes.

Makes 4 servings of 2 crêpes each.

Old-Fashioned Chicken or Turkey Pot Pie

If you have leftover cooked chicken or turkey and any crisp-cooked vegetables such as carrots, green beans, zucchini, or leeks, combine them with sliced fresh mushrooms, frozen peas, and Cream Sauce (page 204). Season with touch of tarragon and sherry; spoon into baking dish.

Cover with mashed potatoes and bake in 375°F/190°C oven for 30 minutes or until hot and bubbly and potatoes are golden.

Note: Using mashed potatoes instead of pastry as a topping for a chicken or meat pie reduces the fat by about half.

Curried Chicken and Tomato

Per Serving	
Calories	208
fat	9 g
saturated fat	2 g
cholesterol	76 mg
sodium	116 mg
potassium	569 mg
carbohydrate	12 g
fiber	2 g
protein	22 g
9% Vitamin A • 25% Vitamin C	
11% Calcium • 19% Iron	
10% Thiamine • 18% Riboflavin	
39% Niacin • 21% Vitamin B-6	
9% Folate • 14% Vitamin B-12	
28% Zinc	

*Buy garam masala at specialty food shops, or make this version: in a spice grinder, combine 4 peppercorns, 2 cardamom seeds, 2 cloves, ¼-in/1 cm piece cinnamon stick, pinch each of cumin seeds and grated nutmeg (or add 1 tsp/5mL ground cinnamon, pinch each of ground nutmeg, ground cloves, and ground allspice). If you use a coffee grinder, check the manufacturer's instructions concerning grinding moist, gummy, or oily spices.

Make Ahead

Recipe can be prepared in advance, cooled, covered, and refrigerated for up to 2 days. To reheat, cook over medium heat, stirring occasionally, for about 20 minutes, or place uncovered in 350°F/180°C oven for 35 to 45 minutes or until heated through.

My friend and good cook Martha Lemieux showed me this wonderful dish. For an easy yet elegant dinner, serve small dishes of raisins, peanuts, coconut, chutney, and yogurt, plus rice, along with this curry. For a particularly delicious fresh flavor, grind the cumin and coriander seeds just before using, or add 1 tbsp/15 mL each of the spices previously ground. You can, however, substitute 2 tbsp/25 mL curry powder or paste (or more to taste), for the cumin and coriander seeds, turmeric, anise seed, and hot pepper flakes. Don't substitute canned tomatoes. The Sliced Cucumbers with Chives, Yogurt, and Basil (page 99) is particularly nice with this.

3 lb	skinless chicken pieces (thighs and legs)	1.5 kg
2 tbsp	canola oil	25 mL
4	medium onions, chopped	4
3 tbsp	minced fresh gingerroot	45 mL
5	cloves garlic, minced	5
2 tbsp	cumin seeds, ground	25 mL
2 tbsp	coriander seeds, ground	25 mL
1 tsp	turmeric	5 mL
1 tsp	anise seed	5 mL
¼ tsp	(approx.) hot pepper flakes	1 mL
4	large tomatoes, seeded and coarsely chopped	4
1½ cups	low-fat plain yogurt	375 mL
	Salt and pepper	
1 tsp	garam masala*	5 mL
⅓ cup	chopped fresh coriander	75 mL

In large Dutch oven or skillet, heat oil over medium-high heat; brown chicken pieces a few at a time and remove to plate. Add onions and cook for 5 to 10 minutes or until tender, stirring often. Add gingerroot, garlic, cumin, coriander, turmeric, anise seed, and hot pepper flakes; mix well and simmer for 1 minute. Add tomatoes and simmer for 2 minutes. Stir in yogurt.

Return chicken, including any juices, to pan and stir gently. Add more hot pepper flakes if desired. Cover and simmer for 25 to 30 minutes or until chicken is tender and cooked through. Season with salt and pepper to taste.

Just before serving, stir in garam masala and chopped coriander.

Makes 10 servings.

Compare (per serving)	g fat	calories
This recipe including chicken skin	20	305
This recipe without chicken skin	9	208

Winter Sunday-Dinner Menu
Tarragon-Roasted Chicken
Cranberry sauce
Baked Parsnips and Carrots
  (page 182)
Garlic-Parsley Potatoes
  (page 179)
Pear Streusel Cake
  (page 222)

Tarragon-Roasted Chicken

This is a delicious and easy way to cook chicken. Be sure to remove the skin when carving, as it has a large amount of fat.

2	cloves garlic	2
1	chicken (about 3 lb/1.5 kg)	1
2 tsp	dried tarragon	10 mL
3/4 cup	white wine	175 mL
1 tbsp	olive oil	15 mL

Per Serving	
Calories	176
fat	10 g
saturated fat	2 g
cholesterol	69 mg
sodium	61 mg
potassium	249 mg
carbohydrate	trace
fiber	0 g
protein	19 g
2% Vitamin A • 0% Vitamin C	
1% Calcium • 6% Iron	
4% Thiamine • 9% Riboflavin	
49% Niacin • 32% Vitamin B-6	
2% Folate • 7% Vitamin B-12	
17% Zinc	

Cut 1 garlic clove in half. Rub cut sides on outside of chicken; place garlic in chicken cavity. Sprinkle half the tarragon in chicken cavity. Truss chicken (page 112) with string and place in roasting pan.

Mince remaining garlic and combine with remaining tarragon, wine, and oil; drizzle over chicken. Roast in 350°F/180°C oven, basting frequently, for 1 1/4 hours or until juices run clear when chicken is pierced and meat thermometer inserted in thigh registers 185°F/85°C.

Makes 6 servings.

Mushroom-Onion Stuffing

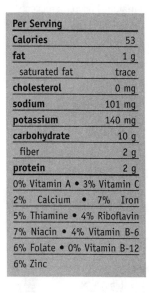

Per Serving	
Calories	53
fat	1 g
saturated fat	trace
cholesterol	0 mg
sodium	101 mg
potassium	140 mg
carbohydrate	10 g
fiber	2 g
protein	2 g
0% Vitamin A • 3% Vitamin C	
2% Calcium • 7% Iron	
5% Thiamine • 4% Riboflavin	
7% Niacin • 4% Vitamin B-6	
6% Folate • 0% Vitamin B-12	
6% Zinc	

This stuffing is good with chicken or turkey. Serve with cranberry sauce, and nobody will notice if you don't have gravy. I always make breadcrumbs using my food processor.

3 cups	fresh whole-wheat breadcrumbs*	750 mL
1 1/2 cups	coarsely chopped mushrooms	375 mL
1 cup	finely chopped celery	250 mL
2	small onions, finely chopped	2
1 tsp	dried thyme	5 mL
1 tsp	dried sage	5 mL
1/4 tsp	freshly ground pepper	1 mL

In large bowl, combine breadcrumbs, mushrooms, celery, onions, thyme, sage, and pepper.

Makes 6 cups (1.5 L), enough for a 6 lb/3 kg chicken (about 8 servings).

*These breadcrumbs are homemade in a food processor. They are not the fine store-bought crumbs.

Stuffing a Chicken or Turkey
Stuff a bird just before cooking. If you stuff it in advance, even if you refrigerate it, the center will take time to become cold and you run the risk of contamination. Fill cavity but don't pack it in, it will expand during cooking. Fasten closed with skewers or sew closed using a needle and string or thread.

To Truss a Chicken or Turkey
Use a cotton string to tie the legs and wings close to the body. This prevents the legs and wings from becoming overcooked and dried out before the rest of the bird is cooked.

Variations
Instead of mushrooms or celery, add chopped apple or pear, cooked cranberries, or chopped dried apricots; or replace half of the breadcrumbs with cooked wild rice.

Chicken and Shrimp Creole

Monda Rosenberg, food editor of Chatelaine *magazine was the source of inspiration for this recipe. I've served it at buffet dinners at my home and taken it to potlucks. If preparing in advance, use parboiled (converted) rice, as some kinds of rice get mushy when reheated. Cooked, sliced Italian sausage is a tasty addition or substitute for shrimp in this dish.*

Per Serving	
Calories	396
fat	5 g
saturated fat	1 g
cholesterol	160 mg
sodium	705 mg
potassium	833 mg
carbohydrate	47 g
fiber	3 g
protein	39 g

18% Vitamin A • 95% Vitamin C
10% Calcium • 27% Iron
13% Thiamine • 13% Riboflavin
91% Niacin • 38% Vitamin B-6
15% Folate • 58% Vitamin B-12
28% Zinc

1½ lb	boneless, skinless chicken	750 g
1 tbsp	canola oil	15 mL
2	onions, coarsely chopped	2
3	cloves garlic, minced	3
1	each sweet red and green pepper, coarsely chopped	1
1	can (28 oz/796 mL) diced tomatoes (undrained)	1
3½ cups	chicken stock	875 mL
1 tsp	dried thyme	5 mL
2 tsp	dried oregano	10 mL
¼ tsp	each cayenne and black pepper	1 mL
2 cups	parboiled (converted) rice	500 mL
1 lb	large shrimp, peeled and deveined	500 g
½ cup	chopped fresh parsley	125 mL
	Hot pepper sauce to taste (optional)	

Buffet Dinner for 16
(Double or triple recipes when needed.)
Spinach-Onion Dip with fresh vegetables (page 63)
Spiced Meatballs with Coriander Dipping Sauce (page 68)
Chicken and Shrimp Creole
Tossed Seasonal Greens (page 100)
Hot French bread
Oranges in Grand Marnier (page 236)
Strawberry Mousse (page 242)

Cut chicken into 1-in/2.5-cm cubes. In large nonstick skillet or heavy pan, heat oil over medium-high heat; cook chicken in batches for about 3 minutes or until lightly browned. Add onions and garlic; cook for 5 minutes or until softened. Stir in peppers; add tomatoes. Add stock, thyme, oregano, cayenne, and pepper; bring to boil. Stir in rice; cover, reduce heat and simmer for 15 minutes or until most of the liquid is absorbed.

Add shrimp to rice mixture; cover and cook for 5 minutes or until shrimp are pink. Stir in parsley and hot pepper sauce (if using).

Makes 8 servings.

Szechuan Orange-Ginger Chicken

This popular recipe is much easier and faster to make than it looks. Asian dishes from the Szechuan region of China usually have a spicy, hot flavor; if you prefer a milder taste, use less chili paste—the dish is delicious either way. Serve with rice.

1 lb	boneless, skinless chicken breasts	500 g
1	sweet green pepper	1
1	sweet red pepper	1
1	orange	1
1 tsp	bottled chili paste* or	5 mL
	¼ tsp/1 mL dried hot pepper flakes	
2 tbsp	sherry	25 mL
1 tbsp	soy sauce	15 mL
1 tsp	granulated sugar	5 mL
1 tsp	cornstarch	5 mL
2 tbsp	canola oil	25 mL
3	cloves garlic, minced	3
1 tbsp	minced fresh gingerroot	15 mL

*Bottled chili paste or Asian hot chili sauce is available in some supermarkets and most Asian grocery stores. You can substitute dried chili peppers. The seeds in fresh or dried peppers are very hot; if you want a milder taste, omit seeds.

Cut chicken into 1-in/2.5-cm squares; set aside. Halve green and red peppers and remove ribs and seeds; cut into 1-in/2.5-cm squares.

Finely grate the orange rind. Squeeze orange and reserve ¼ cup/50 mL juice.

In small bowl, combine reserved orange juice, chili paste, sherry, sugar, and cornstarch; stir until smooth.

In wok or large nonstick skillet, heat half the oil over high heat; add chicken and stir-fry for 3 minutes or until browned and no longer pink. Remove chicken. Add remaining oil, orange rind, garlic, and gingerroot; stir-fry for 10 seconds. Add peppers and stir-fry for 1 minute. Add chili paste mixture and bring to boil. Return chicken to wok and stir until heated through.

Makes 4 servings.

Stir-Fried Chicken with Broccoli

Stir-fries are perfect last-minute dishes that can easily be stretched to accommodate extra guests. Just add more broccoli or extra vegetables and cook more rice or noodles. If you have dried Chinese mushrooms on hand, use a few of them (soaked first) instead of fresh.

Per Serving	
Calories	174
fat	5 g
saturated fat	1 g
cholesterol	49 mg
sodium	239 mg
potassium	666 mg
carbohydrate	9 g
fiber	3 g
protein	22 g

49% Vitamin A • 65% Vitamin C
6% Calcium • 11% Iron
8% Thiamine • 14% Riboflavin
58% Niacin • 32% Vitamin B-6
20% Folate • 12% Vitamin B-12
13% Zinc

1½ lb	boned, skinned chicken breasts	750 g
2 tbsp	canola oil	25 mL
2 tbsp	minced fresh gingerroot	25 mL
2	onions, sliced	2
6 cups	broccoli florets	1.5 L
1 cup	thinly sliced carrots	250 mL
3 cups	sliced mushrooms (8 oz/250 g)	750 mL
¾ cup	chicken stock	175 mL
2 tbsp	sherry	25 mL
2 tsp	soy sauce	10 mL
2 tsp	cornstarch	10 mL
2 tbsp	water	25 mL
4 cups	sliced Chinese cabbage or bok choy*	1 L
¼ cup	chopped, toasted almonds (optional)	50 mL

Cut chicken into thin strips about 1½ in/4 cm long; set aside.

In wok or large heavy skillet, heat oil over high heat. Gradually add chicken to wok with half of the gingerroot; stir-fry for 2 minutes. Remove from wok and set aside. Add onion and stir-fry for 2 minutes; set aside with chicken.

Add broccoli, carrots, mushrooms, and remaining gingerroot to wok; stir-fry for 2 minutes, adding a little water to prevent sticking if necessary.

Mix together chicken stock, sherry, and soy sauce; pour over broccoli mixture. Cover and let steam for 2 minutes. Stir in reserved onion and chicken. Mix cornstarch with water; stir into wok and bring to boil. Add Chinese cabbage; stir and cook for 1 minute or until tender-crisp. Sprinkle with almonds before serving (if using).

Makes 8 servings.

*If neither is available, use thinly sliced green cabbage.

When stir-frying, it is very important to heat wok or heavy skillet and have oil very hot before adding any food. If food sticks, either the wok isn't hot enough or you need a little more oil. If food starts to stick after adding vegetables, add a little water to prevent scorching.

Make-Ahead Paella

This is one of my favorite dishes for entertaining—it looks spectacular, tastes delicious and can be mostly prepared in advance. It's great at any time of year for a sit-down dinner or special buffet. There are many versions of this Spanish specialty—so vary the seafood to your own tastes and to what's available. Saffron adds a delicate, delicious flavor and a beautiful yellow color but is expensive and sometimes hard to find. If unavailable, add 1 tsp/5 mL turmeric.

12	littleneck or Manila clams (in shells)	12
1 lb	mussels (in shells)	500 g
1 tsp	saffron threads	5 mL
1 tbsp	olive oil	15 mL
2 lb	skinless chicken thighs	1 kg
½ lb	Chorizo or dry Italian sausage	250 g
4	cloves garlic, minced	4
1½ cups	coarsely chopped tomato	375 mL
1	sweet green pepper, chopped	1
1	bay leaf	1
¼ tsp	ground turmeric	1 mL
¼ tsp	freshly ground pepper	1 mL
1½ cups	long- or medium-grain rice*	375 mL
3 cups	water or clam cooking liquid	750 mL
¾ lb	raw large shrimp, peeled and deveined	375 g
1 cup	peas	250 mL

Chorizo is a highly seasoned pork sausage with garlic, chili powder, and other spices. The Spanish version is made with smoked pork. Remove the casing before using.

*Use medium-grain rice if available. Long-grain parboiled rice is not as authentic but will result in firmer, more separate grains if making in advance.

**Because some clams take much longer to cook than others, I cook them in advance. I cook the mussels in the rice because they cook in a short time, and I want the liquid from them to flavor the dish.

Scrub clams and mussels under cold running water; cut off any hairy beards from mussels. Discard any clams or mussels that do not close when tapped. Refrigerate mussels until needed. Steam clams** over boiling water until shells open (about 5 minutes); reserve cooking liquid, discard any that don't open. Refrigerate until needed.

Place saffron in small bowl and pour 2 tbsp/25 mL boiling water over; set aside.

In paella pan or large deep skillet, heat oil over medium-high heat, cook chicken for about 15 minutes, turning to brown all over; transfer to plate.

Cut sausage into ¼-in/5-mm thick slices, add to pan and cook, stirring, until browned. Add garlic, tomatoes, green pepper, bay leaf, turmeric, and pepper; cook for 5 minutes. Stir in rice to coat, and then water, soaked saffron, and soaking liquid; bring to boil. Reduce heat to low, return chicken to pan, cover and cook for 15 minutes or until rice is nearly tender. (Recipe can be prepared ahead to this point, covered and refrigerated for up to 1 day. Return to stove, cook over medium heat until hot, adding water a few tablespoons at a time if pan is dry.)

Remove bay leaf. Add mussels, cooked clams, and shrimp; cover and simmer for 10 to 15 minutes or until mussels have opened and shrimp are pink (discard any mussels that don't open). Stir in peas until heated through.

Makes 10 servings.

Barbecued Lemon Chicken

This simple way to cook chicken is one of my husband's favorites— the chicken is moist and juicy and very delicious. In the winter, my friend Janet Dey cooks chicken this way in her fireplace barbecue.

4	boneless, skinless chicken breasts	4
	Juice of 1 lemon	
2 tsp	olive oil	10 mL
2	cloves garlic, minced	2
1 tsp	dried oregano	5 mL
Pinch	cayenne pepper	Pinch

In shallow dish, arrange chicken in single layer.

In small dish, combine lemon juice, oil, garlic, oregano, and cayenne; mix well. Pour over chicken and turn to coat both sides. Let stand at room temperature for 20 minutes or cover and refrigerate up to 6 hours.

On greased grill, cook chicken over medium heat for 4 to 5 minutes on each side or until meat is no longer pink inside.

Makes 4 servings.

To store mussels

Mussels will keep for 1 to 2 days in a bowl or paper bag in the refrigerator on top of ice covered with plastic. Cover mussels loosely with wrung out wet towel. Don't store in a plastic bag or submerge in water.

Dinner Party for Eight

Zucchini and Watercress
  Vichyssoise (page 81)
Make-Ahead Paella
Spinach Salad with Sesame
  Seed Dressing (page 101)
Fruit sorbets (pages
  246–247) with fresh fruit
  and Raspberry Sauce
  (page 241)

Per Serving	
Calories	177
fat	4 g
saturated fat	1 g
cholesterol	84 mg
sodium	73 mg
potassium	413 mg
carbohydrate	1 g
fiber	trace
protein	32 g
1% Vitamin A • 7% Vitamin C	
1% Calcium • 4% Iron	
5% Thiamine • 7% Riboflavin	
86% Niacin • 34% Vitamin B-6	
2% Folate • 17% Vitamin B-12	
11% Zinc	

Chicken with Preserved Lemons, Olives, and Coriander

Make-Ahead

Cover and refrigerate up to 1 day. Reheat, covered, in microwave or skillet.

Make-Ahead Dinner Party

Spiced Meatballs with
  Coriander Dipping Sauce
  (page 68)
Tossed Seasonal Greens
  (page 100)
Curried Chicken and Tomato
  (page 110) or Chicken with
  Preserved Lemons, Olives
  and Coriander
Bulgur Pilaf with Apricots
  and Raisins (page 179)
Sliced Cucumbers with
  Chives, Yogurt, and Basil
  (page 99)
Oranges in Grand Marnier
  (page 236)
Easy Cranberry-Chocolate
  Cookies (page 221)

Serve with basmati rice or couscous and a green vegetable or salad. Preserved lemons have a wonderful mellow citrus and salty flavor and a tender texture. They are easy to make or can be bought in specialty food stores. You can make this recipe without the preserved lemons—it is very good—but the lemons add an extra flavor and texture to the dish. (Recipe pictured opposite page 26.)

1 tbsp	extra-virgin olive oil	15 mL
3 lb	skinless chicken legs	1.5 kg
2 tsp	ground cumin	10 mL
2 tbsp	minced fresh gingerroot	25 mL
1/4 cup	fresh lemon juice	50 mL
1/2 tsp	each salt and pepper	2 mL
6	slices preserved lemons, cut in chunks (opposite page)	6
6 to 12	green or black olives	6 to 12
3 tbsp	chopped fresh coriander leaves	45 mL

In large skillet, heat oil over high heat; add chicken and brown on all sides. Stir in cumin and gingerroot; cook 1 minute; add lemon juice, salt, and pepper. Cover and cook over medium-low heat, turning often, until chicken is tender, about 35 to 45 minutes.

Add lemon pieces, olives, and coriander leaves. Cover and simmer 5 minutes.

Makes 6 servings.

Preserved Lemons

Salted preserved lemons are used in Tunisian, Moroccan, and Provençal cooking. They add a subtle and wonderful flavor to chicken, fish, and lamb dishes, as well as salad dressings, soups, and North African tagines. In France, they are often preserved in olive oil; in Tunisia and North Africa, they are preserved in lemon juice or brine.

5	lemons	5
½ cup	sea salt	125 mL
	Freshly squeezed lemon juice	

Wash lemons; quarter each lemon from the top to within ½ inch (2 cm) of the bottom. Sprinkle the inside with salt, then reshape the lemon.

Place 1 tbsp/15 mL of salt in a sterilized 2-cup/500-mL Mason-type jar. Pack in the lemons, salting between each, and packing down firmly to make room for lemons and to release juice.

Add freshly squeezed lemon juice to cover lemons. Fill to within ½ inch/2 cm of the top of the jar. Seal jar.

Let stand in a warm place for 3 weeks. Turn the jar upside down each day to distribute salt and juices. After 3 weeks, the rinds should be tender. Refrigerate up to 3 months.

To use, rinse each lemon under cold water; cut into chunks or slices. A white, lacy film may form, just rinse if off.

Makes 2 cups/500 mL.

Fresh Gingerroot

Fresh gingerroot is far superior to ground ginger. It is available in the fresh-produce section in supermarkets and at Asian grocery stores.

To store: Will keep in the refrigerator for 2 to 3 weeks, or wrap tightly in plastic wrap and freeze for up to 4 weeks.

To use: Peel the skin from the portion to be used with a sharp knife or vegetable peeler, then either chop or finely grate it. I use fresh gingerroot most often in stir-fries such as Szechuan Orange-Ginger Chicken (page 114) and with vegetables such as Broccoli with Ginger and Lemon (page 190).

To substitute ground ginger in recipes calling for gingerroot (only if you can't find gingerroot): Use about ½ tsp/2 mL ground ginger in most recipes in this book. Taste, then add another ½ tsp/2 mL if desired. Use ground ginger where called for in baked recipes.

Leftover Chicken or Turkey

Turkey or chicken leftovers can be used for a lovely lunch or dinner in the following recipes:
Curried Chicken Croustades (page 72)
Turkey Noodle Soup (page 88)
Tarragon Chicken Salad (page 90)
Curried Chicken Crêpes (page 109)
Chicken and Shrimp Creole (page 113)
Old-Fashioned Chicken or Turkey Pot Pie (page 109)
As a pizza topping

Herb-Breaded Chicken

My son John likes to make this when it is his turn to cook dinner. I try to keep chicken breasts and a jar of these seasoned breadcrumbs in my freezer so I can make this in a jiffy. Don't worry if you don't have all the herbs, just use a little more of the ones you have. I also use these crumbs on pork tenderloin, fish fillets, and broiled tomato halves.

1½	slices whole-wheat bread or	1½
	¾ cup/175 mL coarse crumbs	
½ tsp	each dried basil, thyme, oregano,	2 mL
	tarragon, paprika, and salt	
	Freshly ground pepper	
1 lb	boneless, skinless chicken breasts	500 g
	(about 4 breast pieces or	
	2 lb/1 kg bone-in chicken breasts*)	

Other alternatives to takeout chicken:

Barbecued Lemon Chicken (page 117)

Grilled Turkey Scallopini with Herbs and Garlic (page 122)

Stir-Fried Chicken with Broccoli (page 115)

Single Serving

For one boneless chicken breast, use about ¼ cup/50 mL of crumb mixture (freeze remainder for another time). Bake or microwave, uncovered, on high power for 2 minutes; let stand 1 minute.

I always use the leaf form of dried herbs, not the powdered, and find most recipes are better with this form. Also, the more finely ground the herbs, the quicker they will lose flavor under storage.

In food processor or blender, process bread to make crumbs. Add basil, thyme, oregano, tarragon, paprika, salt, and pepper to taste; process to mix.

Rinse chicken under cold running water; shake off water. Transfer crumb mixture to plastic bag; add chicken a few pieces at a time and shake to coat.

Place chicken in single layer in microwave-safe dish or on baking sheet. Bake in 400°F/200°C oven for 18 to 20 minutes for boneless breasts, 40 minutes for bone-in, or until no longer pink inside.

Microwave Method: Microwave, uncovered, at high power for 5 minutes for boneless, 9 minutes for bone-in; let stand for 1 minute.

Makes 4 servings.

*When using bone-in chicken breasts, double the amount of bread and herbs.

Stir-Fry for One

Stir-fries are a quick and easy meal for one or two people and an excellent way to use up a piece of broccoli or half a red pepper lurking in the refrigerator—add a few more vegetables and they can easily be stretched to make an extra serving. Don't be put off by the long list of ingredients—they only take a minute or two to put together and taste delicious. Serve over hot rice or noodles.

	Per Serving	
Calories		320
fat		12 g
saturated fat		1 g
cholesterol		66 mg
sodium		453 mg
potassium		928 mg
carbohydrate		18 g
fiber		5 g
protein		31 g
43% Vitamin A • 353% Vitamin C		
8% Calcium • 16% Iron		
14% Thiamine • 18% Riboflavin		
74% Niacin • 50% Vitamin B-6		
40% Folate • 14% Vitamin B-12		
18% Zinc		

¼ lb	boneless chicken, beef, or pork	125 g
1 tsp	cornstarch	5 mL
1 tbsp	sherry or white wine	15 mL
1	stalk broccoli or celery	1
½	sweet red pepper	½
2 tsp	canola oil	10 mL
1	clove garlic, minced	1
1 tsp	minced fresh gingerroot	5 mL

SEASONING SAUCE

1 tbsp	water	15 mL
1 tbsp	sherry or white wine	15 mL
½ tsp	cornstarch	2 mL
1 tsp	soy sauce	5 mL

Cut meat into thin strips about 2 in/5 cm long. In bowl, mix cornstarch and sherry; stir in meat and let stand for 10 minutes or up to 2 hours. Cut vegetables into florets or thin strips. In small bowl, combine water, sherry, cornstarch, and soy sauce; mix well.

In wok or non-stick skillet, heat oil over high heat. Add garlic, gingerroot, and meat and stir-fry for 1 minute. Add broccoli and red pepper and stir-fry 2 minutes or until tender-crisp; add water if necessary to prevent scorching. Stir in seasoning sauce and stir-fry for another minute.

Makes 1 serving.

Spring Barbecue
Grilled Turkey Scallopini
  with Herbs and Garlic
  (page 121)
Asparagus
Wild rice and mushrooms
Spinach Salad with Sesame
  Seed Dressing (page 101)
Rhubarb-Strawberry Sorbet
  (page 246)

Grilled Turkey Scallopini with Herbs and Garlic

Per Serving	
Calories	206
fat	10 g
saturated fat	2 g
cholesterol	62 mg
sodium	201 mg
potassium	294 mg
carbohydrate	2 g
fiber	trace
protein	27 g
0% Vitamin A • 7% Vitamin C	
2% Calcium • 11% Iron	
5% Thiamine • 8% Riboflavin	
49% Niacin • 29% Vitamin B-6	
3% Folate • 17% Vitamin B-12	
21% Zinc	

This is a favorite dish of mine for summer entertaining. It's extremely fast and easy, and very tasty. Because turkey is tender and this is a fairly strong-flavored marinade, it doesn't need hours of marinating and can be prepared at the last minute or an hour or two in advance. Veal scallopini can be used instead of turkey.

3	cloves garlic, minced	3
1/2 tsp	each dried thyme, rosemary, and oregano	2 mL
2 tbsp	olive oil	25 mL
2 tbsp	lemon juice	25 mL
1/4 tsp	salt	1 mL
	Freshly ground pepper	
1 lb	turkey scallopini*	500 g

30-Minute Summer Barbecue

Grilled Turkey Scallopini with
  Herbs and Garlic
Corn on the cob
French bread
Sliced tomatoes
Strawberries with Raspberry
  Sauce (page 241)

In small bowl, combine garlic, thyme, rosemary, oregano, oil, lemon juice, salt, and pepper to taste; mix well. Brush over both sides of turkey. (Grill immediately or cover and let stand at room temperature for 30 minutes or refrigerate for up to 2 hours.) On lightly greased grill over high heat, grill turkey for 2 minutes on each side or just until cooked through.

Makes 4 servings.

*If turkey scallopini aren't available in your store, slice partially frozen turkey breast meat thinly, then pound between two pieces of waxed paper into 1/4-in/5-mm-thick slices or use veal scallopini.

FISH AND SEAFOOD

Fish is an original fast food that's easy to cook at home. Not only does it taste good but it is very nutritious. It is an excellent source of high-quality protein, is high in Vitamins A, D, and B-complex, and is low in fat, particularly saturated fat. Fish contains the beneficial Omega-3 type of fat, which according to the latest research, helps to reduce the incidence of heart disease. Most fish is lower in cholesterol than meat and poultry.

For many years, shellfish were banned from diets prescribed to lower blood cholesterol because of a supposed high sterol count. But better testing techniques can now discriminate between the different sterols and show that cholesterol isn't present in shellfish in so large an amount as to be of concern. Shrimp is the shellfish that is highest in cholesterol, but as long as you don't have it too often or are on a low-cholesterol diet, it can still be enjoyed.

The two most important factors in preparing tasty fish are, above all, to buy good-quality fish, either fresh or frozen, and to not overcook it. You can substitute one kind of fish for another in the recipes here. Buy whatever kind is freshest and use in the recipe that appeals most to you.

Fish Fillets with Herbed Crumbs

Per Serving	
Calories	136
fat	4 g
saturated fat	2 g
cholesterol	75 mg
sodium	128 mg
potassium	382 mg
carbohydrate	2 g
fiber	trace
protein	22 g

6% Vitamin A • 7% Vitamin C
5% Calcium • 13% Iron
4% Thiamine • 4% Riboflavin
36% Niacin • 17% Vitamin B-6
7% Folate • 62% Vitamin B-12
6% Zinc

Here's an easy-to-make and tasty way to serve fish fillets. It's really quick if you make your breadcrumbs and chop the parsley in a blender or food processor, then cook the fish in a microwave.

1 lb	fish fillets	500 g
⅓ cup	fresh breadcrumbs	75 mL
1 tbsp	olive oil or canola oil	15 mL
¼ cup	chopped fresh parsley	50 mL
1 tsp	dried thyme	5 mL
¼ tsp	freshly ground pepper	1 mL

In shallow baking dish or microwave-safe dish, arrange fillets in single layer. Combine breadcrumbs, oil, parsley, thyme, and pepper; mix well and sprinkle over fish.

Bake uncovered in 450°F/230°C oven for 10 minutes per inch of thickness (5 to 7 minutes per cm) for fresh fish, 20 minutes per inch (10 to 12 minutes per cm) for frozen, or until fish flakes easily when tested with fork.

Microwave Method: Microwave, uncovered, at high (100%) power for about 4 minutes for fresh fish or until fish flakes easily when tested with fork.

Makes 4 servings.

Cod is higher in cholesterol than many other fish. In sole, the cholesterol drops to about 60 g; in halibut, it's about 55 g per serving.

Tilapia is a mild-flavored fish that young children usually enjoy.

Buying Fish

Odor and appearance are the clues to the freshness of seafood. There should be no strong fishy odor, the eyes should be bright and bulging, not sunken into the head. The skin should spring back when pressed lightly. When I buy fish, I ask the salesperson what fish came in that day and choose from these.

Storing Fish

Wash, pat dry, and cover with an airtight wrapper. Fish can be refrigerated for about two days or in a freezer as long as three months.

Fish Fillets with Basil and Lemon

This is so simple and easy yet results in the best-tasting fish. If buying frozen fillets, try to buy those that have been frozen in a single layer or individually wrapped. If using the kind that has been frozen in a block, defrost the fish and separate into fillets before cooking. If buying fresh, choose whatever kind of fillet is freshest. About 1 tbsp/15 mL of any fresh herbs, such as chopped fresh dill, thyme or tarragon, can be substituted for the basil.

1 lb	fish fillets	500 g
1 tbsp	lemon juice	15 mL
2 tsp	olive oil	10 mL
1/2 tsp	dried basil or 1 tbsp/15 mL fresh	2 mL
	Freshly ground pepper	
	Fresh herbs or chopped fresh parsley for garnish	

Per Serving	
Calories	130
fat	5 g
saturated fat	1 g
cholesterol	52 mg
sodium	96 mg
potassium	348 mg
carbohydrate	trace
fiber	0 g
protein	20 g

12% Vitamin A • 3% Vitamin C
1% Calcium • 1% Iron
15% Thiamine • 6% Riboflavin
27% Niacin • 24% Vitamin B-6
3% Folate • 110% Vitamin B-12
10% Zinc

In microwave-safe or conventional baking dish, arrange fillets in a single layer. In small dish, combine lemon juice, oil, and basil; drizzle over fish. Sprinkle lightly with pepper to taste.

Bake, uncovered, in 450°F/230°C oven for 8 to 10 minutes (10 minutes per inch/2.5 cm thickness for fresh fish) or until fish is opaque and flakes easily with fork. Sprinkle with fresh herbs or parsley.

Microwave Method: Cover with plastic wrap and turn back corner to vent. Microwave at high (100%) power for 3 1/2 to 4 1/2 minutes or until fish is opaque and flakes easily with fork.

Makes 4 servings.

Cooking Fish

Fish and shellfish are naturally tender. They should be cooked for a short time at a high temperature. To determine the length of cooking time, measure the thickness of the fish at its thickest part. Cook fresh fish 10 minutes per inch of thickness, adding five minutes if wrapped in foil; frozen fish requires 20 minutes per inch, plus 10 minutes if wrapped in foil. Cooking time may vary depending on the cooking method used. Don't overcook. Overcooked fish becomes dry, tough, and rubbery and loses its flavor. Fish is cooked when the flesh is opaque and it flakes easily.

Sole with Tomatoes

This is a delicious and easy-to-make dish for one. Serve with a green vegetable along with potatoes, rice or bread. For two servings, double the ingredients and place on one plate before microwaving for 4 to 5 minutes.

1	medium tomato, thickly sliced	1
1	fillet sole, about 5 oz/140 g	1
1/2 tsp	olive oil	2 mL
1/2 tsp	lemon juice	2 mL
2 tsp	chopped fresh basil, dill or parsley (or 1/4 tsp/1 mL dried)	10 mL
	Freshly ground pepper	

On microwave-safe plate, arrange tomato slices in single layer. Arrange fish to cover tomatoes; drizzle with oil and lemon juice. Sprinkle with basil and pepper to taste. Cover with vented plastic wrap; microwave at high (100%) power for 3 minutes or until fish is almost opaque and flakes easily when tested with fork. Remove from oven and let stand for 1 minute. If necessary, pour off excess liquid from plate.

Conventional Oven Method: In shallow baking dish, arrange fish; cover with sliced tomato. Drizzle with oil and lemon juice. Sprinkle with basil and pepper to taste. Bake in 400°F/200°C oven for 12 minutes or until fish is almost opaque and flakes easily when tested with a fork.

Makes 1 serving.

Steamed Fish

Instead of grilling, fish can be cooked in a fish steamer. If you don't have a fish steamer, you can:
- *Use a wok with a lid. Place fish on a heatproof plate. Add a small amount of water to the bottom of a wok and bring to a boil. Set two chopsticks above water level in the wok and place the plate on the chopsticks. Cover. The steam will circulate around the fish and cook it gently.*
- *Use a roasting pan. Place a rack in the roaster and a heatproof plate on top of the rack. Add water to below the level of the plate. To prevent the fish from falling apart, wrap in cheesecloth or lettuce leaves. Cover with a lid or foil. Cook until fish is opaque and flakes easily when tested with a fork.*

Dilled Trout Fillets with Cucumber-Yogurt Sauce

Any kind of fish fillets—snapper, sole, sea bass—can be used; just choose whatever is freshest. If at all possible, try to use fresh dill instead of dried because the flavor is quite different.

1¼ lb	rainbow trout fillets	625 g
1 tbsp	lemon juice	15 mL
1	clove garlic, minced	1
2 tbsp	chopped fresh dill	25 mL
	(or 1 tsp/5 mL dried)	

CUCUMBER-YOGURT SAUCE

½ cup	low-fat plain yogurt or	125 mL
	light sour cream	
½ cup	finely chopped cucumber	125 mL
1 tbsp	chopped green onion	15 mL
1 tbsp	chopped fresh dill, basil or parsley	15 mL
½	clove garlic, minced	½
	Salt and freshly ground pepper	

Per Serving	
Calories	212
fat	8 g
saturated fat	3 g
cholesterol	77 mg
sodium	69 mg
potassium	604 mg
carbohydrate	3 g
fiber	trace
protein	29 g

11% Vitamin A • 15% Vitamin C
14% Calcium • 4% Iron
22% Thiamine • 10% Riboflavin
65% Niacin • 27% Vitamin B-6
16% Folate • 284% Vitamin B-12
10% Zinc

On broiler pan or in microwave-safe dish, arrange fillets in single layer with thickest part to outside. Brush with lemon juice; sprinkle with garlic and dill. Broil for 6 to 8 minutes or microwave, covered loosely with waxed paper, at high (100%) power for 4 to 5 minutes or until fish is opaque and flakes easily when tested with fork.

Cucumber-Yogurt Sauce: Meanwhile, in small dish, combine yogurt, cucumber, onion, dill, garlic, salt, and pepper to taste; mix well. Spread over fish and broil for 2 minutes or microwave at high (100%) power for 1 minute or until sauce is hot.

Makes 4 servings.

Sauces to serve over grilled, poached or microwaved fish:
Tomato-Shallot Dressing
  (page 92)
Tomato Salsa Sauce
  (page 129)
Watercress Sauce (page 130)
Yogurt Béarnaise Sauce
  (page 205)
Quick Tzatziki Sauce
  (page 143)

Teriyaki Cod Fillets

These fillets are absolutely delicious. Any kind of fish can be used in this recipe, but I like cod and salmon the best.

1 lb	cod fillets, ¾ in/2 cm thick	500 g
2 tsp	finely grated gingerroot	10 mL
1 tbsp	dry sherry, wine or lemon juice	15 mL
1 tbsp	honey	15 mL
1 tbsp	soy sauce*	15 mL
1 tsp	sesame oil	5 mL
1	large clove garlic, minced	1
1 tbsp	chopped green onions	15 mL
1 tsp	sesame seeds	5 mL

Arrange fillets in single layer in shallow 4-cup/2 L glass baking dish.

Microwaving Fish

One of the best reasons for owning a microwave is to cook fish. It takes only minutes to cook and is very moist. Arrange fish in a microwave dish with the thickest part facing the outside of the dish. Season with pepper, lemon juice or herbs (always add salt after microwaving, not before). Place plastic wrap over dish with a small corner turned back for steam to escape. One pound of fresh or thawed fillets in a single layer at high setting takes about 4 to 5 minutes (10 to 12 for frozen). Times will vary depending on thickness. Rotate dish during cooking.

In small bowl, whisk together gingerroot, sherry, honey, soy sauce, sesame oil, and garlic; pour over fillets and marinate at room temperature for 20 minutes or refrigerate for up to 4 hours, turning once or twice.

Sprinkle fillets with green onions and sesame seeds; bake in 450°F/230°C oven for 8 to 10 minutes or until fish is opaque and flakes easily when tested with fork.

Microwave Method: Cover dish (fish and marinade) with vented plastic wrap and microwave at high (100%) power for 5 minutes or until fish is opaque and flakes easily when tested with fork.

Makes 4 servings.

*Naturally brewed soy sauce is lower in sodium than chemically brewed.

Grilled Halibut Steaks with Tomato Salsa Sauce

As well as its delicious taste when barbecued, halibut is a good choice for grilling because it doesn't fall apart as some fish does. However, other kinds of firm-fleshed fish, such as salmon, can be substituted. Instead of using a rich cream sauce, dress grilled fish with a light, fresh Mexican salsa. This fairly mild tomato and cucumber salsa does not overpower the delicate flavor of fish. For extra spiciness, add chopped hot peppers to taste.

Per Serving	
Calories	207
fat	5 g
saturated fat	1 g
cholesterol	54 mg
sodium	94 mg
potassium	859 mg
carbohydrate	3 g
fiber	1 g
protein	36 g
16% Vitamin A • 48% Vitamin C	
8% Calcium • 11% Iron	
9% Thiamine • 9% Riboflavin	
71% Niacin • 32% Vitamin B-6	
12% Folate • 91% Vitamin B-12	
9% Zinc	

1½ lb	halibut steaks, about ¾ in/2 cm thick	750 g

TOMATO SALSA SAUCE

⅓ cup	finely diced cucumber	75 mL
⅓ cup	finely diced sweet red pepper	75 mL
2 tbsp	finely diced red onion	25 mL
1	small ripe tomato, finely diced	1
2 tsp	red wine vinegar	10 mL
2 tsp	chopped fresh coriander (optional)	10 mL
Dash	hot pepper sauce	Dash
1 tsp	olive oil	5 mL
	Salt and pepper to taste	

Tomato Salsa Sauce: In bowl, combine cucumber, red pepper, onion, tomato, vinegar, coriander (if using), hot pepper sauce, and oil; stir to mix. In food processor, purée half of the salsa mixture; combine with remaining salsa.

On greased grill over medium heat or in broiler, grill fish, turning once, for about 4 minutes on each side or until fish is opaque and flakes easily when tested with fork. Place on serving platter or plates and spoon salsa over.

Microwave Method: Place steaks in single layer in microwave-safe dish; cover with vented plastic wrap and microwave at high (100%) power for 4 to 5 minutes or until opaque.

Makes 4 servings (1¼ cups/300 mL sauce).

Serve with Carrots and Leeks with Parsley (page 193) and boiled new potatoes or couscous.

Oven-Steaming Fish

This method is the easiest and requires the least cleanup. Place fish on the shiny side of foil and season with lemon juice and/or herbs. Wrap fish in foil and place on cookie sheet. Bake in 450°F/230°C oven for required time (page 125), depending on thickness.

Quick and Easy Salmon Steaks
with Watercress Sauce

Per Serving	
Calories	263
fat	13 g
saturated fat	3 g
cholesterol	66 mg
sodium	347 mg
potassium	491 mg
carbohydrate	3 g
fiber	trace
protein	31 g
5% Vitamin A • 15% Vitamin C	
9% Calcium • 4% Iron	
28% Thiamine • 18% Riboflavin	
60% Niacin • 38% Vitamin B-6	
22% Folate • 162% Vitamin B-12	
10% Zinc	

Fresh salmon steaks or fillets are a wonderful treat and I like them best when simply cooked—either grilled, broiled, or wrapped in foil. In summer, dress them up with this Watercress sauce; in winter, serve with the Fresh Dill Cream Sauce (page 204). (Recipe pictured opposite page 154.)

4	salmon fillets or steaks,	4
	1 in/2.5 cm thick (5 oz/150 g each)	
1 tbsp	lemon juice	15 mL
	Freshly ground pepper	
	Watercress sprigs	

WATERCRESS SAUCE

1 cup	light sour cream	250 mL
¼ cup	low-fat plain yogurt	50 mL
½ cup	finely chopped fresh	125 mL
	watercress leaves	
2 tbsp	chopped fresh parsley	25 mL
1 tbsp	chopped fresh chives or green onions	15 mL
2 tsp	grated Parmesan cheese	10 mL
	Salt and freshly ground pepper to taste	

The watercress sauce also makes a wonderful dip for fresh vegetables.

The only way to ruin good-quality fish is to overcook it. If fillets or steaks are ¾ to 1 in (2–2.5 cm) thick, you'll be much less likely to over-cook them than if they are thin. Cooking times in this recipe are based on 1-in/2.5-cm-thick steaks.

On large, lightly oiled piece of foil, or microwave-safe dish, arrange salmon in single layer. Sprinkle with lemon juice, and pepper to taste. Fold foil over salmon and seal; place on baking sheet. Bake in 400°F/200°C oven for about 15 minutes. Or, in microwave-safe dish, cover with plastic wrap; fold back corner to vent. Microwave at high (100%) power for 5 minutes or until fish is opaque and flakes easily with fork.

Watercress Sauce: Combine sour cream, yogurt, chopped watercress, parsley, chives, Parmesan, salt, and pepper to taste; stir until well mixed. Sauce can be made up to 1 day in advance.

Arrange salmon on plates and garnish with sprig of watercress. Pass sauce separately.

Makes 4 servings.

The New Lighthearted Cookbook

Barbecued Skewered Salmon with Red Peppers and Snow Peas

These easy-to-make kabobs look festive, taste great and, as an added bonus, make the fish go further. Serve over rice along with Tomato Salsa Sauce (page 129) or Cucumber-Yogurt Sauce (page 127). Be sure to soak the wooden skewers in water for at least 30 minutes to prevent charring.

1 lb	center-cut salmon or swordfish steaks	500 g
	Juice of 1 lime or lemon	
1 tbsp	olive oil	15 mL
2 tbsp	chopped fresh coriander, parsley, or dill	25 mL
	Salt and freshly ground pepper	
1	sweet red pepper	1
20	snow peas	20

Per Serving	
Calories	198
fat	11 g
saturated fat	2 g
cholesterol	49 mg
sodium	50 mg
potassium	423 mg
carbohydrate	4 g
fiber	1 g
protein	19 g

12% Vitamin A • 112% Vitamin C
2% Calcium • 7% Iron
25% Thiamine • 9% Riboflavin
44% Niacin • 34% Vitamin B-6
18% Folate • 110% Vitamin B-12
6% Zinc

Remove skin from fish if necessary; cut into 1-in/2.5-cm cubes; place in a single layer in a shallow dish. Sprinkle with lime juice, oil, coriander, salt, and pepper; cover and refrigerate for 30 minutes, turning once or twice.

Seed and cut red pepper into 1-in/2.5-cm squares. String snow peas and blanch in boiling water for 1 minute or until bright green and easily bent.

Thread fish on water-soaked wooden skewers, alternating with red pepper and snow peas folded in half. Grill over medium heat, turning once or twice, for 5 to 10 minutes or until fish is opaque.

Makes 4 servings.

Mussel, Clam, and Fish Stew

Serve this wonderfully warming seafood soup-stew for lunch, dinner or as late-night party fare. If fresh mussels and clams aren't available, use canned or bottled ones. Shrimp can be added instead of clams. Some fish markets sell fresh fish pieces, often called chowder bits or pieces. These are usually inexpensive and ideal for this recipe; remove any skin and bones.

2 tsp	canola oil	10 mL
1	onion, chopped	1
1	stalk celery, chopped	1
1	carrot, chopped	1
2	cloves garlic, minced	2
1 tsp	fennel or anise seed	5 mL
1/2 tsp	dried thyme	2 mL
1 tsp	dried basil	5 mL
1	can (28 oz/796 mL) diced tomatoes	1
2 cups	water	500 mL
2	potatoes, diced	2
1 lb	mussels	500 g
1 lb	small clams (or one 5-oz/142-g can)	500 g
1 lb	fresh white-flesh fish (cod, haddock, monkfish)	500 g
1/2 cup	white wine	125 mL
	Salt and freshly ground pepper	
1/2 cup	chopped fresh parsley	125 mL

Make-Ahead Winter Lunch or Late-Night Dinner

Parsley-Onion Dip with fresh
  vegetables (page 63)
Mussel, Clam, and Fish Stew
Five-Grain Soda Bread
  (page 226)
Winter Fruit Compote
  with Figs and Apricots
  (page 235)

In large saucepan, heat oil over medium heat; cook onion, celery, and carrot, stirring, for 5 minutes. Add garlic, fennel, thyme, basil, tomatoes, water, and potatoes; bring to simmer. Cover and cook over low heat for 20 minutes or until vegetables are tender. Remove bay leaf.

Meanwhile, scrub mussels and clams under cold running water; cut off any hairy beards from mussels. Discard any clams or mussels that do not close when tapped. Add clams to saucepan; simmer for 5 minutes. Add mussels, fish (if using monkfish, cut into chunks), and wine. Simmer for 5 minutes or until clams and mussels open; discard any that don't open. Season with salt and pepper to taste. (Stew can be prepared up to 1 day in advance, refrigerated, and reheated.) Just before serving, sprinkle with parsley.

Makes 6 servings, 1³⁄₄ cups/425 mL each.

Swordfish Steaks with Lime and Coriander

Fresh lime juice and coriander complement the flavor of most fish. Swordfish is particularly good for barbecuing because its firm flesh doesn't fall apart. Other fresh fish steaks, such as halibut or salmon, are also delicious cooked this way. If fresh coriander isn't available, substitute other herbs, such as fresh parsley, dill, rosemary or oregano. Serve with Tomato Salsa Sauce (page 129).

Per Serving	
Calories	169
fat	8 g
saturated fat	2 g
cholesterol	44 mg
sodium	102 mg
potassium	339 mg
carbohydrate	1 g
fiber	0 g
protein	22 g
4% Vitamin A • 5% Vitamin C	
1% Calcium • 6% Iron	
3% Thiamine • 6% Riboflavin	
64% Niacin • 19% Vitamin B-6	
1% Folate • 89% Vitamin B-12	
14% Zinc	

1 lb	swordfish or halibut steaks	500 g
	(about ³⁄₄ in/2 cm thick)	
	Juice of 1 lime	
1 tbsp	olive oil	15 mL
2 tbsp	chopped fresh coriander	25 mL
	(or ¹⁄₂ tsp/2 mL ground)	
	Freshly ground pepper	
	Lime wedges, fresh coriander	
	sprigs for garnish	

Place fish in single layer in shallow dish. Sprinkle with lime juice, oil, and coriander; cover and refrigerate for at least 15 minutes or up to 2 hours, turning once or twice.

Broil or grill fish for 5 to 8 minutes or until fish is opaque and flakes easily when tested with fork. If grilling, turn halfway through. (Time will vary depending upon thickness of fish, about 10 minutes per in/2.5 cm of thickness.) Sprinkle with pepper to taste. Garnish each serving with lime wedges and sprigs of fresh coriander.

Makes 4 servings.

Fish Barbecue Dinner
Swordfish Steaks with Lime
  and Coriander
Peas with Green Onions
  (page 196)
New Potatoes with Herbs
  (page 181)
Peaches and Blueberries with
  Easy Grand Marnier Sauce
  (page 239)

Coconut Shrimp Curry

This recipe is a favorite of mine for a dinner party—it's quick, easy to make, looks great, and has a fabulous flavor. Serve over basmati or jasmine rice along with green beans or snow peas. (Recipe pictured opposite page 59.)

1 tsp	canola oil	5 mL
1	onion, chopped	1
3	cloves garlic, minced	3
3 tbsp	minced gingerroot	45 mL
1 tsp	ground cumin	5 mL
1 tsp	garam masala*	5 mL
1 to 2 tbsp	mild Indian curry paste	15 to 25 mL
1 tsp	grated lemon rind	5 mL
1	sweet red pepper, chopped	1
1	tomato, diced	1
1 cup	light coconut milk	250 mL
1 lb	jumbo shrimp, peeled, deveined	500 g
2 tbsp	lemon juice	25 mL
¼ cup	chopped fresh coriander, mint or basil	50 mL
	Salt and pepper	

If you make this recipe with regular coconut milk instead of light, there will be 262 calories and 17 g of fat per serving.

In nonstick skillet, heat oil over medium heat; add onion and cook, stirring often, until tender, about 5 minutes. Stir in garlic, gingerroot, cumin, garam masala, curry paste, and lemon rind; cook 1 minute; add red pepper and tomato; cook, stirring, for 2 minutes. Add coconut milk and bring to a simmer. (Can be prepared to this point, then reheated.)

Stir in shrimp and cook 3 to 4 minutes until shrimp is pink and cooked. Stir in lemon juice, coriander, salt, and pepper to taste. Serve over hot rice.

Makes 4 servings.

*See page 110.

MEAT

People often tell me how heathfully they are eating and how their diet has changed over the years. One of the first things they say is that they don't eat red meat anymore.

Red meat has been given bad press; there is no reason to eliminate it from your diet completely. Meat is an important source of complete protein, useable iron, B vitamins (thiamin, niacin, and B12), and minerals, but it also contains a high proportion of saturated fats. For this reason, the selection of meats, the size of the servings, and the method of cooking become very important.

Ginger-Garlic Marinated Flank Steak

This steak can marinate for two days and, once cooked, it is good hot or cold. (In other words, if no one arrives home for dinner—your kids get invited out and your partner has to work late—you can cook it the next day. Or if only one person shows up, you can cook it and serve the rest the next day.) If you're cooking for two, have it hot the first night and cold the second. (Recipe pictured opposite page 187.)

1	flank steak (about 1 lb/500 g)	1
	Ginger-Garlic Marinade or Italian Herb Marinade (recipes follow)	

Lightly score (cut) beef about ⅛-in/3 mm deep in diagonal slashes. Place in shallow dish or plastic bag. Pour marinade over; cover and refrigerate for at least 2, or up to 48 hours, turning meat once or twice.

Remove meat from marinade and broil or grill over medium-high heat for 4 to 5 minutes on each side or until desired doneness. Cut diagonally across the grain into thin slices. Serve hot or cold.

Makes 4 servings.

If you're cooking for one, buy a flank steak and cut it into three portions. Use one portion for the Ginger-Garlic Marinated Flank Steak, one for the Beef and Tomato Stir-Fry (page 138); cut recipe in half) and one for the Stir-Fry for One (page 121).

Most marinade recipes call for more oil than necessary. Even though the marinade is poured off before cooking, I recommend keeping the oil at a minimum.

Ginger-Garlic Marinade

Use with fish, shrimp, chicken, turkey, beef, pork, or lamb.

2 tbsp	rice or cider vinegar	25 mL
2 tbsp	water	25 mL
1 tbsp	canola oil	15 mL
1 tbsp	grated fresh gingerroot	15 mL
	(or 1 tsp/5 mL ground ginger)	
1 tsp	granulated sugar	5 mL
3	cloves garlic, minced	3

Combine vinegar, water, oil, gingerroot, sugar, and garlic; mix well.

Makes about ⅓ cup/75 mL, enough for one 1-lb/500 g steak.

Italian Herb Marinade

Use with beef, pork, lamb, chicken, or turkey.

¹/₄ cup	red wine vinegar	50 mL
1 tbsp	canola oil	15 mL
2 tbsp	chopped fresh parsley	25 mL
1 tsp	dried marjoram or oregano (or 1 tbsp/15 mL chopped fresh)	5 mL
1 tsp	dried thyme (or 1 tbsp/15 mL chopped fresh)	5 mL
1	bay leaf	1
¹/₂	small onion, minced	¹/₂
2	cloves garlic, minced	2
	Freshly ground pepper	

In small bowl, mix together vinegar, oil, parsley, marjoram, thyme, bay leaf, onion, garlic, and pepper to taste.

Makes about ¹/₃ cup/75 mL, enough for one 1-lb/500 g steak.

Beware of Cross-Contamination

Bacteria spread when raw meat juices come into contact with other foods. Be careful when handling raw meats, poultry, and seafood:

- *Keep raw meats away from other foods in the grocery cart and during storage, preparation, and cooking.*
- *Wash your hands after handling raw meats and before touching other foods.*
- *Keep raw meats covered.*
- *Have one cutting board for raw meats and another for vegetables only.*
- *Thaw frozen meat, poultry, and seafood in the refrigerator, on a plate, pan or tray. Store on bottom shelf so juices won't drip onto other foods.*
- *Never put cooked food on plate that had raw meat, poultry, or seafood on it. Take a clean plate out to the barbecue for the cooked meat when it's ready.*

Per Serving (with flank steak)	
Calories	220
fat	11 g
saturated fat	4 g
cholesterol	46 mg
sodium	57 mg
potassium	393 mg
carbohydrate	2 g
fiber	trace
protein	26 g

1% Vitamin A • 5% Vitamin C
1% Calcium • 16% Iron
7% Thiamine • 10% Riboflavin
39% Niacin • 17% Vitamin B-6
5% Folate • 133% Vitamin B-12
67% Zinc

Father's Day Barbecue
Ginger-Garlic Marinated Flank
  Steak (opposite)
Yogurt Béarnaise Sauce
  (page 205)
New Potatoes with Herbs
  (page 181)
Asparagus
Strawberry Mousse
  (page 243) or Berries
  with Orange-Honey Yogurt
  (page 234)
Applesauce-Raisin Squares
  (page 216)

Flank steak is one of the leanest cuts of beef. It's delicious when marinated, then grilled or broiled, and cut diagonally across the grain into thin slices. When served this way, it's also an economical cut of beef because 1 lb/500 g will serve four people.

Beef and Tomato Stir-Fry

Make this easy, tasty dish in the summer and fall when garden-fresh tomatoes are plentiful. Serve over rice or noodles. In winter, substitute green peppers, broccoli, or snow peas for tomatoes and cook until tender-crisp, adding water if necessary to prevent burning.

³/₄ lb	inside round or flank steak	375 g
2 tbsp	cornstarch	25 mL
2 tbsp	sherry, wine or brandy	25 mL
1 tbsp	soy sauce	15 mL
2 tbsp	canola oil	25 mL
1	onion, thinly sliced	1
2	cloves garlic, minced	2
4	tomatoes, cut in wedges	4
4	green onions, cut in thin 2-in/5 cm-long strips	4

Cut beef across the grain into thin strips; cut strips into 2-in/5-cm lengths. In bowl, combine cornstarch, sherry, and soy sauce; mix until smooth. Add beef and toss to coat.

In wok or nonstick skillet, heat oil over high heat. Add beef and stir-fry for 2 minutes; add onion and stir-fry for 1 minute or until beef is browned. Add garlic and tomatoes; stir-fry until tomatoes are heated through, 1 to 2 minutes, adding 1–2 tbsp/15–25 mL water if necessary to prevent burning. Stir in green onions and serve immediately.

Makes 4 servings.

Compare Roast Beef Dinners	g fat*
10-oz/284-g serving rib roast, including fat	47
1 tbsp/15-mL butter or margarine (for a roll)	12
1 tbsp/15-mL oil and vinegar salad dressing	6
Total	65
3-oz/88-g serving top round steak (lean only)	6
1 tsp/5-mL butter or margarine (for a roll)	4
1 tbsp/15-mL low-calorie dressing (for a salad)	.5
Total	10.5

*The average woman's daily fat requirement is about 70 grams a day; for an average man, it's about 100 g of fat a day.

The New Lighthearted Cookbook

Recommended Cuts of Meat

Beef: round, flank, sirloin-tip roast, sirloin steak (if well trimmed), tenderloin, and rump; all cuts trimmed of all visible fat are lean except short ribs

Pork: choose lean cuts or those easy to trim—sirloin roast, tenderloin, loin chops, and pork steaks (choose ham and bacon less often because of their high salt and fat content)

Lamb: cuts from leg and loin section

Veal: lower in fat than beef and other red meats but slightly higher in cholesterol; all cuts are lean except those from the breast, i.e., stewing veal

If you do buy cuts higher in fat, then choose a lower-fat cooking method. For example, when using regular ground beef in spaghetti sauce, brown the meat first, then pour off the fat before adding other ingredients. If making stews or pot roast, make the dish ahead and refrigerate it. The next day, you can easily remove the fat that will have hardened on top of the dish.

Choose lean or extra-lean ground beef for recipes such as meatloaf and cabbage rolls. Medium and regular grinds are best used in burgers and meatballs because fat can drip out during cooking. Extra-lean or lean ground beef, chicken, turkey, and pork all have the same amount of fat. They contain no more than 10% fat for extra-lean, and 17% for lean.

Compare Beef Cuts and Portion Sizes

Cut	3-oz/88 g portion			6-oz/176 g portion		
	g fat	g saturated fat	calories	g fat	g saturated fat	calories
Rib roast, roasted lean and fat	17	7	245	34	14	489
Rib roast, roasted lean only	9	4	187	18	7	374
Steak inside (top) round (lean and fat)	9	4	190	19	7	379
Steak inside (top) round (lean only)	6	2	164	12	4	327

Family Favorite Shepherd's Pie

My mother always made shepherd's pie from leftover Sunday roast beef, gravy, and mashed potatoes. However, since we seldom have roasts, I make shepherd's pie using ground meat—either beef, pork or lamb. If you don't have leftover mashed potatoes, boil 5 medium potatoes; drain and mash with milk.

1 lb	lean ground beef, pork or lamb, or a combination of these	500 g
2	onions, chopped	2
2	large cloves garlic, minced	2
1	carrot, minced	1
1/3 cup	tomato paste	75 mL
2/3 cup	water	150 mL
1 tsp	dried thyme	5 mL
1 tbsp	Worcestershire sauce	15 mL
	Salt and freshly ground pepper	
2 cups	mashed potatoes	500 mL
	Paprika	

This dish is equally good made with 1 can (7½ oz/213 mL) tomato sauce instead of tomato paste and water, but it is higher in sodium.

Which meat has the most fat: beef, pork, lamb, or chicken? Whether or not beef has more fat than pork is not really the issue. *What is most important is the kind of cut you buy, the way you cook it, and the amount you eat.* A lean cut of pork has less fat than a prime rib roast. Pork spareribs have more fat than top round steak. Try to choose a lean cut, remove all visible fat, and cook it without adding any fat.

In skillet over medium heat, cook beef, stirring to break up meat, until brown; pour off fat. Add onions, garlic, and carrot; cook until tender. Add tomato paste, water, thyme, Worcestershire sauce, salt, and pepper to taste. Simmer for 5 minutes, stirring up any brown bits on bottom of pan.

Spoon meat mixture into 8-cup/2 L baking or microwave-safe dish; spread mashed potatoes evenly on top. Sprinkle with paprika to taste. Bake in 375°F/190°C oven for 35 minutes or until heated through, or microwave at high (100%) power for 9 minutes.

Makes 5 servings.

Compare Shepherd's Pie (per serving)	*mg sodium*
Made with tomato paste plus water	*113*
Made with tomato sauce	*396*

Easy Oven Beef and Vegetable Stew

This is the easiest stew to make and tastes wonderful. Make it on the weekend, and you'll probably have enough left over for a meal during the week. Or make it during the week to transport to ski cabin or cottage.

1½ lb	stewing beef	750 g
¼ cup	all-purpose flour	50 mL
6	small onions, halved	6
2	large potatoes, cut in chunks (1 lb/500 g)	2
4	large carrots, peeled and cut in chunks	4
3	cloves garlic, minced	3
2 cups	peeled, diced rutabaga	500 mL
3 cups	water	750 mL
1¼ cups	beef stock or canned bouillon	300 mL
1	can (7½ oz/213 mL) tomato sauce	1
1 tsp	dried thyme	5 mL
1 tsp	dried oregano	5 mL
¼ tsp	each salt and freshly ground pepper	1 mL
1	bay leaf	1
½ tsp	grated orange rind (optional)	2 mL

Per Serving	
Calories	252
fat	7 g
saturated fat	2 g
cholesterol	42 mg
sodium	455 mg
potassium	959 mg
carbohydrate	26 g
fiber	4 g
protein	22 g

118% Vitamin A • 25% Vitamin C
6% Calcium • 22% Iron
14% Thiamine • 14% Riboflavin
34% Niacin • 29% Vitamin B-6
16% Folate • 81% Vitamin B-12
60% Zinc

Remove all visible fat from beef; cut beef into 1-in/2.5-cm cubes.

In large casserole or Dutch oven, toss beef with flour. Add onions, potatoes, carrots, garlic, rutabaga, water, beef stock, tomato sauce, thyme, oregano, salt, pepper, bay leaf, and orange rind; stir to mix.

Bake, covered, in 325°F/160°C oven for 2½ to 3 hours, stirring occasionally (if you remember). Remove bay leaf.

Makes 8 servings.

The flavor of a stew is usually better the second day. Make it a day in advance and refrigerate. Any fat will solidify on top and can easily be removed.

Compare	mg sodium per serving
This recipe	*455*
Canned beef and vegetable stew	*995*

Frozen Hamburger Patties

Until I was assigned an article on using frozen hamburger patties for Canadian Living *magazine, I didn't realize what a convenience it would be to have these on hand. It doesn't take long to make hamburger patties, and they are much easier to use than a block of frozen meat. Lean ground pork or lamb also make tasty patties, and they can be combined with beef.*

4 lb	lean ground beef	2 kg
3	onions, finely chopped	3
1	sweet green pepper,	1
	finely chopped (optional)	
1	egg	1
1 tsp	dry mustard	5 mL
2 tsp	Worcestershire sauce	10 mL
½ tsp	freshly ground pepper	2 mL
Dash	hot pepper sauce	Dash

To broil, place frozen patties on grill 3 to 4 inches (8 to 10 cm) from broiler. Broil for about 5 minutes on each side or until browned and no longer pink inside.

In large bowl, combine beef, onions, green pepper (if using), egg, mustard, Worcestershire sauce, pepper, and hot pepper sauce; with spoon or hands, mix just until combined.

Using ice-cream scoop or hands, divide mixture into 20 portions; shape each portion into round patty. Place patties on baking sheets and freeze until solid, 4 to 5 hours. Stack patties with foil or paper plates between them. Package in freezer bags and store up to 4 months in freezer.

Makes 20 patties.

Middle-Eastern Burgers

For a nice change, try beef or lamb patties in whole-wheat pita bread pockets topped with garlicky Greek Tzatziki Sauce, which is so delicious any extra can be used as a dip with pita bread.

QUICK TZATZIKI SAUCE

1 cup	low-fat plain yogurt	250 mL
1/2	English cucumber, finely chopped or grated	1/2
1 tbsp	chopped fresh mint (optional)	15 mL
1	large clove garlic, minced	1
Pinch	salt	Pinch
4	hamburger patties (opposite)	4
4	whole-wheat pita rounds (6 in/15 cm)	4
	Shredded lettuce	

Quick Tzatziki Sauce: In small bowl, combine yogurt, cucumber, mint (if using), garlic, and salt; mix well.

Broil or grill hamburger patties until no longer pink inside. Cut slice off each pita bread about 1 in/2.5 cm from edge; pull apart to form opening. Heat pitas in microwave or oven until warm. Place hot hamburger patty and shredded lettuce inside pita; divide Tzatziki Sauce over each hamburger patty.

Makes 4 servings.

Per Serving	
Calories	333
fat	10 g
saturated fat	4 g
cholesterol	54 mg
sodium	393 mg
potassium	426 mg
carbohydrate	38 g
fiber	5 g
protein	24 g

2% Vitamin A • 5% Vitamin C
9% Calcium • 24% Iron
22% Thiamine • 19% Riboflavin
42% Niacin • 18% Vitamin B-6
26% Folate • 66% Vitamin B-12
56% Zinc

Best Tzatziki Sauce

If you have time to make tzatziki sauce in advance, use this method for a longer lasting, thicker sauce. Line a sieve with cheesecloth or muslin; add yogurt* and let drain for 2 to 4 hours. Place chopped cucumber in a colander and sprinkle with 1/4 tsp/1 mL salt, let stand for 30 minutes then pat dry. Combine drained yogurt, cucumber, and garlic; mix well. Cover and refrigerate up to 4 days.

*Buy plain yogurt made without gelatin.

Mexican Beef Tacos or Tostadas

A tostada is a flat tortilla with toppings. A taco is a folded tortilla filled with a variety of foods such as grated cheese, shredded lettuce, and meat sauce. Use this meat sauce as a basis for either.

1 lb	lean ground beef	500 g
1	medium onion, chopped	1
1	clove garlic, minced	1
1/3 cup	tomato paste	75 mL
1 cup	water	250 mL
2 tsp	chili powder	10 mL
1 tsp	dried oregano	5 mL
1/2 tsp	cumin	2 mL
1/4 tsp	hot red pepper flakes	1 mL
	Salt and freshly ground pepper	
12	6-in/15-cm corn tortillas (tacos or tostadas)	12

TOPPINGS
Shredded lettuce, chopped tomato, chopped sweet green pepper, bottled or homemade taco sauce or Tomato Salsa Sauce (page 129), yogurt or light sour cream, grated part-skim mozzarella

In large skillet, cook beef over medium heat until brown; pour off fat. Add onion and garlic; cook until tender. Stir in tomato paste, water, chili powder, oregano, cumin, and hot red pepper flakes. Simmer for 5 to 10 minutes. Taste and add salt and pepper to taste. (If mixture becomes dry, add a little water.) Spoon into serving dish.

Place bowls of various toppings on table. Serve packaged crisp tortillas cold, or warm in 300°F/150°C oven for 5 minutes. Soft tortillas are usually fried in hot oil, but to keep fat content down, crisp them in a 400°F/200°C oven for 10 minutes.

Let each person spoon some meat mixture into tortilla then top with cheese, lettuce, and other toppings of their choice.

Makes 6 servings, 2 tacos each.

Grilled Butterflied Leg of Lamb with Lemon and Garlic

I love lamb, and this is one of my favorite ways to cook it. I either barbecue or broil this cut; when it's cooked medium-rare, lamb is delicious cold the next day. Serve with chutney or tzatziki (page 143) or Coriander Dipping Sauce (page 68).

3	cloves garlic, minced	3
1 tsp	grated lemon rind	5 mL
1 tsp	dried crushed rosemary	5 mL
	(or 1 tbsp/15 mL chopped fresh)	
½ tsp	freshly ground pepper	2 mL
¼ cup	lemon juice	50 mL
2 tbsp	olive oil	25 mL
1	boned and butterflied* leg of lamb	1
	(about 3 lb/1.5 kg boned)	

Per Serving	
Calories	206
fat	9 g
saturated fat	3 g
cholesterol	105 mg
sodium	48 mg
potassium	210 mg
carbohydrate	1 g
fiber	trace
protein	29 g

0% Vitamin A • 7% Vitamin C
1% Calcium • 18% Iron
10% Thiamine • 33% Riboflavin
59% Niacin • 9% Vitamin B-6
0% Folate • 139% Vitamin B-12
48% Zinc

In small bowl or food processor, combine garlic, lemon rind, rosemary, pepper, and lemon juice. Gradually pour in oil and mix until blended.

Trim fat from lamb. Place lamb in shallow dish or resealable plastic bag; pour marinade over, turning to coat both sides. Cover and let stand at room temperature for 1 hour or refrigerate overnight. Remove from refrigerator 30 minutes before cooking.

Remove lamb from marinade, reserving marinade. On greased grill over high heat, or under broiler, grill or broil lamb for 15 minutes, brushing with marinade several times. Turn and cook for 12 minutes longer or until meat is pink inside.

Remove from heat and let stand for 10 minutes. To serve, slice thinly across the grain.

Makes 8 servings.

*Butterflied legs of lamb are boned then cut open, but not all the way through, so the meat can be spread apart like two butterfly wings. Be sure to trim all fat from lamb.

Cooking Methods to Reduce Fat

Most of the time, don't fry meats—instead, grill, broil, stew, stir-fry, braise or roast on a rack.

If you are going to fry, use a nonstick skillet and use as little vegetable oil (such as canola) as possible.

Make a stew one day in advance; cover and refrigerate. When cold, remove fat that has solidified on top.

Compare 4 oz/125 g servings of this recipe:	g fat	calories
Lamb leg, lean and fat	24	359
Lamb leg, lean only	9	206

Lamb Tenderloins with Rosemary and Peppercorns

Fork-tender lamb tenderloins or loins, often available in the frozen food section of the supermarket, are a special treat and one of the leanest cuts of lamb.

1 lb	lamb tenderloins or loins	500 g
1½ tsp	dried peppercorns, crushed (¼ tsp/mL freshly ground)	7 mL
1 tbsp	fresh rosemary (or 1 tsp/5 mL dried)	15 mL
2 tbsp	chopped fresh mint	25 mL
2	cloves garlic, minced	2
2 tbsp	dry sherry or red wine vinegar	25 mL
1 tbsp	soy sauce	15 mL

Lamb tenderloins and loins cook quickly and are best served rare or medium-rare. Be careful not to overcook, as they will be too dry and sometimes tough.

Place lamb in shallow dish or resealable plastic bag.

In small bowl, combine peppercorns, rosemary, mint, garlic, sherry, and soy sauce; mix well and pour over lamb. Cover and marinate at room temperature for 30 minutes or refrigerate for at least 1, or up to 6, hours.

Remove from marinade. Broil or grill over medium heat 3 to 4 minutes for tenderloins, 6 minutes for loins or until meat is pink inside, turning once or twice. Cut diagonally into thin slices.

Makes 4 servings.

Pork Chops with Rosemary and Orange

This fast and easy recipe also works well for veal or turkey scallopini. My son doesn't like sauces, so I don't pour any over his serving. My daughter quietly scrapes the rosemary off hers. My husband and I like it the way it is, so everyone is happy.

1 lb	fast-fry or thinly sliced pork chops	500 g
2	oranges	2
2 tsp	canola or olive oil	10 mL
2 tsp	dried rosemary, crumbled	10 mL
	Salt and freshly ground pepper	

Trim fat from pork chops. Peel and slice one orange; squeeze juice from other and set aside. Sprinkle chops with rosemary, salt, and pepper.

Heat heavy-bottomed or nonstick skillet over high heat; add oil and heat until sizzling. Add pork chops and cook in batches for about 2 minutes or until brown on bottom; turn. Cook until brown on other side and a hint of pink remains inside. Remove chops to side plate.

Add reserved orange juice and slices; cook for 1 to 2 minutes, stirring to scrape up brown bits on bottom of pan. To serve, arrange chops on plates and pour juice and orange slices over.

Makes 4 servings.

Per Serving	
Calories	179
fat	7 g
saturated fat	2 g
cholesterol	58 mg
sodium	75 mg
potassium	375 mg
carbohydrate	6 g
fiber	1 g
protein	22 g

4% Vitamin A • 43% Vitamin C
4% Calcium • 7% Iron
55% Thiamine • 14% Riboflavin
38% Niacin • 17% Vitamin B-6
7% Folate • 22% Vitamin B-12
18% Zinc

Grey Cup Buffet

Ginger-Garlic Marinated Flank
  Steak (cold) (page 136)
Tossed Seasonal Greens
  (page 100)
Whole-Wheat Oatmeal Bread
  (page 224)
Streusel Plum Cake
  (page 222)

Amount to Serve

How do I know what a 50- or 100-g portion of meat is? The easiest way is to buy only that much. For example, if you are cooking for 4 people, buy only 500 g of ground meat, stewing beef, pork chops or boneless chicken breasts. For 4 servings, buy about 750 g of bone-in meats, 1 kg of chicken.

When you are cooking roasts or bone-in cuts, it is more difficult to judge amounts; for a rough estimate, consider a 100 g serving of meat to be about the size of a deck of playing cards. Many adults, especially men, are used to larger meat portions than 100 g.

Brochette of Pork with Lemon and Herb Marinade

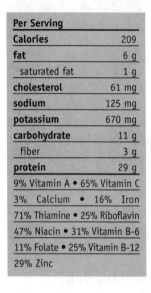

Herbs and lemon add tangy flavor to this easy-to-prepare pork dish. Use pork tenderloin or any other lean cut of pork. Zucchini or blanched slices of carrot can be used instead of the vegetables here.

1 lb	boneless lean pork	500 g
	Grated rind and juice of 1 lemon	
2	large cloves garlic, minced	2
2 tsp	dried basil (or 2 tbsp/25 mL fresh)	10 mL
1 tsp	dried thyme (or 1 tbsp/15 mL fresh)	5 mL
2 tbsp	chopped fresh parsley	25 mL
1 tbsp	olive or canola oil	15 mL
1	sweet green pepper, cut in squares	1
2	onions, quartered and separated into pieces	2
16	cherry tomatoes or fresh pineapple chunks	16

Pineapple chunks packed in their own juice can be used instead of fresh pineapple.

Cut pork into 1-in/2.5-cm cubes. In bowl, combine lemon rind and juice, garlic, basil, thyme, parsley, and oil. Add pork and toss to coat well. Cover and marinate in refrigerator for 4 hours or overnight.

Alternately thread pork, green pepper, onions, and cherry tomatoes or pineapple onto soaked wooden skewers. On greased grill over medium heat or under broiler, grill brochettes, turning often, for 15 minutes or until just a hint of pink remains inside.

Makes 4 servings.

The New Lighthearted Cookbook

Cauliflower and Ham Gratin

Ham and cauliflower are a wonderful combination. Dill adds extra flavor, and red pepper adds color and crunch.

1/2	head cauliflower	1/2
1 1/2 tbsp	soft non-hydrogenated margarine	20 mL
2 tbsp	all-purpose flour	25 mL
1 cup	1% milk	250 mL
1/4 cup	freshly grated Parmesan cheese	50 mL
1/4 cup	grated Danbo or part-skim (16% m.f.) mozzarella cheese	50 mL
1/4 cup	packed chopped fresh dill* Freshly ground pepper	50 mL
1/2 cup	diced cooked ham (2 oz/60 g)	125 mL
1/2	sweet red pepper, coarsely chopped	1/2
1/3 cup	fresh breadcrumbs	75 mL

Per Serving	
Calories	170
fat	8 g
saturated fat	3 g
cholesterol	16 mg
sodium	528 mg
potassium	310 mg
carbohydrate	12 g
fiber	2 g
protein	12 g

16% Vitamin A • 92% Vitamin C
20% Calcium • 6% Iron
15% Thiamine • 15% Riboflavin
17% Niacin • 13% Vitamin B-6
20% Folate • 13% Vitamin B-12
11% Zinc

Cut cauliflower into florets, about 2-in/5-cm pieces. In large pot of boiling water, blanch cauliflower for 5 minutes or until tender-crisp; drain and set aside.

In saucepan, melt margarine; add flour and cook over low heat, stirring, for 1 minute. Pour in milk and bring to simmer, stirring constantly. Simmer, stirring, for 2 minutes. Add Parmesan and mozzarella cheeses, dill, and pepper to taste; cook, stirring, until cheese melts.

In lightly greased 8 cup/2 L shallow baking dish, arrange cauliflower, ham, and sweet pepper; pour sauce evenly over. Sprinkle with breadcrumbs. Bake in 375°F/190°C oven for 30 minutes or until bubbly.

Makes 4 servings.

*If fresh dill is unavailable, use 1/4 cup/50 mL fresh parsley plus 1 tsp/5 mL dried dillweed.

Because ham is very high in sodium, it shouldn't be eaten often. When you do use it, try to make a little go a long way, as in this cauliflower dish. Don't add any salt. (See ham dinner comparison on page 150).

Use the remaining cauliflower in stir-fries, salads or soups.

Compare

Ham Dinner 1

(29% of calories from fat)	g fat	g saturated fat	mg sodium	calories
Cauliflower and Ham Gratin (page 149)	8	3	528	170
Green beans	0	0	2	19
Sliced tomatoes	0	0	11	26
Whole-wheat bun	2	0	167	93
Margarine (1 tsp/5 mL)	4	1	51	34
Milk, skim (8 oz/250 mL)	0	0	121	82
Totals	14	4	829	424

Ham Dinner 2

(44% of calories from fat)	g fat	g saturated fat	mg sodium	calories
Ham steak	9	3	1570	187
Cauliflower	0	0	7	11
with cheese sauce (2 tbsp/25 mL)	4	3	142	56
Green beans	0	0	2	19
Whole-wheat bun	2	0	167	93
Butter (1 tsp/5 mL)	4	2	39	34
Milk, whole (8 oz/250 mL)	8	5	115	145
Totals	27	13	2042	545

How to present the recommended serving size of meat (50 to 100 g)

The meat portion should only take up $^1/_4$ of the dinner plate. Increase the amount and variety of vegetables you serve.

Slice meat thinly: it will look like more. For example, 100 g of thinly sliced flank steak will look as if there is more meat than the same weight of sirloin steak in a single piece 1-in/2.5-cm thick.

Choose dishes in which meat is combined with vegetables, such as stews, stir-fries, and casseroles.

Serve in a sauce over pasta—see All-Purpose Quick Spaghetti Sauce, page 168.

Canada's Food Guide recommends that we have two servings (50 to 100 g per serving) of meat or meat alternatives a day. If one serving is small—for example, a thin slice of meat in a sandwich at lunch—then the serving size at dinner can be larger.

PASTA

Tortellini with Tuna Salad

Shell Pasta Salad with Salmon and Green Beans

Pasta and Fresh Vegetable Salad

Tomato, Broccoli, and Pasta Salad

Penne and Mussel Salad

Curried Vermicelli Noodle Salad

Beef and Pasta Casserole for a Crowd

Last-Minute Pasta Casserole

Penne with Herbed Tomato-Tuna Sauce

Rotini with Fresh Tomatoes, Basil, and Parmesan

Tuscan-Style Capellini with Clams and Garlic

Fettuccine with Mussels, Leeks, and Tomatoes

Fettuccine with Pesto Sauce

Fettuccine with Basil and Parsley

Linguine with Salmon and Chives

Vegetable Lasagna

All-Purpose Quick Spaghetti Sauce

Tofu Alfredo

Tortellini with Tuna Salad

Pasta salads are great for lunches, picnics, buffets, and light suppers. You don't really need a recipe; just add any of the usual salad ingredients such as cooked or raw vegetables (except for lettuces) to cooked noodles or any type of pasta and toss with a dressing.

12 oz	tortellini	375 g
1 cup	frozen peas	250 mL
1/2	sweet red pepper, diced	1/2
1/2 cup	chopped red onion	125 mL
1	can (6 oz/170 g) tuna, packed in water, drained	1
1	can (14 oz/398 mL) artichokes, drained and quartered (optional)	1
1/2 cup	chopped fresh parsley	125 mL
1/4 cup	chopped fresh basil (or 2 tsp/10 mL dried)	50 mL

DRESSING

1	clove garlic, minced	1
1 tsp	Dijon mustard	5 mL
3 tbsp	lemon juice or white wine vinegar	45 mL
1/4 cup	orange juice	50 mL
3 tbsp	olive oil	45 mL
1/4 cup	low-fat plain yogurt	50 mL
1/4 cup	finely chopped fresh basil	50 mL
	Salt and freshly ground pepper	

In large pot of boiling water, cook tortellini until al dente (tender but firm); drain and rinse under cold water. Drain thoroughly. Thaw peas under cold water.

In salad bowl, combine pasta, peas, sweet pepper, onion, tuna, artichokes (if using), parsley, and basil; toss lightly to mix.

Dressing: In blender, food processor or bowl, combine garlic, mustard, lemon, and orange juice; mix well. With machine running or while mixing, gradually add oil. Add yogurt, basil, salt, and pepper to taste; mix. Pour over salad and toss to mix.

Cover and refrigerate for up to 2 days.

Makes 8 servings, 3/4 cup/175 mL each.

Shell Pasta Salad with Salmon and Green Beans

I love the flavor of fresh dill in this salad, but if it is not available, use fresh basil to taste. In a pinch, use 1 tsp/5 mL dried basil or dill plus ¹/₂ cup/125 mL finely chopped fresh parsley. If you have it, use leftover or fresh cooked salmon instead of canned.

	Per Serving	
	Calories	221
	fat	6 g
	saturated fat	2 g
	cholesterol	17 mg
	sodium	405 mg
	carbohydrate	26 g
	fiber	2 g
	protein	15 g

3% Vitamin A • 12% Vitamin C
15% Calcium • 10% Iron
12% Thiamine • 9% Riboflavin
25% Niacin • 7% Vitamin B-6
25% Folate • 7% Vitamin B-12
11% Zinc

8 oz	small pasta shells or macaroni	250 g
4 oz	green beans	125 g
¹/₄ cup	light sour cream or low-fat plain yogurt	50 mL
¹/₄ cup	light mayonnaise	50 mL
¹/₄ cup	fresh lemon juice	50 mL
1 cup	chopped cucumber or fennel	250 mL
¹/₄ cup	capers, drained	50 mL
³/₄ cup	coarsely chopped fresh dill	175 mL
2	cans (7.5 oz/213 g) salmon, drained*	2
	Salt and freshly ground pepper	
	Boston or red leaf lettuce	

In large pot of boiling water, cook pasta until al dente (tender but firm). Drain, reserving ¹/₂ cup (125 mL) cooking liquid, and rinse under cold water; drain again and set aside.

Cut green beans into 1¹/₂-inch/4-cm lengths (approx 1 cup/ 250 mL) and blanch in boiling water for 2 minutes. Drain and rinse under cold water; drain thoroughly and set aside.

In a large bowl, combine sour cream, mayonnaise, ¹/₄ cup/50 mL pasta cooking liquid, and lemon juice; mix well. Stir in pasta, green beans, cucumber, capers, and dill; stir to mix. Discard skin from salmon and break into chunks; add to salad and stir gently to mix; add remaining pasta water as needed. Add salt and pepper to taste. Line serving plates with lettuce leaves and mound salad on top.

Makes 8 servings.

*Be sure to crush salmon bones and include in salad because they are an excellent source of calcium.

Salmon is an excellent source of Omega-3 polyunsaturated fatty acids, which some studies have found help to lower blood pressure and reduce the risk of heart disease.

Ladies' Lunch Buffet
Shell Pasta Salad with
    Salmon and Green Beans or
    Curried Chicken Crêpes
    (page 109)
Sliced Cucumbers with
    Chives, Yogurt, and Basil
    (page 99)
Whole-Wheat Zucchini Bread
    (page 227)
Lemon Roll with Berries
    (page 244)

Pasta and Fresh Vegetable Salad

This is the kind of salad I often make during the summer using whatever vegetables I have on hand. It's great with cold meats, salmon or tuna salad, poached fish or chicken, and sliced tomatoes. It keeps well for a few days in the refrigerator and is fine for lunches or picnics.

8 oz	macaroni or rotini or any pasta (about 3 cups/750 mL)	250 g
1	sweet green pepper, chopped	1
1 cup	coarsely grated carrots	250 mL
4	green onions, chopped	4
6	radishes, sliced	6
½	head cauliflower, cut in small florets	½
1 cup	coarsely chopped fresh parsley	250 mL

ITALIAN VINAIGRETTE DRESSING

¼ cup	cider or tarragon vinegar	50 mL
¼ cup	canola oil	50 mL
¼ cup	orange juice	50 mL
2 tsp	Dijon mustard	10 mL
1 tbsp	grated Parmesan cheese	15 mL
1	clove garlic, minced	1
1 tsp	each dried basil and oregano	5 mL
2 tbsp	prepared pesto sauce (optional)	25 mL
½ tsp	salt	2 mL
¼ tsp	freshly ground pepper	1 mL

In large pot of boiling water, cook pasta until al dente (tender but firm). Drain and rinse under cold water; drain thoroughly.

In large bowl, combine cooked pasta, green pepper, carrots, onions, radishes, cauliflower, and parsley.

Italian Vinaigrette Dressing: In bowl or food processor, combine vinegar, oil, orange juice, mustard, cheese, garlic, basil, oregano, pesto sauce to taste (if using), salt, and pepper; mix well. (Dressing can be covered and refrigerated for up to 1 week.) Pour over salad and toss to mix. Cover and refrigerate for up to 2 days.

Makes 10 servings.

Photo:
Quick and Easy Salmon Fillets with Watercress Sauce (page 130) with Skillet Greens with Ginger and Celery (page 202)

The New Lighthearted Cookbook

Tomato, Broccoli, and Pasta Salad

This salad is perfect for buffets, with a green salad or soup for a main course. I like it with rigatoni, the large, tubular-shaped pasta, because it goes well with large chunks of tomato and broccoli; however, any other pasta can be substituted.

4 oz	rigatoni or other pasta	125 g
3 cups	broccoli florets	750 mL
1 cup	chopped green onions	250 mL
3	tomatoes, cut in wedges	3
4 oz	part-skim mozzarella cheese, 16% m.f., cubed	125 g
1/3 cup	minced fresh parsley	75 mL

MUSTARD VINAIGRETTE

3 tbsp	lemon juice	45 mL
3 tbsp	water	45 mL
2	cloves garlic, minced	2
1 tsp	Dijon mustard	5 mL
1/4 cup	olive oil	50 mL
	Salt and freshly ground pepper	

Per Serving	
Calories	233
fat	13 g
saturated fat	3 g
cholesterol	10 mg
sodium	128 mg
potassium	318 mg
carbohydrate	21 g
fiber	3 g
protein	9 g

13% Vitamin A • 68% Vitamin C
16% Calcium • 10% Iron
12% Thiamine • 12% Riboflavin
13% Niacin • 8% Vitamin B-6
30% Folate • 9% Vitamin B-12
12% Zinc

In large pot of boiling water, cook pasta until al dente (tender but firm). Drain and rinse under cold water; drain again and set aside.

In another pot of boiling water, blanch broccoli for 2 minutes. Drain and rinse under cold water. Drain again and wrap in paper towel; set aside.

In salad bowl, combine pasta, green onions, tomatoes, cheese, and parsley.

Mustard Vinaigrette: Combine lemon juice, water, garlic, mustard, and oil; mix well. Pour over salad and toss to mix. Add salt and pepper to taste.

Cover and refrigerate for 30 minutes or up to 4 hours. Just before serving, add broccoli and toss to mix.

Makes 6 servings.

The broccoli is added just before serving because the acid in the salad dressing will cause the broccoli to lose its bright green color.

For other main-course salads, see salad section (page 89).

When in season, cherry tomatoes would suit this salad well.

Photo:
Beef and Pasta Casserole for a Crowd (page 158)

Penne and Mussel Salad

This easy-to-make salad with Asian flavours is delicious with any kind of cooked pasta, from rotini to fusilli noodles to shells. Serve as a first course or with soup for a light dinner or as part of a buffet supper.

8 oz	penne	250 g
2 lb	mussels	1 kg
1/4 cup	water or white wine	50 mL
1 1/2 cups	frozen peas, thawed	375 mL
1	sweet red pepper or tomato, diced	1
4	green onions, chopped	4
1/4 cup	each chopped fresh parsley, coriander, and mint	50 mL
1/4 cup	lemon juice	50 mL
3 tbsp	canola oil	45 mL
1 tbsp	sesame oil	15 mL
2	cloves garlic, minced	2
	Salt and freshly ground pepper	

8 oz/250 g uncooked penne is about 3 cups/750 mL.

Before the Concert Light Supper
Penne and Mussel Salad
Sliced tomatoes with fresh basil
Crisp Flatbread (page 228)
Fresh strawberries

In large pot of boiling water, cook penne until al dente (tender but firm). Drain and rinse under cold water; drain thoroughly and set aside.

Scrub mussels under cold running water and remove any hairy beards. Discard any that do not close when tapped. In large heavy saucepan, combine water and mussels. Cover and bring to boil over high heat; reduce heat and simmer for 5 to 8 minutes or until mussels open. Discard any that do not open. Let cool; reserve 1/2 cup/125 mL cooking liquid and remove meat from shells.

In large salad bowl, combine penne, mussels, peas, sweet pepper, green onions, parsley, coriander, and mint.

In small bowl, combine reserved mussel cooking liquid, lemon juice, oil, and garlic; mix well. Pour over pasta mixture and toss to mix. Season with salt and pepper to taste. Serve or cover and refrigerate up to 24 hours.

Makes 8 servings, 1 cup/250 mL each.

Curried Vermicelli Noodle Salad

I love this elegant salad. It's easy to prepare, especially in large quantities, and is perfect for buffets or hot-weather dining.

8 oz	vermicelli noodles*	250 g
1/2 cup	pine nuts	125 mL
1 cup	coarsely chopped fresh parsley	250 mL

CURRY DRESSING

1 cup	pearl onions	250 mL
1/4 cup	olive oil	50 mL
1 tbsp	curry powder or paste	15 mL
2 tsp	ground coriander	10 mL
1 tsp	ground cardamom	5 mL
1/4 tsp	turmeric	1 mL
1	clove garlic, minced	1
1 1/2 cups	beef or chicken or vegetable stock	375 mL
1/2 cup	golden raisins	125 mL

Per Serving	
Calories	210
fat	10 g
saturated fat	1 g
cholesterol	0 mg
sodium	137 mg
carbohydrate	28 g
fiber	3 g
protein	4 g

3% Vitamin A • 17% Vitamin C
2% Calcium • 13% Iron
7% Thiamine • 3% Riboflavin
7% Niacin • 3% Vitamin B-6
9% Folate • 1% Vitamin B-12
8% Zinc

In large pot of boiling water, cook vermicelli according to package directions or for 3 to 5 minutes, just until al dente (tender but firm). Don't overcook, because noodles become mushy. Rinse under cold water; drain well and set aside.

In a small skillet over medium heat, cook pine nuts for 5 minutes or until golden, shaking pan often. Set aside.

Curry dressing: In saucepan of boiling water, blanch pearl onions for 3 minutes; drain. Let cool slightly, then peel.

In saucepan, heat oil over medium heat. Add curry powder, coriander, cardamom, and turmeric; cook for 3 minutes, stirring occasionally. Add garlic, pearl onions, stock, and raisins. Simmer for 5 minutes or until onions are tender. Remove from heat and let cool.

Toss noodles with dressing. (Salad can be covered and refrigerated for up to 1 day.) Just before serving, add pine nuts and parsley; toss well.

Makes 10 servings.

*Vermicelli, very thin noodles, are available in the pasta section of most supermarkets. I prefer rice vermicelli, sometimes called rice sticks, which are clear, very thin noodles often sold in the Asian food section of the supermarket. If unavailable, use 4 cups/1 L cooked thin noodles.

Beef and Pasta Casserole for a Crowd

Per Serving	
Calories	373
fat	12 g
saturated fat	5 g
cholesterol	54 mg
sodium	356 mg
potassium	718 mg
carbohydrate	37 g
fiber	4 g
protein	30 g

31% Vitamin A • 40% Vitamin C
32% Calcium • 29% Iron
22% Thiamine • 28% Riboflavin
51% Niacin • 20% Vitamin B-6
44% Folate • 75% Vitamin B-12
57% Zinc

This recipe can be made with other short pasta such as fusilli or rotini.

Make Ahead

May be prepared up to two days in advance, covered and refrigerated. Remove from refrigerator 1 hour before baking.

Unbaked dish can also be covered and frozen for up to 1 month. Defrost in refrigerator 2 days or in microwave, if in glass dish.

After the Ball Game Supper

Beef and Pasta Casserole for
  a Crowd
Tossed Seasonal Greens
  (page 100)
French bread
Iced Raspberry Mousse
  (page 243)

This crowd-pleasing recipe from my friend Sue Zacharias is pictured opposite page 155.

1 lb	penne (5 cups/1.25 L uncooked)	500 g
1 tsp	canola oil	5 mL
2 lb	lean ground beef	1 kg
3	onions, finely chopped	3
2	cloves garlic, minced	2
1/2 lb	mushrooms, sliced	250 g
2	stalks celery, sliced	2
1	sweet green pepper, chopped	1
1	large can (13 oz/369 mL) tomato paste	1
4 cups	water	1 L
2 tsp	each dried oregano and basil	10 mL
1	pkg (10 oz/284 g) fresh spinach, cooked, drained and chopped	1
1 lb	part-skim (16% m.f.) mozzarella cheese, cut in small cubes	500 g
1 cup	fresh breadcrumbs	250 mL
1/4 cup	chopped fresh parsley	50 mL
1/2 cup	freshly grated Parmesan cheese	125 mL

In large pot of boiling water, cook pasta until al dente (tender but firm), about 10 minutes or according to package directions. Drain and rinse under cold running water; drain and set aside.

In large nonstick skillet or Dutch oven, heat oil over medium heat. Add beef, onions, and garlic; cook, stirring, for a few minutes or until beef is no longer pink. Drain off fat. Add mushrooms, celery, and green pepper; cook for 5 minutes, stirring occasionally. Stir in tomato paste, water, oregano, and basil; simmer, covered, for 30 minutes.

Combine meat sauce, spinach, pasta, and mozzarella cheese; season to taste with salt and pepper. Spoon into lightly greased 16-cup/4 L casserole. Sprinkle with breadcrumbs, parsley, then Parmesan. Bake, uncovered, in 350°F/180°C oven for 45 minutes or until bubbly. **Makes 14 servings.**

Last-Minute Pasta Casserole

This is another of my kids' favorites. If there are any leftovers, my son John heats them up in the microwave for breakfast or snacks. It's a good dish for small children who don't like to chew meat. I never seem to make this exactly the same way twice, and I add whatever vegetables I have on hand: fresh tomatoes and zucchini in the summer, celery and carrots in the winter. Add fresh basil if you have it.

4 oz	macaroni (1 cup/250 mL) or shell pasta	125 g
2 cups	All-Purpose Quick Spaghetti Sauce (page 168)	500 mL
1	small sweet green or yellow pepper, chopped	1
4	large mushrooms, sliced	4
	Salt and pepper to taste	
1 cup	kernel corn or green peas	250 mL
2 tbsp	grated Parmesan cheese	25 mL

In large pot of boiling water, cook macaroni until al dente (tender but firm); drain, reserving ¼ cup/50 mL cooking water.

Meanwhile, in flameproof casserole or heavy saucepan over medium heat, combine spaghetti sauce, sweet pepper, mushrooms, salt, and pepper; simmer, covered, for 5 minutes. Stir in hot cooked pasta, corn, and reserved cooking water, if needed; sprinkle each serving with Parmesan cheese.

Makes 4 servings, about 1¼ cups/300 mL each.

Starchy foods or complex carbohydrates, such as whole-wheat breads, pastas, rice, potatoes, are not high in fat or calories. They are a good source of B vitamins, iron, and trace minerals. It's what we add to these starchy foods that increases the fat and calorie content in our diet.

Compare (per tbsp/15 mL)

Potato toppings	g fat	calories
Yogurt (1-2% m.f.)	trace	10
Butter	12	102
Non-hydrogenated margarine	11	102

Per Serving	
Calories	258
fat	5 g
saturated fat	2 g
cholesterol	23 mg
sodium	263 mg
potassium	617 mg
carbohydrate	40 g
fiber	5 g
protein	15 g

10% Vitamin A • 67% Vitamin C
8% Calcium • 21% Iron
20% Thiamine • 17% Riboflavin
34% Niacin • 19% Vitamin B-6
32% Folate • 36% Vitamin B-12
31% Zinc

Fresh Tomato Sauce

One of my favorite meals in August and September is a fresh tomato sauce made with plum tomatoes and fresh herbs served over pasta. Sometimes I add some cooked Italian sausage. I don't follow a recipe, and the result is slightly different every time.

Cook a few pounds of small plum tomatoes (chopped) in a spoonful or two of olive oil (sometimes I add a chopped onion and garlic) until they are soft, nearly smooth, thick, and of a sauce-like consistency. This should take about 30 minutes. Add a handful of chopped fresh basil or a pinch of dried rosemary or oregano, and you will have a wonderful Italian tomato sauce to toss with pasta. Top with freshly grated Parmesan cheese.

Penne with Herbed Tomato-Tuna Sauce

Per Serving	
Calories	331
fat	5 g
saturated fat	1 g
cholesterol	10 mg
sodium	416 mg
potassium	649 mg
carbohydrate	54 g
fiber	5 g
protein	18 g
15% Vitamin A • 58% Vitamin C	
9% Calcium • 24% Iron	
26% Thiamine • 9% Riboflavin	
44% Niacin • 22% Vitamin B-6	
46% Folate • 51% Vitamin B-12	
17% Zinc	

You'll probably have all the ingredients for this popular economical family dish right in your own cupboard. My kids gobble it up and, at first, didn't know if it was tuna or chicken in the sauce.

1 tbsp	olive oil	15 mL
1	small onion, chopped	1
4	cloves garlic, minced	4
1	can (28 oz/796 mL) diced tomatoes	1
2 tsp	dried basil (or 2 tbsp/25 mL chopped fresh)	10 mL
1/4 tsp	hot pepper flakes	1 mL
	Salt and freshly ground pepper	
1/3 cup	chopped fresh parsley or fresh basil	75 mL
8 oz	penne or macaroni (about 3 cups/750 mL dried pasta)	250 g
1	can (6 oz/170 g) tuna, packed in water, drained	1

Easy Summer Dinner

Rotini with Fresh Tomatoes, Basil, and Parmesan (opposite)

Tossed Seasonal Greens (page 100) with Ranch-Style Buttermilk Dressing (page 106)

Hot bread

Blueberries with Orange-Honey Yogurt (page 234)

In heavy saucepan, heat oil over medium heat; cook onion and garlic for 5 minutes or until tender, stirring occasionally.

Add tomatoes, basil, and hot pepper flakes; simmer, uncovered, for 10 minutes. Season with salt and pepper to taste; add parsley.

Meanwhile, in large pot of boiling water, cook penne until al dente (tender but firm); drain. Toss with tomato mixture and tuna and serve immediately.

Makes 4 servings, 1 1/2 cups/375 mL each.

Rotini with Fresh Tomatoes, Basil, and Parmesan

You can use any kind of pasta in this easy recipe. To preserve the fresh flavor and texture of the tomatoes, they are quickly cooked over high heat. Once you have cooked the pasta, the whole mixture cooks in less than five minutes.

8 oz	rotini (corkscrew shape) or any tubular pasta (about 3 cups)	250 g
2 tbsp	olive or canola oil	25 mL
4	green onions, chopped	4
4	tomatoes, coarsely chopped	4
3	cloves garlic, minced	3
1 cup	strips or cubes cooked ham, turkey, chicken (optional)	250 mL
½ cup	coarsely chopped fresh parsley	125 mL
½ cup	coarsely chopped fresh basil (or 1 tsp/5 mL dried)	125 mL
½ cup	grated Parmesan cheese	125 mL
	Salt and pepper	

Per Serving	
Calories	365
fat	12 g
saturated fat	3 g
cholesterol	10 mg
sodium	255 mg
potassium	460 mg
carbohydrate	51 g
fiber	5 g
protein	14 g

24% Vitamin A • 62% Vitamin C
21% Calcium • 23% Iron
25% Thiamine • 11% Riboflavin
21% Niacin • 9% Vitamin B-6
52% Folate • 9% Vitamin B-12
18% Zinc

In large pot of boiling water, cook pasta until al dente (tender but firm); drain. (If sauce isn't ready, rinse pasta under warm water for a few seconds to prevent it from sticking together.)

Meanwhile, in large heavy saucepan or Dutch oven, heat oil over high heat. Add onions, tomatoes, and garlic; cook, stirring, for 2 to 3 minutes or until tomatoes are just heated through but still hold their shape. Stir in rotini, ham (if using), parsley, basil, and Parmesan. Reduce heat to medium; cook, stirring gently, for about 2 minutes or until heated through. Season with salt and pepper to taste.

Makes 4 servings.

Adding shrimp, chicken, turkey, or ham to this dish will increase the protein. Adding ham will also increase the sodium (to 703 mg).

Tuscan-Style Capellini with Clams and Garlic

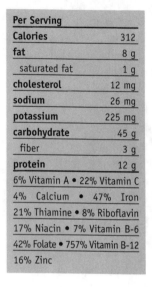

Per Serving	
Calories	312
fat	8 g
saturated fat	1 g
cholesterol	12 mg
sodium	26 mg
potassium	225 mg
carbohydrate	45 g
fiber	3 g
protein	12 g
6% Vitamin A • 22% Vitamin C	
4% Calcium • 47% Iron	
21% Thiamine • 8% Riboflavin	
17% Niacin • 7% Vitamin B-6	
42% Folate • 757% Vitamin B-12	
16% Zinc	

In Italy, this popular pasta dish is made with tiny tender clams that have about 1-in/2.5-cm shells. They are available in Canada on the West Coast, but they're harder to find elsewhere. Capellini is the very thin, angel-hair noodle; however, any type can be used.

2 lb	small clams (in shells)	1 kg
6	cloves garlic, minced	6
2 tbsp	olive oil	25 mL
¼ cup	white wine	50 mL
8 oz	capellini or spaghetti noodles	250 g
½ cup	coarsely chopped fresh parsley	125 mL
	Salt and freshly ground pepper	

Scrub clams under cold running water; discard any that do not close when tapped.

Try to time cooking of pasta so it is ready when the clams are. If using dried pasta, start it before cooking clams; if using fresh or very fine pasta, cook clams first.

In large heavy saucepan, cook garlic and oil over medium-high heat for 1 minute; add wine and clams. Cover and cook until clams open (time will vary from 2 to 10 minutes depending on size of clams); discard any that do not open. Meanwhile, in large pot of boiling water, cook capellini until al dente (tender but firm); drain.

Recent research has shown that not all shellfish are high in cholesterol. Mollusks—oysters, scallops, clams, and mussels—are not as high in cholesterol as crustaceans—shrimp, crab, and lobster.

Pour clam mixture over hot pasta and toss with parsley. Season with salt and pepper to taste.

Makes 4 servings.

Fettuccine with Mussels, Leeks, and Tomatoes

3 lb	mussels	1.5 kg
2	large leeks	2
8 oz	fettuccine	250 g
1 tbsp	olive oil	15 mL
4	cloves garlic, minced	4
1/2 tsp	dried thyme	2 mL
Pinch	hot pepper flakes	Pinch
4	large tomatoes, coarsely chopped, or 1 can (28 oz/796 mL) diced tomatoes	4
1/4 cup	dry white wine	50 mL
1/2 cup	chopped fresh parsley, basil or coriander	125 mL
	Salt and freshly ground pepper	

Per Serving	
Calories	393
fat	7 g
saturated fat	1 g
cholesterol	28 mg
sodium	310 mg
potassium	859 mg
carbohydrate	60 g
fiber	6 g
protein	21 g

28% Vitamin A • 75% Vitamin C
8% Calcium • 53% Iron
38% Thiamine • 20% Riboflavin
32% Niacin • 17% Vitamin B-6
68% Folate • 533% Vitamin B-12
30% Zinc

Scrub mussels under cold running water; cut off any hairy beards. Discard any that do not close when tapped. Place in large pot, cover and cook over medium-high heat for 5 to 7 minutes or until mussels open. Discard any that do not open. Drain and reserve liquid.

Trim leeks, discarding dark green parts. Slice into quarters lengthwise and wash under running water. Cut into 1 1/2-in/4-cm-long pieces. In large pot of boiling water, cook fettuccine until al dente (tender but firm); drain.

Meanwhile, in nonstick skillet, heat oil over medium heat; cook leeks for 5 minutes or until tender, stirring often; add garlic, thyme, hot pepper flakes, tomatoes, and wine. Bring to boil; stir in parsley.

To serve, divide fettuccine between four pasta bowls or plates, spoon cooked mussels over fettuccine, then spoon tomato mixture over each. (Alternatively, pour tomato sauce over mussels, then spoon mixture over fettuccine.) If dish is dry, add some reserved mussel cooking liquid.

Makes 4 servings.

Storing Mussels

Don't refrigerate mussels wrapped in plastic; instead remove from plastic bag and place in bowl, on top of ice covered in plastic and refrigerate.

Easy Friday-Night Seafood Dinner for Four

Mushroom Bisque with Tarragon (page 75)
Fettuccine with Mussels, Leeks, and Tomatoes
French bread
Fresh Pineapple Slices with Rum (page 237) or Berries with Orange-Honey Yogurt (page 234)

Fettuccine with Pesto Sauce

Per Serving	
Calories	361
fat	8 g
saturated fat	2 g
cholesterol	7 mg
sodium	158 mg
potassium	107 mg
carbohydrate	57 g
fiber	4 g
protein	13 g
4% Vitamin A • 3% Vitamin C	
13% Calcium • 14% Iron	
25% Thiamine • 6% Riboflavin	
17% Niacin • 6% Vitamin B-6	
50% Folate • 6% Vitamin B-12	
16% Zinc	

Pesto sauce is a fragrant fresh basil sauce that is absolutely perfect over pasta. This version has a full, pungent basil flavor yet omits the pine nuts and is much lower in oil than the classic recipe.

1 lb	fettuccine	500 g
	Freshly ground pepper	
	Grated Parmesan cheese	

PESTO SAUCE

2	cloves garlic	2
1 cup	fresh basil leaves, lightly packed	250 mL
½ cup	grated Parmesan cheese	125 mL
2 tbsp	olive oil	25 mL

Freeze pesto sauce in ice-cube containers; when frozen, transfer to plastic bag. Use a cube to flavor soups, salad dressings, and sauces.

For varations, add strips of roasted red pepper, rehydrated sundried tomato cut into strips, or strips of grilled chicken.

In large pot of boiling water, cook fettuccine until al dente (tender but firm). While pasta is cooking, prepare sauce.

Pesto Sauce: In food processor, combine garlic and basil; process until chopped. Add Parmesan and olive oil, process until smooth. Remove ½ cup/125 mL of the pasta cooking liquid and add to sauce; process until smooth.

Drain pasta and toss with pesto sauce. Sprinkle with pepper and Parmesan to taste.

Makes 6 servings.

Compare	*g fat per serving*
This recipe	*8*
Fettucine with regular pesto sauce	*27*

Fettuccine with Basil and Parsley

Serve this as a side dish with any meats or as part of a meatless meal. Keep a pot of fresh parsley on the windowsill or a bunch in a plastic bag in the refrigerator to give a fresh flavor to this dish. Use any other fresh herbs you have, such as sage, rosemary, or thyme (start with 1 tbsp/15 mL and add more to taste), before adding dried.

4 oz	fettuccine or any pasta	125 g
1 tbsp	olive oil	15 mL
2	cloves garlic, minced	2
1/3 cup	chopped fresh parsley	75 mL
1/4 cup	chopped fresh basil	50 mL
	(or 1 tsp/5 mL dried)	
	Salt and freshly ground pepper	
	Parmesan cheese (optional)	

Per Serving	
Calories	140
fat	4 g
saturated fat	1 g
cholesterol	0 mg
sodium	78 mg
potassium	69 mg
carbohydrate	22 g
fiber	1 g
protein	4 g

3% Vitamin A • 10% Vitamin C
2% Calcium • 7% Iron
9% Thiamine • 2% Riboflavin
5% Niacin • 3% Vitamin B-6
21% Folate • 0% Vitamin B-12
6% Zinc

In large pot of boiling water, cook noodles according to package directions or until al dente (tender but firm). Drain in colander, reserving 1/2 cup/125 mL cooking liquid.

Add oil and garlic to pot; cook, stirring, for 1 minute over medium heat. Add hot noodles, parsley, basil, salt, and pepper to taste; toss to mix. Sprinkle with Parmesan (if using). Add a little reserved cooking liquid to moisten. Serve hot.

Makes 4 small servings.

Variation

Add one large tomato, chopped, along with herbs. Sprinkle each serving with grated Parmesan cheese. Make with capellini or vermicelli noodles and serve as a first course.

Easy July Supper

Fettuccine with Pesto Sauce (opposite)
Sliced Cucumbers with Chives and Yogurt (omit basil) (page 99)
Raw baby carrots
Whole-wheat pita bread
Strawberries with Orange-Honey Yogurt (page 234)

Linguine with Salmon and Chives

Tender-crisp cooked vegetables, such as asparagus, green peas, or mushrooms, can be added to this quick-and-easy supper dish. Green onions can be used instead of chives, and shrimp, scallops or cooked fresh salmon instead of canned. Serve with wedges of lemon.

8 oz	linguine or any noodles	250 g
4 tsp	soft non-hydrogenated margarine	20 mL
1	small onion, chopped	1
2 tbsp	all-purpose flour	25 mL
1 cup	1% milk	250 mL
1/3 cup	chopped fresh chives or fresh dill	75 mL
	Salt and freshly ground pepper	
1	can (7 1/2 oz/213 g) salmon	1
2 tbsp	grated Parmesan cheese	25 mL

Recipe includes juices from canned salmon. Although this adds to the fat content, these juices are an excellent source of Omega-3 fatty acids, which may help to reduce heart disease.

In large pot of boiling water, cook linguine until al dente (tender but firm); drain, reserving 1/2 cup/125 mL cooking liquid. Return linguine to pan.

Meanwhile, in saucepan, melt margarine over medium heat; add onion and cook until tender. Stir in flour; mix well. Add milk and cook, whisking, until mixture comes to boil and thickens. Stir in chives, salt, and pepper to taste, and add reserved cooking liquid.

Flake salmon and add along with juices and chive mixture to pot with linguine; mix lightly. Sprinkle Parmesan cheese over each serving.

Makes 4 servings.

Vegetable Lasagna

This is light and easy to make. It can be prepared a day or two in advance and refrigerated.

2 tsp	canola oil	10 mL
1	onion, chopped	1
3	cloves garlic, minced	3
2	carrots, chopped	2
2	stalks celery, chopped	2
2 cups	sliced mushrooms	500 mL
1	can (28 oz/796 mL) diced tomatoes	1
1	can (7½ oz/213 mL) tomato sauce	1
1½ tsp	each dried basil and oregano	7 mL
	Salt and freshly ground pepper	
3 cups	small broccoli florets	750 mL
9	lasagna noodles	9
2 cups	low-fat cottage cheese	500 mL
3 cups	shredded part-skim (16% m.f.) mozzarella cheese	750 mL
⅓ cup	grated Parmesan cheese	75 mL

Per Serving	
Calories	355
fat	12 g
saturated fat	6 g
cholesterol	29 mg
sodium	898 mg
potassium	638 mg
carbohydrate	36 g
fiber	4 g
protein	27 g
66% Vitamin A • 52% Vitamin C	
43% Calcium • 16% Iron	
18% Thiamine • 26% Riboflavin	
35% Niacin • 19% Vitamin B-6	
35% Folate • 43% Vitamin B-12	
29% Zinc	

In large nonstick saucepan, heat oil over medium heat; add onion and cook until tender. Stir in garlic, carrot, celery, and mushrooms; cook, stirring often, for 5 minutes. Add tomatoes, tomato sauce, basil, oregano; season with salt and pepper to taste. Simmer, uncovered, for 10 minutes or until thickened slightly. Let cool; stir in broccoli.

In large pot of boiling water, cook noodles until al dente (tender but firm); drain and rinse under cold water.

In 13- x 9-in/3.5 L baking dish, cover bottom with thin layer of vegetable-tomato sauce; arrange 3 noodles evenly over top. Spread another cup of sauce and then half of the cottage cheese; sprinkle with ⅓ of the mozzarella cheese.

Repeat noodle, sauce, cottage, and mozzarella cheese layers once. Arrange remaining noodles; spread remaining sauce on top; sprinkle with remaining mozzarella and Parmesan. Bake in 350°F/180°C oven for 35 to 45 minutes or until hot and bubbly.

Makes 8 servings.

Meatless Buffet Dinner

Salmon Spread with Capers (page 62)

Marinated Mushrooms (page 70)

Vegetable Lasagna

Tossed Seasonal Greens (page 100)

Strawberry Mousse (page 242) or Fresh Pineapple Slices with Rum (page 237)

Oatmeal-Apricot Cookies (page 220)

All-Purpose Quick Spaghetti Sauce

Per cup/250 mL	
Calories	188
fat	7 g
saturated fat	2 g
cholesterol	41 mg
sodium	266 mg
potassium	832 mg
carbohydrate	16 g
fiber	3 g
protein	18 g
15% Vitamin A • 55% Vitamin C	
7% Calcium • 24% Iron	
12% Thiamine • 17% Riboflavin	
39% Niacin • 20% Vitamin B-6	
10% Folate • 67% Vitamin B-12	
44% Zinc	

I make this sauce in large amounts then freeze it in 2-cup/500 mL containers. You can double or triple this recipe. Sometimes I add chopped carrot, green pepper, celery, or mushrooms. My kids like it best over spaghetti noodles sprinkled with Parmesan cheese. It's also good as a base for lasagna, tacos, chili, or casseroles.

1 lb	lean ground beef	500 g
2	onions, chopped	2
1	large clove garlic, minced	1
1	can (5½ oz/156 mL) tomato paste	1
1	can (28 oz/796 mL) diced tomatoes	1
2 tsp	granulated sugar	10 mL
1 tsp	dried oregano	5 mL
1 tsp	dried basil	5 mL
½ tsp	dried thyme	2 mL
¼ tsp	each salt and freshly ground pepper	1 mL

Quick Chili

In saucepan, combine 2 cups/500 mL All-Purpose Quick Spaghetti Sauce, one 19 oz/540 mL can each kidney beans (drained and rinsed), and beans with pork, and 1 tbsp/15 mL chili powder.

Bring to a simmer over medium heat, stirring occasionally. Add chili powder and hot pepper flakes to taste.

* For 1 lb/500 g pasta use about 4 cups/1 L sauce to make 4 to 6 servings.

In large heavy skillet, cook beef over medium heat until no longer pink, breaking up with spoon. Pour off fat. Stir in onion and garlic; cook until softened. Stir in tomato paste, tomatoes, sugar, oregano, basil, thyme, salt, and pepper.

Bring to boil, reduce heat and simmer for 10 minutes; thin with water if desired. Taste and adjust seasonings if necessary.

Makes 6 cups (1.5 L) sauce.

How Much Pasta to Cook?

For a main-course pasta dish that includes a number of ingredients besides the pasta, I usually plan on about ½ lb/250 g for 4 servings. If it is a dish with only a light sauce such as pesto with pasta, I use more. One-half pound/250 g of spaghetti noodles yields about 4 cups/1 L when cooked.

The easiest way to measure it is to weigh the uncooked pasta. If you don't have scales, you can estimate by dividing up the package according to total weight (i.e. divide a 1 lb/500 g package in half to get ½ lb/250 g). Another method is to wrap a tape measure around a bundle of pasta, about 4½ inches/11 cm equals 8 oz/250 g of pasta.

I usually try to cook more pasta than I need and use the extra to make a pasta salad, or I mix it with any extra sauce and reheat it for breakfast or lunch.

Tofu Alfredo

It's easy to slip some tofu into your diet with this tasty pasta recipe from Susan Van Hezewijk, a talented home economist who retested many of the recipes in this new edition of The Lighthearted Cookbook.

8 oz	spaghetti	250 g
1	pkg (300 g) soft silken tofu	1
2 tsp	extra-virgin olive oil	10 mL
4	cloves garlic, minced	4
1/4 tsp	each salt and freshly ground pepper	1 mL
1/2 cup	chopped fresh basil	125 mL
1/4 cup	freshly ground Parmesan cheese (optional)	50 mL

Per Serving	
Calories	278
fat	5 g
saturated fat	1 g
cholesterol	0 mg
sodium	328 mg
potassium	219 mg
carbohydrate	46 g
fiber	3 g
protein	11 g

2% Vitamin A • 2% Vitamin C
4% Calcium • 15% Iron
24% Thiamine • 5% Riboflavin
14% Niacin • 6% Vitamin B-6
37% Folate • 0% Vitamin B-12
14% Zinc

In large pot of boiling salted water, cook pasta for 8 to 10 minutes or until al dente (tender but firm); drain, reserving 1/3 cup (75 mL) of the cooking water.

Meanwhile, purée tofu in food processor or blender; set aside.

In saucepan, heat oil over low heat. Add garlic and cook, stirring, until softened but not colored. Stir in tofu, reserved cooking liquid, salt, and pepper just until warmed through.

Toss pasta in sauce; place on serving plate and top with basil and Parmesan cheese.

Makes 4 servings, 1 cup/250 mL each.

This would also be nice served with a few grilled shrimp on top. A garlic-flavored oil could be used for a shortcut.

Tofu Primer

Tofu, made from soybeans, is one of the best sources of soy protein, a high-quality vegetable protein. Soybeans are a rich source of isoflavones, which are linked to reducing our risk of heart disease by helping to lower our LDL (bad) cholesterol. Phytosterols, found in soybeans, may prevent cholesterol absorption from foods.

Add firm tofu to salads, soups, pastas, and stir-fries; add soft tofu to spreads, dips, or salad dressings. When choosing soy beverages, read the label and choose ones fortified with calcium and vitamin D.

VEGETABLES AND GRAINS: MAINS AND SIDES

Beans with Tomatoes and Spinach

Barley, Green Pepper, and Tomato Casserole

Mexican Rice and Bean Casserole

Quick Lentils with Coriander and Mint

Barley and Mushroom Pilaf

Bulgur Pilaf with Apricots and Raisins

Cabbage and Potato Pie

New Potatoes with Herbs

Oven-Baked French Fries

Baked Parsnips and Carrots

Rutabaga and Apple Purée

Stir-Fry Ratatouille

Middle-Eastern Eggplant Baked with Yogurt and Fresh Mint

Spaghetti Squash with Parsley and Garlic

Gratin of Fall Vegetables

Mushroom, Broccoli, and Onion Pizza

Vegetable Taco Sauce

Broccoli with Ginger and Lemon

Broccoli and Red Pepper Casserole

Steamed Fresh Vegetables

Carrots and Leeks with Parsley

Green Beans with Sautéed Mushrooms

Skillet Zucchini with Chopped Tomatoes

Peas with Green Onions

Asian-Style Vegetables

Cherry Tomatoes and Mushroom Sauté

Tomatoes Broiled with Goat Cheese and Basil

Brussels Sprouts with Peppers and Potatoes

Mushroom-Stuffed Zucchini Cups

Skillet Greens with Ginger and Celery

When my daughter asks what's for dinner, she can't understand why I often answer by mentioning only the meat course; to her, the vegetables are as important and most enjoyable. I, too, love vegetables but often plan meals around the meat or fish because they usually take more time to prepare or cook. For healthy eating, vegetables should cover at least three-quarters of your dinner plate.

Vegetables are an important source of vitamins, minerals, carbohydrates, protein, and fiber. They are cholesterol-free and low in fats and calories. Choose locally grown fresh vegetables that are in season for the best flavor and nutritive value. When out of season, frozen vegetables are often higher in nutritive value than fresh because imported vegetables lose nutrients during transportation and storage. For example, lettuce loses half its Vitamin C in one week after it is picked. Canned vegetables are often higher in sodium than fresh or frozen.

When we serve a meatless meal, we can use some cheese and eggs and still keep our saturated-fat intake down to the recommended level. It's important to consider your diet over a day or a week. It's when we eat meats, high-fat cheese, and eggs on a daily basis that the fat and cholesterol amounts will be too high. Check the Soups, Pasta, Salads and Dressings sections of this book for more meatless main-course dishes.

Beans with Tomatoes and Spinach

It seems that something that tastes as good as this should be harder to make. My son, Jeff, really likes this and says the Five-Grain Soda Bread (page 226) is perfect with it. Serve as a quick dinner or lunch along with a green salad. Sometimes I cook a pound (500 g) of ground beef along with the onions and add chili powder.

1 tbsp	olive oil	15 mL
2	cloves garlic, minced	2
2	onions, sliced	2
1	can (28 oz/796 mL) diced tomatoes	1
1	can (19 oz/540 mL) red kidney beans, drained and rinsed	1
1	can (19 oz/540 mL) romano beans, drained and rinsed	1
½ tsp	dried oregano	2 mL
1	pkg (10 oz/284 g) fresh spinach (or 1 bunch) stems removed	1
	Freshly ground pepper	

To make our diet healthier, we need to rely more on vegetable protein and less on animal protein. Legumes (beans, peas, lentils), nuts, seeds, and grains can also provide protein, vitamins, and minerals and are higher in fiber and lower in saturated fat than animal protein.

In large non-stick or heavy saucepan or casserole, heat oil over medium heat; cook garlic and onions, stirring occasionally, for 5 minutes or until softened.

Add tomatoes, kidney beans, romano beans, and oregano; simmer 5 minutes.

Stir in spinach. Season with pepper to taste.

Makes 4 large servings, 1½ cups/375 mL each.

Barley, Green Pepper, and Tomato Casserole

Serve this as a main course along with a tossed salad and whole-wheat toast or pita bread. Crumbled feta cheese is a nice addition.

1 cup	pot barley	250 mL
3 cups	hot vegetable or chicken stock or water	750 mL
2	onions, chopped	2
1	sweet green pepper, chopped	1
2	large tomatoes, cut in chunks	2
1 tsp	dried oregano	5 mL
	Salt and freshly ground pepper	
2 cups	shredded light old Cheddar cheese	500 mL
	Fresh basil, coriander or parsley to taste	

Per Serving	
Calories	269
fat	8 g
saturated fat	5 g
cholesterol	24 mg
sodium	652 mg
potassium	343 mg
carbohydrate	36 g
fiber	4 g
protein	15 g
8% Vitamin A • 40% Vitamin C	
29% Calcium • 14% Iron	
11% Thiamine • 6% Riboflavin	
14% Niacin • 12% Vitamin B-6	
12% Folate • 0% Vitamin B-12	
11% Zinc	

In baking dish, combine barley, stock or water, onions, green pepper, tomatoes, oregano, salt, and pepper to taste; stir to mix. Cover and bake in 350°F/180°C oven for 45 minutes. Stir in cheese and bake, uncovered, for 20 minutes longer or until barley is tender and most liquid has been absorbed. Sprinkle with fresh herbs.

Makes 6 servings.

Plant and Animal Protein

Protein is made up of 22 amino acids. Nine of these can't be produced by the body and must be obtained from food. These are called essential amino acids. All animal products contain all the essential amino acids. Plant foods are missing an essential amino acid. Therefore, it is important to combine a plant food with an animal food or two plant foods that together contain all the essential amino acids. Good combinations of plant foods are:
- *legumes and grains (e.g., baked beans and whole-wheat bread)*
- *legumes and nuts (e.g., tossed salad with chick peas and walnuts)*
- *legumes and low-fat dairy products (e.g., bean casserole with low-fat mozzarella topping)*
- *grains and low-fat dairy products (e.g., cereal and skim milk or barley and cheese)*

Cheese is a good source of protein and calcium; however, it (particularly Cheddar) is high in fat. If this is part of a meatless meal, it can fit into a 30% fat diet. If you are serving this with meat, you should reduce the cheese by half and use a lower-fat cheese such as lower-fat mozzarella or feta.

Fall Friday-Night Dinner
Harvest Pumpkin and Zucchini Soup (page 80)
Barley, Green Pepper, and Tomato Casserole
Tossed Seasonal Greens (page 100)
Buttermilk Apple Cake (page 223)

Rice Basics

The Heart and Stroke Foundation of Canada recommends that we reduce the fat, particularly saturated fat, in our diet and increase the complex carbohydrate. One way to do this is to have more fruits, vegetables and whole grains, including rice.

Basmati rice is a nutty, fragrant rice grown in India. It's available white or brown.

Brown rice is the most nutritious because it contains the bran and germ. It's higher in fiber and B vitamins than other rice.

Instant or pre-cooked rice is white rice that has been cooked then dehydrated. It cooks the fastest but is the least nutritious. Follow package directions for cooking.

Parboiled rice is a white rice that has been processed so that when cooked, the grains are firm and separate. It is more nutritious than white rice because the thiamin is retained during processing. One manufacturer's brand name for parboiled rice is "converted" rice.

Short-, medium- or long-grain rice: Short-grain cooked rice is stickiest of the three. The longer the grain, the more firm and separate the rice is after cooking.

Thai Jasmine is a fragrant long-grain rice used in Asian cooking. Rinse it several times before cooking. To cook: For the first cup/250 mL of rice, add 1½ cups/375 mL of boiling water; for each additional cup/250 mL, add 1 cup/250 mL of boiling water or follow package directions. Let stand, covered, for 15 minutes after cooking.

Wild rice is not really a rice but we use it as a rice. It has a wonderful nutty flavor and a chewy texture. It is expensive and is often served mixed with cooked white or brown rice. To cook: Rinse under running water. Place in a saucepan. For each cup/250 mL of rice add 4 cups/1 L cold water; bring to a boil. Cover and boil for 40 minutes or until grains are firm-tender but not mushy or splayed; drain.

White rice is most common in Canada; during processing, the bran is removed.

To Cook Rice

For each cup/250 mL of rice, bring 2 cups/500 mL water or stock to a boil. Stir in rice; reduce heat, cover and simmer for 20+ minutes for white, 45 minutes for brown or until water is absorbed and rice is tender. One cup/250 mL of raw rice yields about 3 cups/750 mL when cooked.

Compare (per 1 cup/250 mL, cooked)

	g fat	mg cholesterol	mg sodium	g fiber	g protein	g carbohydrate	calories
Bulgur, or cracked wheat	1	0	2	4	6	41	191
Rice, parboiled (converted)	0	0	5	0.5	4	41	186
Rice, regular white	0	0	4	0.6	4	50	223
Rice, brown	1	0	6	2	5	50	232
Macaroni	0.5	0	1	1	5	31	150
Spaghetti	0.5	0	1	1	5	31	150

Mexican Rice and Bean Casserole

This is a well-liked dish at our house. You may want to add a little less chili or cayenne if you have young children. Serve with a green vegetable, salad, and toast.

1 tsp	canola oil	5 mL
1	onion, chopped	1
2	cloves garlic, minced	2
1½ cups	mushrooms, sliced (¼ lb/125 g)	375 mL
2	sweet green peppers, chopped	2
¾ cup	long-grain rice	175 mL
1	can (19 oz/540 mL) red kidney beans, drained and rinsed	1
1	can (28 oz/796 mL) diced tomatoes	1
¼ cup	water	50 mL
1 tbsp	chili powder	15 mL
2 tsp	cumin	10 mL
¼ tsp	cayenne pepper	1 mL
¾ cup	shredded Cheddar cheese	175 mL
2 tbsp	chopped fresh coriander or parsley	25 mL

For variety and to increase the amount, add a small can of black beans or any other kind of beans.

In large nonstick skillet or Dutch oven, heat oil over medium heat. Add onion, garlic, mushrooms, and green peppers; cook, stirring often, until onion is tender, about 10 minutes.

Add rice, beans, tomatoes, water, chili powder, cumin, and cayenne; cover and simmer for about 25 minutes or until rice is tender and most of the liquid is absorbed.

Transfer to baking dish and sprinkle with cheese. Bake in 350°F/180°C oven for 15 minutes or microwave at high (100%) power for 1 to 2 minutes or until cheese melts. Sprinkle with coriander.

Makes 6 servings, 1 cup/250 mL each.

Quick Lentils with Coriander and Mint

This is by far one of the best-tasting and easiest-to-make lentil dishes. Keep a can of lentils on your shelf, and you can have a quick vegetable dish in minutes. Fresh mint and coriander add a special flavor. You could use fresh basil instead of coriander. Serve with chicken, fish, or meat or as part of a meatless meal.

2 tsp	canola oil	10 mL
1	small onion, chopped	1
2 tsp	mild Indian curry paste	10 mL
1	tomato, chopped	1
1	can (19 oz/540 mL) lentils, drained and rinsed or 2 cups/500 mL cooked lentils	1
2 tbsp	each chopped fresh coriander and mint	25 mL
	Salt and pepper to taste	

In nonstick skillet, heat oil over medium heat; add onions and cook until tender, about 5 minutes. Stir in curry paste until well mixed. Stir in tomato and lentils; cook until hot. Stir in coriander, mint, salt, and pepper to taste.

Makes 5 servings, ½ cup/125 mL each.

Per Serving	
Calories	128
fat	3 g
saturated fat	trace
cholesterol	0 mg
sodium	193 mg
potassium	379 mg
carbohydrate	19 g
fiber	4 g
protein	8 g

4% Vitamin A • 10% Vitamin C
2% Calcium • 21% Iron
12% Thiamine • 5% Riboflavin
10% Niacin • 9% Vitamin B-6
68% Folate • 0% Vitamin B-12
12% Zinc

Types of Lentils

Split red lentils are used in most soups and cook in 10 to 15 minutes.

Green or brown whole lentils retain their shape when cooked and take about 45 minutes to cook.

How to Cook Dried Lentils

Lentils are a good source of iron and an excellent source of fiber and vegetable protein. Serve with complementary cereal protein such as bread or rice. One cup/250 mL of dried lentils will yield about 2 to 2½ cups/500 to 625 mL cooked lentils.

Wash and drain dried lentils. In saucepan, combine lentils with 3 times the amount of water (add a quartered onion and bay leaf if desired). Bring to a boil; reduce heat and simmer, covered, for 10 to 45 minutes, depending on type, or until tender; drain. Use in salads, casseroles, and soups or as a vegetable.

Barley and Mushroom Pilaf

I like to serve this as an alternative to rice or potatoes. Sometimes I vary it by adding chopped almonds, chopped celery or green onion, chopped fresh dill, thyme or basil. It's nice for a buffet and can be prepared in advance.

1 tbsp	soft non-hydrogenated margarine	15 mL
1	onion, chopped	1
12 oz	mushrooms, sliced	375 g
1 cup	pot barley	250 mL
3 cups	hot chicken or vegetable stock	750 mL
½ cup	chopped fresh parsley	125 mL
	Salt and freshly ground pepper	

In nonstick skillet, melt margarine over medium heat; add onion and cook for about 2 minutes or until softened. Add mushrooms and cook, stirring occasionally, for 5 minutes.

Transfer mixture to 8-cup/2 L baking dish; add barley and chicken stock. Bake, covered, in 350°F/180°C oven for 1 hour; uncover and bake for 10 minutes longer (or bake in 325°F/160°C oven for 1½ hours). Stir in parsley, salt, and pepper to taste.

Makes 8 servings, ½ cup/125 mL each.

Rice and Mushroom Pilaf

Substitute 1½ cups/375 mL parboiled (converted) rice or brown rice for the barley. Stir rice into mushroom mixture. Reduce cooking time to about 40 minutes or cook until liquid has been absorbed. Makes 8 cups/2 L.

Pot or Pearl Barley?

What's the difference? Pearl barley is more polished than pot barley. When possible, choose pot barley because it is higher in fiber and more nutritious. They take the same length of time to cook. Use as an alternative to rice or pasta in soups and casseroles.

The New Lighthearted Cookbook

Bulgur Pilaf with Apricots and Raisins

Bulgur's mild, nutty flavor and slightly crunchy texture make it a nice change from rice.

2 tsp	olive oil	10 mL
1	onion, chopped	1
1 cup	bulgur or cracked wheat	250 mL
1/4 cup	raisins	50 mL
1/4 cup	diced dried apricot	50 mL
2 cups	boiling chicken stock	500 mL
1/4 cup	chopped fresh parsley (optional)	50 mL
	Salt and freshly ground pepper	
	Chopped almonds (optional)	

Per Serving	
Calories	214
fat	3 g
saturated fat	1 g
cholesterol	0 mg
sodium	426 mg
potassium	434 mg
carbohydrate	42 g
fiber	6 g
protein	8 g

8% Vitamin A • 3% Vitamin C
3% Calcium • 16% Iron
8% Thiamine • 6% Riboflavin
23% Niacin • 11% Vitamin B-6
15% Folate • 6% Vitamin B-12
12% Zinc

In nonstick skillet, heat oil over medium heat; cook onion, stirring, until softened. Stir in bulgur and cook, stirring, for 1 minute. Stir in raisins, apricot, and stock; cover and simmer over low heat for 15 minutes or until liquid is absorbed. Stir in parsley (if using); season with salt and pepper to taste. Garnish with chopped almonds (if using).

Makes 4 servings.

Bulgur, or cracked wheat, is available in some supermarkets and most health-food stores. It is a good source of fiber.Dish can be prepared a day in advance and refrigerated. Reheat, covered, in 350°F/180°C oven for 30 minutes.

Garlic-Parsley Potatoes

Boil 1 lb/500 g tiny new potatoes, red-skinned potatoes or any you have on hand until tender. Peel only if skins are old and tough, because the skins add flavor, fiber, and vitamins.

In small saucepan or microwave dish, combine 2 tsp/10 mL margarine or oil and 2 cloves minced garlic and cook over medium heat, stirring, for 1 minute or microwave on medium (50%) power for 30 seconds.

Drain potatoes and cut in half or quarters if large; transfer to warm serving dish. Toss with garlic mixture and 1/4 cup/50 mL chopped fresh parsley or dill. Makes 4 servings.

Variation: *Instead of potatoes, use green beans, carrots, cauliflower, broccoli, or peas.*

Cabbage and Potato Pie

Crinkly savoy cabbage, collard greens, kale, chard, or a combination of these in light cream sauce with a mashed potato topping make a delicious vegetable dish.

1 lb	savoy cabbage, collard greens or kale	500 g
4	medium potatoes, peeled and quartered	4
¼ cup	1% milk	50 mL
1 tbsp	soft non-hydrogenated margarine	15 mL
	Salt and freshly ground pepper	
	Paprika	

CREAM SAUCE

1½ tbsp	soft non-hydrogenated margarine	22 mL
1	medium onion, chopped	1
2 tbsp	all-purpose flour	25 mL
1 cup	1% milk	250 mL
½ cup	grated Parmesan cheese	125 mL
	Salt, freshly ground pepper, and nutmeg	

If using leftover mashed potatoes, use 2 cups/500 mL.

Winter Meatless Dinner
Cabbage and Potato Pie
Baked Parsnips and Carrots
(page 182)
Whole-wheat buns with low-
fat mozzarella cheese
Fresh-fruit compote
Milk

Separate and trim cabbage leaves or stems from collard leaves or kale. In large pot of boiling water, cover and cook cabbage for 5 to 10 minutes, collards or kale for 10 to 15 minutes, or until tender. Drain thoroughly; chop coarsely and set aside.

In saucepan of boiling water, cook potatoes until tender; drain. Mash potatoes along with milk, margarine, salt, and pepper to taste.

Cream Sauce: Meanwhile, in small saucepan, melt margarine over medium heat; add onion and cook for 3 to 5 minutes or until tender. Whisk in flour and mix well; cook, stirring, for 1 minute. Add milk and cook, stirring, for 3 to 5 minutes or until mixture comes to simmer and has thickened. Stir in grated cheese until melted. Season with salt, pepper, and nutmeg to taste.

Mix sauce with cabbage; spoon into 4-cup/1 L baking dish. Cover evenly with mashed potatoes; sprinkle lightly with paprika. Bake in 350°F/180°C oven for 20 to 30 minutes or until heated through.

Makes 4 servings.

New Potatoes with Herbs

Small new potatoes, boiled in their skins, are delicious. Instead of butter, top with chopped fresh herbs and a dash of lemon juice and oil. These go well with any meats, poultry or fish.

1 lb	tiny new potatoes (about 20)	500 g
2 tbsp	chopped fresh basil, dill or mint	25 mL
3 tbsp	chopped chives	45 mL
1 tsp	lemon juice	5 mL
1 tsp	olive or canola oil (optional)	5 mL
	Salt and freshly ground pepper	

In saucepan, boil unpeeled potatoes until tender, about 15 minutes; drain. Add basil, chives, lemon juice, oil (if using), salt, and pepper to taste. Mix lightly and serve.

Makes 4 servings.

Per Serving	
Calories	82
fat	trace
saturated fat	trace
cholesterol	0 mg
sodium	5 mg
potassium	370 mg
carbohydrate	19 g
fiber	2 g
protein	2 g
1% Vitamin A • 22% Vitamin C	
1% Calcium • 6% Iron	
8% Thiamine • 1% Riboflavin	
7% Niacin • 16% Vitamin B-6	
5% Folate • 0% Vitamin B-12	
3% Zinc	

Oven-Baked French Fries

These good-tasting French fries are much healthier and easier to make than the ones that you deep-fry in fat.

4	medium baking potatoes (1½ lb/750 g)	4
1 tbsp	canola oil	15 mL
½ tsp	each salt and pepper	2 mL
	Paprika	
	Grated Parmesan cheese (optional)	

Wash potatoes but don't peel; slice into ½-in/1-cm-thick strips. Toss potatoes with oil in a bowl until coated; sprinkle with salt, pepper, and paprika. Spread on baking sheet and bake in 475°F/240°C oven for 25 to 30 minutes, or until golden, turning occasionally.

Toss with Parmesan (if using).

Makes 4 servings.

Per Serving	
Calories	160
fat	4 g
saturated fat	trace
cholesterol	0 mg
sodium	10 mg
potassium	500 mg
carbohydrate	30 g
fiber	3 g
protein	3 g
1% Vitamin A • 25% Vitamin C	
1% Calcium • 11% Iron	
10% Thiamine • 3% Riboflavin	
12% Niacin • 23% Vitamin B-6	
6% Folate • 0% Vitamin B-12	
4% Zinc	

Baked Parsnips and Carrots

As a child, parsnips were one of the few foods I didn't like; now I love them. I'm not sure if it was because of the parsnips themselves or that they might have been overcooked. In any case, parsnips cooked around a roast, baked or microwaved, are really sweet and delicious. Even my children like them this way.

2	parsnips	2
4	carrots	4
1 tbsp	soft non-hydrogenated margarine	15 mL
	Salt and freshly ground pepper	
¼ tsp	cumin	1 mL
1 tbsp	water	15 mL

Peel parsnips and carrots; cut in half crosswise, then cut lengthwise into strips. Place in baking dish and dot with margarine. Sprinkle with cumin, salt, and pepper to taste; add water.

Cover and bake in 375°F/190°C oven for 50 to 60 minutes or until vegetables are tender.

Microwave Method: Prepare as above in a microwave-safe baking dish. Cover and microwave at high (100%) power for 12 to 15 minutes or until vegetables are tender.

Makes 4 servings.

Seasonings to add to mashed squash: nutmeg, cinnamon, maple syrup, brown sugar, minced fresh gingerroot, lemon juice, applesauce, or fruit juice.

Squash

I love winter squash and most often serve it very simply—either in wedges still in its skin or mashed with a small amount of butter and freshly ground pepper. If it is dry, add some orange or apple juice.

Preparation: Cut squash in half and scoop out seeds and interior pulp.

To bake squash: Place cut side down on lightly greased baking sheet. Bake in 375°F/190°C oven 50 minutes for acorn or pepper squash, 70 minutes for butternut or until flesh is tender when pierced with a fork.

To steam squash: Cut prepared squash into halves or quarters (cut hubbard squash into chunks); peel if desired. Arrange on rack in steamer; add boiling water; cover and steam until tender about 15 to 25 minutes, depending on size of pieces. Serve as is or remove squash from skin and mash.

Rutabaga and Apple Purée

Apple adds a mellow, sweet flavor to rutabaga or yellow turnip. For an equally delicious variation, use pear instead of apple. The recipe can be prepared up to a day in advance, but omit the yogurt and add when reheating.

	Per Serving	
	Calories	77
	fat	2 g
	saturated fat	trace
	cholesterol	1 mg
	sodium	51 mg
	potassium	350 mg
	carbohydrate	13 g
	fiber	2 g
	protein	2 g

8% Vitamin A • 30% Vitamin C
6% Calcium • 4% Iron
6% Thiamine • 4% Riboflavin
4% Niacin • 6% Vitamin B-6
6% Folate • 1% Vitamin B-12
4% Zinc

1	small rutabaga (about 1¼ lb/625 g), peeled and cubed	1
1	large apple, peeled, cored and cut in chunks	1
¼ cup	low-fat plain yogurt	50 mL
1 tbsp	soft non-hydrogenated margarine	15 mL
Pinch	nutmeg	Pinch
	Salt and freshly ground pepper	

Steam rutabaga for 15 to 20 minutes or until nearly tender. Add apple and cook for 5 to 10 minutes or until rutabaga and apple are tender. Drain well.

In food processor or blender, purée rutabaga mixture until smooth (or mash or put through food mill). Add yogurt, margarine, and nutmeg; season with salt and pepper to taste and process just until combined. Reheat in saucepan over medium-low heat or in microwave until heated through.

Microwave Method: Place halves or quarters cut side up on microwave-safe baking dish; cover with plastic wrap. Microwave on high (100%) power approximately 7 to 8 minutes per pound or until flesh is tender when pierced with a fork. (One whole acorn squash, halved, will take 12 to 13 minutes, a 14 oz/400 g butternut squash will take 7 minutes.)

Makes 6 servings.

Stir-Fry Ratatouille

This version of the colorful Mediterranean vegetable dish is lower in oil and quicker to make than most and is good hot or cold. It's an attractive fall dish to serve with rice and cold meat or grilled lamb chops; for a meatless meal, cover with grated cheese and place under broiler until cheese melts and is golden brown.

2 tbsp	canola oil	25 mL
1	medium onion, sliced	1
2	cloves garlic, minced	2
8	medium mushrooms, halved	8
1	small sweet yellow or red pepper, cubed	1
2 cups	cubed (½-in/1-cm pieces) unpeeled eggplant	500 mL
1	small zucchini, sliced	1
2	tomatoes, cut in wedges	2
½ tsp	each dried thyme and basil	2 mL
	Salt and freshly ground pepper	

Low-Fat Cooking Tip

In many recipes, vegetables are cooked in margarine or oil to soften and develop flavor. It's important to use as little fat as possible and to use a non-stick saucepan or skillet.

If vegetables stick to the pan, or to prevent scorching, add water a spoonful at a time and cook until water evaporates.

In large nonstick skillet, heat half of oil over medium-high heat; add onion, garlic, mushroom, and sweet pepper and stir-fry until tender, about 4 minutes, adding up to 2 tbsp (25 mL) water if needed to prevent burning. With slotted spoon, remove to side dish and set aside.

Heat remaining oil in skillet; add eggplant and zucchini; stir-fry for 4 minutes or until tender. Return mushroom mixture to pan, add tomatoes, thyme, and basil; cover and simmer for 5 minutes. Add salt and pepper to taste.

Makes 6 servings.

Middle-Eastern Eggplant Baked with Yogurt and Fresh Mint

This is one of the tastiest and easiest ways to prepare eggplant. It's very good with lamb. You can also serve it with pork, beef, or chicken or as part of a buffet or meatless dinner.

3 tbsp	canola oil	45 mL
2 tbsp	water	25 mL
1	large onion, sliced	1
1	medium eggplant, unpeeled (1 ¼ lb/625 g)	1
1 cup	low-fat plain yogurt	250 mL
3 tbsp	chopped fresh mint and/or parsley	45 mL
2	cloves garlic, minced	2
¼ tsp	salt	1 mL
	Freshly ground pepper	
	Paprika	

Per Serving	
Calories	122
fat	8 g
saturated fat	1 g
cholesterol	2 mg
sodium	128 mg
potassium	361 mg
carbohydrate	11 g
fiber	3 g
protein	3 g
2% Vitamin A • 5% Vitamin C	
8% Calcium • 4% Iron	
7% Thiamine • 7% Riboflavin	
5% Niacin • 7% Vitamin B-6	
9% Folate • 4% Vitamin B-12	
7% Zinc	

In large nonstick skillet, heat 1 tsp/5 mL of the oil and water over medium heat; cook onion, stirring, for 5 minutes or until softened. Remove onion and set aside.

Cut eggplant into ¼-in-/5-mm-thick slices. Brush remaining oil over eggplant slices. In skillet over medium heat, cook eggplant (in batches) turning once, until tender, about 10 minutes (or arrange in a single layer on baking sheet and bake in 400°F/200°C oven for 15 minutes or until tender and soft).

In ungreased shallow baking dish, arrange overlapping slices of eggplant alternating with onion.

In small bowl, stir together yogurt, fresh mint or parsley, garlic, salt, and pepper to taste; drizzle over eggplant slices. Sprinkle liberally with paprika. Bake in 350°F/180°C oven until hot and bubbly, 10 to 15 minutes.

Makes 6 servings.

Variation

When tomatoes are in season, add slices of tomato between eggplant slices and onion in baking dish. Sprinkle top with grated low-fat mozzarella cheese.

Spaghetti Squash with Parsley and Garlic

1 tbsp	olive oil or butter	15 mL
3	cloves garlic, minced	3
1	spaghetti squash (4 lb/2 kg)	1
1 cup	coarsely chopped fresh parsley or grated zucchini	250 mL
¼ cup	low-fat plain yogurt or light sour cream (optional)	50 mL
	Salt and freshly ground pepper	

In small skillet, heat oil over medium-low heat; add garlic and cook until tender, about 1 minute. (Or cook garlic and oil in microwave for 30 seconds.)

To Boil: In large pot of boiling water, cook whole spaghetti squash until tender when pierced with skewer, about 30 minutes (some varieties of spaghetti squash may take longer) Drain squash.

Microwave Method: Pierce spaghetti squash in 10 to 15 places with a fork; place in microwave-safe dish and microwave at high (100%) power for 5 to 7 minutes per lb or until tender when pierced with a fork. Turn over halfway through cooking. Let stand 5 minutes.

To Steam: Cut squash in half lengthwise; scoop out seeds. Steam for 15 to 20 minutes or until tender.

To Bake: Cut lengthwise, remove seeds, and pierce skin with fork. Place cut side down in baking dish and bake at 350°F/180°C for 45 minutes. Turn and bake another 10 to 15 minutes or until skin is tender.

Cut cooked squash in half lengthwise. Scoop out seeds. Run tines of fork lengthwise over squash to loosen spaghetti-like strands; scoop out strands into baking dish or serving bowl. Add garlic mixture, parsley, yogurt (if using), salt, and pepper to taste; toss to mix.

Makes 8 servings.

The spaghetti-like strands of this unusual squash are very good tossed with garlic and parsley. Be sure to cut the squash lengthwise, or else you will cut the strands in half.

For a very low-calorie meal, serve spaghetti squash topped with vegetable mixture in lasagna recipe (page 167).

Make Ahead
Recipe can be prepared a day in advance and refrigerated. To serve, bring to room temperature then reheat, covered, in 350°F/180°C oven for 35 minutes, or microwave on high for 8 to 10 minutes or until heated through.

Photo:
Strawberry Meringue Tarts with Strawberry Sauce (page 241)

Gratin of Fall Vegetables

This cheese-topped vegetable casserole dish is good as part of a meatless meal or with roast chicken, turkey, or meats.

2 cups	thin strips of rutabaga (yellow turnip) or peeled white turnip	500 mL
1/2 cup	water	125 mL
1	sweet red pepper, cut in thin strips	1
3/4 cup	thinly sliced onion	175 mL
2 cups	thinly sliced zucchini	500 mL
1 cup	sliced mushrooms (about 8)	250 mL
4	medium tomatoes, cut in chunks	4
1 tsp	dried oregano	5 mL
	Salt and freshly ground pepper	
1 1/4 cups	shredded part-skim mozzarella cheese (16% m.f.) or Danbo	300 mL
2 tbsp	grated Parmesan cheese	25 mL

Per Serving	
Calories	84
fat	2 g
saturated fat	1 g
cholesterol	6 mg
sodium	284 mg
potassium	409 mg
carbohydrate	10 g
fiber	2 g
protein	7 g

16% Vitamin A • 68% Vitamin C
14% Calcium • 6% Iron
8% Thiamine • 9% Riboflavin
9% Niacin • 8% Vitamin B-6
9% Folate • 1% Vitamin B-12
4% Zinc

In large skillet or Dutch oven, cook rutabaga in water, covered, for 10 minutes or until tender, stirring occasionally. If necessary, add more water to prevent burning. Add red pepper, and onions; cook, stirring, for 2 minutes.

Add zucchini and mushrooms; cook, stirring, for 3 minutes. Add tomatoes and increase heat to high; cook, stirring occasionally, 5 to 10 minutes or just until excess moisture has evaporated. Stir in oregano; season with salt and pepper to taste.

Spoon vegetable mixture into shallow heatproof baking dish; sprinkle evenly with mozzarella and Parmesan cheeses. Broil for 3 to 5 minutes or until cheese is melted and slightly browned.

Makes 8 servings.

Photo:
Ginger-Garlic Marinated Flank Steak
(page 136) with Broccoli and Red
Pepper Casserole (page 191)

Make Ahead

Recipe can be prepared in advance, covered, and refrigerated. Reheat in oven at 350°F/180°C for 20 to 25 minutes or microwave on high for 3 to 5 minutes or until heated through.

Try these lighter cheeses to boost flavor:
• Danbo, a Danish cheese traditionally lower in fat
• light Swiss
• light Provolone

Your skillet can go straight from stovetop to oven even if the handle is not oven-proof; simply wrap the handle in foil.

Mushroom, Broccoli, and Onion Pizza

Per Serving (2 pieces)	
Calories	493
fat	15 g
saturated fat	8 g
cholesterol	35 mg
sodium	1036 mg
potassium	438 mg
carbohydrate	63 g
fiber	4 g
protein	26 g
23% Vitamin A • 75% Vitamin C	
43% Calcium • 26% Iron	
26% Thiamine • 33% Riboflavin	
41% Niacin • 11% Vitamin B-6	
28% Folate • 26% Vitamin B-12	
23% Zinc	

Keep some homemade or store-bought pizza dough rounds in your freezer so you can easily make your own fast food. Depending on the toppings you choose, your pizzas can be nutritious as well as delicious.

1	pre-cooked pizza crust* (12-inch/30 cm)	1
½ cup	tomato sauce	125 mL
1 tsp	dried oregano (or 2 tbsp/25 mL fresh)	5 mL
½ tsp	dried basil (or 1 tbsp/15 mL fresh)	2 mL
5	mushrooms, sliced	5
2 cups	small broccoli florets	500 mL
1	small onion, thinly sliced	1
½	sweet red and/or yellow pepper, chopped	½
2 cups	shredded part-skim (16% m.f.) mozzarella cheese	500 mL
Pinch	red pepper flakes (optional)	Pinch
	Black olives (optional)	

Good-tasting pizza can also be very nutritious. If you choose vegetables such as broccoli, onion, sweet peppers, tomatoes, zucchini, mushrooms, and reduced-fat cheese for toppings, your pizza will be a good source of calcium, Vitamins A and C, and fiber.

If, instead, you choose anchovies, olives, pepperoni, and regular mozzarella cheese, you will double the fat and sodium. The pizza will still be a good source of calcium, but it will be low in fiber and vitamins.

If your children don't like broccoli, don't assume they won't like it on pizza. They might be receptive to it in this way.

Place pizza crust on baking sheet. Combine tomato sauce, oregano, and basil; mix well and spread over pizza crust. Arrange mushrooms, broccoli, onion, and red pepper on top. Sprinkle with cheese, red pepper flakes, and olives (if using). Bake in 475°F/240°C oven for 12 minutes or until cheese is bubbling. Cut into 8 pieces.

Makes 4 servings, 2 pieces each.

*Pizza dough: If using fresh or frozen (l lb/500 g) pizza dough, roll out fresh or thawed dough to 12-inch/30-cm round, top with above toppings, and bake on greased baking sheet for 12 to 15 minutes or until crust is golden.

Compare	g fat	mg sodium	calories
This pizza (2 slices)	15	1036	493
Frozen pizza (2 slices)	30	1590	503

Vegetable Taco Sauce

Kidney beans make a tasty and nutritious change from meat in a taco or tostada filling. Add other seasonal vegetables, such as chopped zucchini, broccoli, sweet peppers, or corn that you might have on hand. Use the same toppings and procedure as in Mexican Beef Tacos or Tostadas (page 144).

2 tsp	canola oil	10 mL
2	onions, chopped	2
1	clove garlic, minced	1
2	carrots, grated	2
2	tomatoes, chopped	2
1	can (19 oz/540 mL) red kidney beans, drained and rinsed	1
1	green chili (canned or fresh), chopped (optional)	1
2 tsp	chili powder	10 mL
1 tsp	cumin	5 mL
¼ tsp	hot red pepper flakes	1 mL
	Salt and freshly ground pepper	

Per Serving	
Calories	241
fat	8 g
saturated fat	1 g
cholesterol	0 mg
sodium	354 mg
potassium	437 mg
carbohydrate	37 g
fiber	9 g
protein	7 g

68% Vitamin A • 15% Vitamin C
8% Calcium • 16% Iron
14% Thiamine • 8% Riboflavin
10% Niacin • 13% Vitamin B-6
33% Folate • 0% Vitamin B-12
11% Zinc

In large nonstick skillet or saucepan, heat oil over medium heat; add onions, garlic, and carrots and cook for 5 minutes or until tender, stirring often. Add tomatoes, beans, green chili (if using), chili powder, cumin, and hot pepper flakes. Season to taste with salt, pepper, and more hot pepper flakes, if desired.

Simmer, uncovered, for 15 to 20 minutes or until sauce is thickened and vegetables are tender.

Makes 3½ cups, enough for 12 tacos, along with other toppings.

Variation

Instead of taco shells, serve Vegetable Taco Sauce over toasted whole-wheat bread or hamburger buns.

Broccoli with Ginger and Lemon

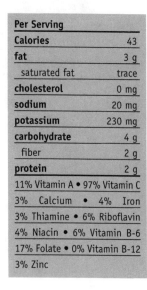

Per Serving	
Calories	43
fat	3 g
saturated fat	trace
cholesterol	0 mg
sodium	20 mg
potassium	230 mg
carbohydrate	4 g
fiber	2 g
protein	2 g
11% Vitamin A • 97% Vitamin C	
3% Calcium • 4% Iron	
3% Thiamine • 6% Riboflavin	
4% Niacin • 6% Vitamin B-6	
17% Folate • 0% Vitamin B-12	
3% Zinc	

Broccoli is an excellent
source of Vitamin C and a
good source of Vitamin A
and fiber.

*Fresh gingerroot is delightful with broccoli; however, using garlic
instead of ginger is equally good.*

1	bunch broccoli (1 lb/500 g)	1
1 tbsp	canola oil or soft margarine	15 mL
2 tsp	minced fresh gingerroot	10 mL
1 to 2 tbsp	lemon juice	15 to 25 mL
	Freshly ground pepper	

Trim broccoli stalks (peel if tough) and cut into ½-in/1-cm-
thick pieces. Separate top into florets. In large pot of boiling
water, cook broccoli for 3 to 5 minutes or until tender-crisp
when pierced with knife; drain.

Meanwhile, in small skillet, heat oil over medium-low heat; cook
gingerroot for 2 minutes. Add lemon juice.

Transfer broccoli to warmed serving dish; pour lemon-juice
mixture over. Sprinkle with pepper to taste and mix lightly.

Makes 6 servings.

Make-Ahead Broccoli or Green Beans

*If you are entertaining, you might want to partially cook a green vegetable in
advance. I find this a big help when serving a first course at a dinner party. It's
hard to judge how long it will take everyone to eat the first course, let alone get
to the table. If you put the broccoli on to cook before everyone sits down, it'll be
overcooked. If you wait until after the first course, it takes too long.*

*Cook prepared green vegetables in boiling water until tender-crisp when pierced
with knife. Immediately drain and plunge into large bowl of ice water. Drain and
wrap in paper towels; refrigerate for up to 1 day.*

*To serve: Blanch vegetable in large pot of boiling water for 1 minute or until
heated through; drain thoroughly. Toss with margarine and lemon juice or other
seasonings.*

*Note: Don't add lemon juice to a green vegetable until just before serving. The
acid will cause it to turn yellowish.*

Broccoli and Red Pepper Casserole

This dish works equally well with cauliflower in place of broccoli, or use half of each. I like to serve it with turkey for Thanksgiving dinner. (Recipe pictured opposite page 187.)

2	bunches broccoli	2
1	sweet red pepper, sliced	1
1½ cups	milk	375 mL
3 tbsp	all-purpose flour	45 mL
	Grated rind of 1 lemon	
1 tsp	dried basil	5 mL
½ tsp	each salt and pepper	2 mL
4 oz	cream cheese, cubed	125 g

TOPPING

1 tbsp	soft non-hydrogenated margarine	15 mL
1 cup	coarse fresh whole-wheat breadcrumbs*	250 mL
¼ cup	freshly grated Parmesan cheese	50 mL
¼ tsp	dried basil	1 mL

Per Serving	
Calories	162
fat	9 g
saturated fat	5 g
cholesterol	21 mg
sodium	349 mg
potassium	474 mg
carbohydrate	15 g
fiber	4 g
protein	8 g
32% Vitamin A • 183% Vitamin C	
16% Calcium • 12% Iron	
9% Thiamine • 18% Riboflavin	
12% Niacin • 13% Vitamin B-6	
31% Folate • 8% Vitamin B-12	
11% Zinc	

Cut broccoli tops into florets; peel and slice stalks to make about 8 cups/2 L. In large pot of boiling water, cook broccoli for about 3 minutes or until tender-crisp. Drain well and blot with paper towels to dry. Transfer to 9- x 13-in/2.5 L baking dish; sprinkle with red pepper.

In microwave-safe bowl, whisk together milk, flour, lemon rind, basil, salt, and pepper. Cook at high (100%) power for 3 minutes, stopping every minute to whisk, or until bubbling and thickened; whisk in cream cheese until smooth. (Alternately, cook milk mixture in saucepan over medium heat, whisking for 5 minutes or until boiling and thickened; whisk in cream cheese.) Spread sauce over broccoli.

Topping: Melt margarine; mix with breadcrumbs, Parmesan, and basil; sprinkle over top.

Bake, uncovered, in 375°F/190°C oven for about 20 minutes or until bubbling and topping is golden. Let stand for 5 minutes before serving. **Makes 8 servings.**

Make Ahead

After cooking, chill broccoli under cold running water and drain well. Combine broccoli and red peppers in baking dish. Whisk together and cook milk mixture; cover separately and refrigerate for up to 1 day. Just before baking, warm milk mixture to soften, then spread over vegetables; sprinkle with topping. Increase baking time to about 40 minutes.

*If you buy ready-made fine, dry breadcrumbs, reduce the amount to ½ cup/125 mL.

Steamed Fresh Vegetables

Per Serving	
Calories	124
fat	3 g
saturated fat	trace
cholesterol	0 mg
sodium	88 mg
potassium	632 mg
carbohydrate	22 g
fiber	5 g
protein	4 g

104% Vitamin A • 107% Vitamin C
7% Calcium • 12% Iron
10% Thiamine • 13% Riboflavin
13% Niacin • 16% Vitamin B-6
39% Folate • 0% Vitamin B-12
9% Zinc

It's easy to add interest and flavor to a dinner by serving a combination of four colorful vegetables. It takes the same amount of time to peel two carrots and two parsnips as it does to peel four carrots. It's also a great way to use up the four mushrooms or half a stalk of broccoli lurking in the back of your refrigerator. Other vegetables to substitute or add: celery, fennel, sweet red or green pepper, snow peas, cauliflower, zucchini, cabbage, and Brussels sprouts.

2	medium carrots, peeled and sliced	2
2	medium parsnips, peeled and sliced	2
1	stalk broccoli, cut in florets	1
8	mushrooms	8
1 tbsp	soft non-hydrogenated margarine	15 mL
	Salt and freshly ground pepper	

Steamed Fennel with Zucchini and Green Onions

The mild licorice flavor of fennel makes a pleasing addition to zucchini and carrots.

Cut about 6 green onions in half lengthwise, then cut into 2-inch/5-cm lengths. Steam onions and 2 cups/500 mL each julienne (thin strips) carrots, fennel, and zucchini for 6 to 8 minutes or until tender-crisp.

Transfer to warm serving platter and toss with a small amount of margarine, salt, and freshly ground pepper to taste. Makes 6 servings.

Steam carrots and parsnips for 3 to 5 minutes or until tender-crisp. Add broccoli and mushrooms; steam for 3 minutes or until broccoli is bright green. Transfer to warm serving dish and add margarine. Sprinkle lightly with salt and pepper to taste; toss to mix.

Microwave Method: In microwave-safe dish, combine carrots, parsnips, broccoli, and mushrooms. Add 1 tbsp/15 mL water. Dot with margarine; sprinkle with pepper to taste. Cover with lid or vented plastic wrap; microwave at high (100%) power for 6 minutes or until vegetables are tender; rotate dish once or twice during cooking. Add salt to taste.

Makes 4 servings.

Compare Sodium Content

per (¹/₂/125 mL)	Fresh	Canned	Frozen
Peas	3 mg	197 mg	73 mg
Green beans	2 mg	188 mg	6 mg
Corn	15 mg	186 mg	4 mg

Carrots and Leeks with Parsley

Choose tender young carrots to combine with delicate-flavored leeks. Chopped fresh dill, thyme, or basil is a lovely addition to this dish.

1 lb	carrots (6 medium)	500 g
4	medium leeks	4
2 tsp	water (for microwave method)	10 mL
1 tbsp	soft non-hydrogenated margarine	15 mL
1/4 cup	chopped fresh parsley or dill	50 mL
	Salt and freshly ground pepper	

Per Serving	
Calories	65
fat	2 g
saturated fat	trace
cholesterol	0 mg
sodium	74 mg
potassium	211 mg
carbohydrate	11 g
fiber	3 g
protein	1 g
158% Vitamin A • 12% Vitamin C	
4% Calcium • 9% Iron	
3% Thiamine • 3% Riboflavin	
3% Niacin • 13% Vitamin B-6	
12% Folate • 0% Vitamin B-12	
3% Zinc	

Scrape carrots and cut diagonally into 1/4-in/5-mm-thick slices. Clean leeks, discarding tough green parts. Slice white and tender green parts in half lengthwise; cut crosswise into 1/2-in/1-cm-thick slices. (You should have about 4 cups/1 L.)

Microwave Method: In microwave-safe dish, combine carrots and water; cover with lid or vented plastic wrap and microwave at high (100%) power for 5 minutes. Stir in leeks; dot with margarine. Cover and microwave at high (100%) power for 5 minutes or until vegetables are tender. Stir in parsley; season with salt and pepper to taste.

To Steam: Place carrots in steamer over boiling water; cover and steam for 5 to 8 minutes or nearly tender-crisp. Add leeks and steam another 5 minutes. Transfer to warmed serving dish; toss with margarine, parsley, salt, and pepper.

Makes 6 servings.

To Clean Leeks

Trim base and tough green leaves from leeks, leaving tender green and white parts.

If you want to use leeks whole, cut lengthwise in half partway down leek; otherwise cut in half lengthwise. Wash under cold running water, spreading leaves apart.

To Bake Leeks

Place leeks on lightly oiled foil, dot with a small amount of soft margarine, salt, and pepper. Wrap in foil. Bake in 350°F/180°C oven for 25 minutes or until tender.

Green Beans with Sautéed Mushrooms

Mushrooms and herbs dress up green beans and add extra flavor. If you want to be fancy, use wild mushrooms or a variety of mushrooms.

12 oz	green beans, trimmed	375 g
1 tbsp	soft non-hydrogenated margarine	15 mL
1	clove garlic, minced	1
2 tbsp	chopped fresh basil	25 mL
	(or ½ tsp/2 mL dried)	
¼ tsp	dried crumbled rosemary	1 mL
8	medium mushrooms, sliced	8
Dash	hot pepper sauce	Dash

In saucepan of boiling water, cook beans for 6 to 8 minutes or until tender-crisp; drain.

Sunday Family Dinner
Tarragon-Roasted Chicken
 (page 111)
Cranberry sauce
Green Beans with Sautéed
 Mushrooms
Potatoes
Berries with Orange-Honey
 Yogurt (page 234) or
 Apple and Raspberry Crisp
 (page 232)

Meanwhile, in small saucepan or microwave-safe dish, melt margarine, add garlic, basil (if using dried), rosemary, mushrooms, and hot pepper sauce; cook over medium heat for 3 to 4 minutes, or cover and microwave at high (100%) power for 1 minute, or until mushrooms are tender.

Transfer beans to warm serving dish; pour mushroom mixture over; add basil if using fresh, and toss to mix.

Makes 4 servings.

Skillet Zucchini with Chopped Tomatoes

In the summer and fall, when tomatoes are everywhere, this is the way I often prepare zucchini.

1 tsp	olive oil	5 mL
2	small onions, chopped	2
4	small (6-in/15-cm) zucchini, thinly sliced	4
2	medium tomatoes, chopped	2
	Freshly ground pepper and salt	
1 to 2 tbsp	chopped fresh herbs	15 to 25 mL
	(basil, oregano, parsley)	

Per Serving	
Calories	53
fat	1 g
saturated fat	trace
cholesterol	0 mg
sodium	22 mg
potassium	487 mg
carbohydrate	11 g
fiber	3 g
protein	2 g
11% Vitamin A • 27% Vitamin C	
2% Calcium • 6% Iron	
8% Thiamine • 6% Riboflavin	
5% Niacin • 9% Vitamin B-6	
13% Folate • 0% Vitamin B-12	
4% Zinc	

In large nonstick skillet, heat oil over medium heat; add onions and cook, stirring, until softened. Add zucchini and cook for 2 minutes. Add tomatoes and cook for 3 to 5 minutes or until zucchini is tender-crisp. Season to taste with pepper and salt; sprinkle with fresh herbs and toss to mix.

Makes 4 servings.

Is it necessary to peel and seed tomatoes?
The skin and seeds of tomatoes are high in fiber. I peel tomatoes only if the skin is very tough. When making a sauce using the small plum tomatoes, peeling isn't necessary.

The easiest way to peel tomatoes is to put them in a pot or bowl and cover with boiling water; let stand for about 30 seconds, then drain. The skin can easily be removed with a knife.

Peas with Green Onions

Onions and green peas are a nice flavor combination. I use the white part of green onions, chopped Spanish, or regular cooking onions. Tiny pearl onions are lovely if you have the time it takes to peel them.

2 tsp	soft non-hydrogenated margarine or olive oil	10 mL
1 cup	chopped green onions (white parts) or Spanish or cooking onion	250 mL
3 cups	frozen peas, thawed and drained Freshly ground pepper	750 mL

In nonstick skillet, melt margarine over medium heat; add onions and cook, stirring often, until tender, about 3 minutes.

To thaw peas quickly, place in colander and run hot water over them.

Add peas to skillet to heat through. Sprinkle with pepper to taste and mix gently.

Makes 6 servings, about ½ cup/125 mL each.

Asian-Style Vegetables

Any seasonal vegetables can be added to this colorful stir-fry.
Consider celery, onion, sweet peppers, mushrooms, green peas,
beans, snow peas, tomatoes, asparagus, and Brussels sprouts.
Instead of red or green cabbage, consider using napa cabbage.

1 tbsp	canola oil	15 mL
2 cups	cauliflower florets	500 mL
2 cups	broccoli florets	500 mL
4	medium carrots, sliced	4
½ cup	chicken stock	125 mL
4 oz	snow peas	125 g
1	clove garlic, minced	1
2 tbsp	minced fresh gingerroot	25 mL
4 cups	chopped bok choy* or red or green cabbage	1 L
2 tsp	soy sauce	10 mL
	Cashews (optional)	

Per Serving	
Calories	56
fat	2 g
saturated fat	trace
cholesterol	0 mg
sodium	137 mg
potassium	352 mg
carbohydrate	8 g
fiber	3 g
protein	3 g

103% Vitamin A • 62% Vitamin C
6% Calcium • 8% Iron
5% Thiamine • 6% Riboflavin
6% Niacin • 13% Vitamin B-6
19% Folate • 1% Vitamin B-12
3% Zinc

In wok or large nonstick skillet, heat oil over medium–high
heat. Add cauliflower, broccoli, and carrots; stir-fry for 3
minutes. Add chicken stock; cover and steam for 2 minutes.

Add snow peas; stir-fry for 1 minute. Add garlic, gingerroot, and
bok choy; stir-fry for 1 minute. Stir in soy sauce. Sprinkle with
cashews to garnish (if using).

Makes 8 servings.

*Bok choy (sometimes called Chinese white cabbage) has long, white, celery-
like stalks and large, dark green leaves. Trim the base and pull stalks apart,
wash, then slice or chop. Its mild flavor is a pleasing addition to a stir-fry,
soup, or salad. Napa cabbage (sometimes called Chinese cabbage) is a crinkly
leafed, oblong-shaped, light green cabbage also good in stir-fries and salads.

Cherry Tomatoes and Mushroom Sauté

This dish is good at any time of year but especially in the winter, when cherry tomatoes are usually less expensive and have better color and flavor than larger ones. Most fresh herbs can be used instead of dried.

1 tbsp	soft non-hydrogenated margarine or olive oil	15 mL
1	large clove garlic, minced	1
8 oz	medium mushrooms, halved	250 g
2 cups	cherry tomatoes, stems removed	500 mL
1 tsp	dried oregano (or 1 tbsp/15 mL fresh)	5 mL
1/2 tsp	dried thyme (or 1 tsp/5 mL fresh)	2 mL
1/4 cup	chopped fresh parsley or basil	50 mL
	Salt and freshly ground pepper	

In large nonstick skillet, melt margarine over medium-high heat; cook garlic and mushrooms, shaking pan, for 3 minutes.

Add tomatoes, oregano, and thyme; cook for 3 to 5 minutes or until tomatoes are heated through and mushrooms are tender. (Can be prepared an hour or two in advance and reheated.) Sprinkle with parsley; season with salt and pepper to taste.

Makes 6 servings.

Tomatoes Broiled with Goat Cheese and Basil

This simple dish is one of my favorites for entertaining. It goes well with any meat or poultry and is good as part of a buffet or meatless meal. It tastes best when made in the summer or fall, when tomatoes are juicy and full of flavor.

3	tomatoes	3
3 oz	soft goat cheese (chèvre)	90 g
	Freshly ground pepper	
3 tbsp	chopped fresh basil	45 mL

Slice each tomato into about 4 thick slices. Arrange in single layer in shallow baking dish or microwave-safe dish.

Thinly slice cold goat cheese; arrange over tomatoes. Sprinkle with pepper to taste, then basil. Broil for 2 to 3 minutes or microwave at high (100%) power for 2 minutes (or grill over medium-low heat for 5 minutes) or until cheese melts.

Makes 6 servings.

Per Serving	
Calories	50
fat	3 g
saturated fat	2 g
cholesterol	7 mg
sodium	57 mg
potassium	137 mg
carbohydrate	3 g
fiber	1 g
protein	3 g

11% Vitamin A • 15% Vitamin C
2% Calcium • 4% Iron
4% Thiamine • 5% Riboflavin
4% Niacin • 4% Vitamin B-6
3% Folate • 2% Vitamin B-12
2% Zinc

A soft or cream goat cheese, or chèvre, has a distinctive flavor that is lovely with tomatoes. If not available, use fresh mozzarella instead.

Cut cold rounds of goat cheese into thin slices using dental floss.

Before the Theater Light Dinner

Fettuccine with Pesto Sauce (page 164)
Tomatoes Broiled with Goat Cheese and Basil
Multigrain Date Quickbread (page 230)
Strawberries with almonds and Amaretto

Compare Fresh and Processed Foods for Sodium Content

Fresh Food	mg sodium	Processed Food	mg sodium
Tomatoes, 2 medium	22	Canned tomatoes (1 cup/250 mL)	354
		Tomato juice (1 cup/250 mL)	854
		Ketchup (1 tbsp/15 mL)	202
Pork chop (3 oz/88 g)	56	Ham, lean (3 oz/88 g)	1128
Beef, round steak (3 oz/88 g)	44	Canned beef and vegetable stew (1 cup/250 mL)	995
Beets, sliced, boiled (1 cup/250 mL)	131	Beets, sliced, canned (1 cup/250 mL)	330
Potatoes, boiled (1)	7	Scalloped potatoes (prepared from a dry mix)	416
Oatmeal, regular or quick cooking, cooked (½ cup/125 mL)	1	Oatmeal, apple cinnamon, ready to serve (1 pouch)	273
		Oatmeal, cinnamon spice, ready to serve (1 pouch)	330
		Oatmeal, maple and brown sugar, ready to serve (1 pouch)	404

Brussels Sprouts with Peppers and Potatoes

Per Serving	
Calories	63
fat	2 g
saturated fat	trace
cholesterol	0 mg
sodium	53 mg
potassium	297 mg
carbohydrate	11 g
fiber	3 g
protein	2 g
12% Vitamin A • 103% Vitamin C	
3% Calcium • 6% Iron	
8% Thiamine • 4% Riboflavin	
5% Niacin • 12% Vitamin B-6	
19% Folate • 0% Vitamin B-12	
3% Zinc	

Thanksgiving Dinner Menu

Tarragon-Roasted Chicken
(page 111)
Brussels Sprouts with
Peppers and Potatoes
Rutabaga and Apple Purée
(page 183)
Pear Streusel Cake
(page 222)
Whole-Berry Blueberry Sorbet
(page 246)

Wonderful with turkey or roast chicken, this is a tasty, colorful vegetable dish to serve for Sunday or Thanksgiving dinner.

1 tbsp	soft non-hydrogenated margarine or canola oil	15 mL
1	onion, chopped	1
1	large potato, cut in small cubes	1
1	bay leaf	1
1 lb	Brussels sprouts, halved if large	500 g
1	sweet red pepper, cut in ½-in/1-cm pieces	1
¼ cup	vegetable or chicken stock	50 mL
	Freshly ground pepper	
2 tbsp	chopped fresh parsley or green onions	25 mL

In large nonstick skillet, melt margarine over medium heat; cook onion, potato, and bay leaf, stirring often, for 2 to 3 minutes or until onion is softened.

Add Brussels sprouts, red pepper, and stock; cover and cook for 8 to 10 minutes or until sprouts and potatoes are tender (add water if necessary to prevent scorching).

Remove bay leaf. Season with pepper to taste. Serve sprinkled with parsley.

Makes 8 servings.

The Best Brussels Sprouts

When buying: Look for small, compact, firm, bright-green Brussels sprouts. Avoid ones with blemishes or yellowing or a brownish or slimy base.

When cooking: Prepare Brussels sprouts by trimming outer leaves and base. Cut shallow "X" in base for even cooking. Boil, steam, stir-fry or microwave, but remember that it's very important to cook for only a short time—just until tender-crisp. Overcooked Brussels sprouts become strong-flavored and lose their bright green color.

Mushroom-Stuffed Zucchini Cups

This is a delicious vegetable dish for a special dinner. It can be prepared early in the day, then reheated in the oven or microwave just before serving.

2	medium zucchini	2
	(about 8–10 in/20–25 cm in length)	
2 tsp	soft non-hydrogenated margarine	10 mL
	or olive oil	
2 cups	finely chopped mushrooms	500 mL
2 tbsp	minced onion or shallots	25 mL
2 tbsp	minced fresh parsley	25 mL
	Salt and freshly ground pepper	
1 tbsp	grated Parmesan cheese	15 mL

Per Serving	
Calories	50
fat	3 g
saturated fat	1 g
cholesterol	1 mg
sodium	33 mg
potassium	320 mg
carbohydrate	5 g
fiber	2 g
protein	2 g
3% Vitamin A • 12% Vitamin C	
3% Calcium • 6% Iron	
5% Thiamine • 8% Riboflavin	
8% Niacin • 6% Vitamin B-6	
10% Folate • 1% Vitamin B-12	
4% Zinc	

Trim ends from zucchini; cut crosswise into 1-in/2.5-cm-thick pieces. Steam zucchini for about 5 minutes or until tender-crisp; let cool. Scoop out small hollow from one end of each piece; set aside.

In nonstick skillet, melt margarine over medium-high heat; cook mushrooms and onion or shallots, stirring, for 2 minutes or until tender. Stir in parsley; season with salt and pepper to taste. Spoon mushroom mixture into zucchini cavities. Arrange in microwave-safe dish or baking dish. Sprinkle with Parmesan cheese.

Just before serving, microwave at high (100%) power for 1 to 2 minutes or bake in 350°F/180°C oven for 15 to 20 minutes or until heated through.

Makes 4 servings.

Skillet Greens with Ginger and Celery

Per Serving	
Calories	77
fat	3 g
saturated fat	trace
cholesterol	0 mg
sodium	64 mg
potassium	411 mg
carbohydrate	12 g
fiber	2 g
protein	2 g
44% Vitamin A • 97% Vitamin C	
9% Calcium • 9% Iron	
6% Thiamine • 6% Riboflavin	
5% Niacin • 11% Vitamin B-6	
12% Folate • 0% Vitamin B-12	
3% Zinc	

*Nutrient analysis is based on 1 cup/250 mL of each of the vegetables listed. The sodium is mainly from the Swiss chard.

Fresh gingerroot is a fabulous seasoning for many vegetables, such as in the Skillet Greens recipe presented here. Other vegetables to stir-fry with gingerroot are broccoli, snow peas, carrots, and celery.

Cabbage, kale, and collards belong to the brassica genus of vegetables. It's now thought that these vegetables may help to reduce the risk of cancers of the colon, stomach, and esophagus.

Kale, Swiss chard, spinach, and cabbage are all delicious cooked this way, either on their own or in a combination. Some tougher greens, such as collard or beet greens, should first be blanched. Rice vinegar is particularly good because it is mild flavored. (Recipe pictured opposite page 154.)

2 tbsp	cider, rice, or white wine vinegar	25 mL
2 tbsp	water	25 mL
2 tsp	cornstarch	10 mL
1 tsp	granulated sugar	5 mL
1 tbsp	canola oil	15 mL
1	onion, chopped	1
2 cups	sliced celery	500 mL
4 cups	thinly sliced kale, Swiss chard, spinach, or cabbage*	1 L
1 tbsp	finely grated fresh gingerroot	15 mL

In small dish, mix together vinegar, water, cornstarch, and sugar; set aside.

In large wok or nonstick skillet, heat oil over medium-high heat. Add onion and stir-fry for 1 minute. Add celery, greens, and gingerroot; stir-fry for 1 minute. Add about 2 tbsp/25 mL water; cover and steam for 3 minutes or until greens are wilted and celery is tender-crisp.

Pour in vinegar mixture and stir-fry for 1 minute or until liquid comes to boil. Serve immediately.

Makes 5 servings.

The New Lighthearted Cookbook

SAUCES AND ACCOMPANIMENTS

Cheese Sauce

Yogurt Béarnaise Sauce

Old-Fashioned Pickled Beets

Fresh-Tasting Cucumber Relish

Red Pepper Jelly

Fresh Mint Sauce

Homemade Ketchup

Sauces are like jewelry: They add the finishing touch to a meal, can dress it up and pull it all together. Many traditional sauces contain large amounts of saturated fat, cholesterol, and calories from the butter, cream, and egg yolks used.

To reduce fat, calories, and cholesterol in sauces

- Use skim or 1% milk.
- Use yogurt or milk or evaporated milk instead of cream.
- Use recommended oil or soft non-hydrogenated margarine instead of butter, and use as little as possible.
- Use lower-fat or part-skim cheese.
- Use flour or cornstarch to thicken instead of egg yolk.
- Use meat drippings (fat removed) instead of fatty gravies.
- Use cranberry sauce, applesauce, or a relish instead of gravy.
- Use the sauce recipes in this book.

Cheese Sauce

Cream Sauce

Prepare Cheese Sauce recipe, omitting grated cheese.

Fresh Dill Cream Sauce

Prepare Cheese Sauce recipe, omitting grated cheese. Instead, add ⅓ cup/75 mL (not packed) chopped fresh dill, ¼ tsp/1 mL salt, ¼ tsp/1 mL dried mustard, and freshly ground pepper to taste. Serve with salmon, sole or other fish either whole or in fillets or steaks. It's also very good with cauliflower.

Fresh dill makes this sauce delicious. If unavailable, use ⅓ cup/75 mL chopped fresh parsley and 1 tsp/5 mL dried dill. Other fresh herbs such as basil are also good, but the amounts will vary. Add a tablespoon at a time and taste.

Cheese sauce is a traditional favorite to serve over cauliflower, broccoli, or other steamed vegetables or to toss with pasta. Using skim milk and a low-fat or part-skim cheese keeps the saturated-fat content at a minimum.

1 cup	skim milk	250 mL
2 tbsp	all-purpose flour	25 mL
1 cup	shredded light old Cheddar cheese (21% m.f.)	250 mL
	Salt and cayenne pepper to taste	

In saucepan, whisk together milk and flour. Cook over medium heat, whisking for about 5 minutes or until boiling and thickened. Whisk in cheese, salt, and cayenne.

Microwave Method: In microwave-safe dish, whisk together milk and flour. Microwave at high (100%) power for 3 minutes, stopping every minute to whisk, until bubbling and thickened. Whisk in cheese, salt, and cayenne.

Makes about 1½ cups/375 mL.

Compare (per serving)	g fat	calories
Cheese sauce made with:		
Skim milk and part-skim cheese	3.7	80
2% milk and part-skim cheese	4.4	86
Whole milk and Cheddar cheese	7.6	110

Macaroni and Cheese

Cook 1 cup/250 mL macaroni until tender; drain. Prepare cheese sauce but increase milk to 1½ cups/375 mL, add 2 tsp/10 mL Dijon mustard, and 1 chopped green onion. Toss with hot macaroni.

Yogurt Béarnaise Sauce

In this version of a Béarnaise sauce, the classic accompaniment to steak, I use yogurt instead of butter and half the usual number of egg yolks—so I call it a halfway healthy sauce. Margie Glue, a cooking-school teacher, gave me the idea of using yogurt in a Béarnaise sauce. It's also delicious with grilled chicken, turkey, lamb or fish.

	Per 2 tbsp/25 mL Serving	
	Calories	40
	fat	2 g
	saturated fat	1 g
	cholesterol	53 mg
	sodium	24 mg
	carbohydrate	3 g
	fiber	trace
	protein	2 g

3% Vitamin A • 0% Vitamin C
6% Calcium • 2% Iron

4 tsp	minced shallots or onions	20 mL
¼ cup	white wine	50 mL
1	small clove garlic, minced	1
1 tbsp	chopped fresh tarragon	15 mL
	(or 1¼ tsp/6 mL dried)	
1 cup	2% plain yogurt*	250 mL
2	egg yolks	2
1 tsp	cornstarch	5 mL
¼ tsp	granulated sugar	1 mL
	Salt, cayenne, and freshly	
	ground pepper	

In small saucepan, combine shallots, wine, garlic, and dried tarragon (if using); bring to boil over medium heat. Boil until liquid is reduced to 1 tbsp/15 mL.

In top of non-aluminum double boiler or saucepan, beat together yogurt, egg yolks, cornstarch, and sugar; add wine mixture.

Cook over simmering water, stirring often, until sauce has thickened, about 20 minutes. Remove from heat, add fresh tarragon (if using), and season to taste with salt, cayenne, and pepper. Serve warm.

Makes about 1 cup/250 mL, enough for 8 people.

*For best results, use 2% or richer yogurt; 1% or fat-free yogurt isn't as good.

Herb Shaker

The Ontario Heart and Stroke Foundation's Cooking for a Healthy Heart Program has a great suggestion for reducing sodium. Instead of salt, keep a mixture of herbs handy and use to season meats, poultry, soups, salads, and salad dressings.

One pleasing combination is 1 tsp/5 mL each of dried thyme, sage, and rosemary mixed with 1½ tsp/7 mL each of dried marjoram and savory.

Make Ahead

Sauce can be prepared in advance and refrigerated for up to 1 week. Reheat over hot water or at low (10%) power in microwave.

Compare (per 2 tbsp/25 mL)

	g fat	g saturated fat	calories
This recipe	*2*	*1*	*40*
Regular béarnaise sauce	*12*	*8*	*122*

Old-Fashioned Pickled Beets

Beets are one of my husband's favorite vegetables. He particularly likes the tartness of these pickled beets; however, you can add more sugar to taste if you prefer a sweeter pickled beet. These are extremely easy to make, especially if you have any leftover cooked beets. They are a colorful addition to appetizer trays, salad plates, buffets, and potluck dinners and are good with hot or cold meats.

9	medium beets (or 1½ lb/750 g trimmed baby beets)	9
1 cup	water	250 mL
1 cup	cider vinegar	250 mL
3 tbsp	granulated sugar	45 mL

Cooking Beets

Beets can be steamed, baked or microwaved as well as boiled. Don't peel beets before cooking, for they will "bleed" too much. Boiling and steaming take about the same time. Baking takes longer. Large old beets take twice as long to cook as young beets.

To microwave 1½ lb/750 g medium-to-small beets: Place beets in microwave-safe dish; add ¼ cup/50 mL water. Cover with lid or vented plastic wrap and microwave on high (100%) power for 12 to 15 minutes or until tender.

Trim beets, leaving at least 1 in/2.5 cm of the stems attached. Place in saucepan and cover with warm water; bring to boil and simmer for 40 minutes or until tender.

Drain and rinse under cold running water. Using fingers, slip off skins. Quarter or cut into thick slices and place in clean 4-cup/1-L jar.

In saucepan, combine water, vinegar, and sugar; heat until sugar dissolves. Pour over beets; cover and let cool. Refrigerate for up to 1 month.

Makes about 4 cups/1 L.

The Heart and Stroke Foundation of Canada recommends that we limit our sodium intake to 3000 mg per day. Pickles, especially dill pickles, can be very high in sodium; instead, choose homemade pickled beets.

Compare:	*mg sodium*
Pickled beets (¼ cup/50 mL)	*25*
Dill pickle, 1 (9.5 cm/157 g)	*2013*

Fresh-Tasting Cucumber Relish

This recipe from my friend Evelyn Barrigar in Victoria, B.C., makes the best relish I've ever tasted. Serve it with cold meats, chops or hamburgers.

4 cups	coarsely shredded peeled cucumbers*	1 L
2 cups	chopped onions	500 mL
1	sweet red pepper, chopped	1
½	bunch celery, chopped	½
2½ cups	packed brown sugar	625 mL
1½ tsp	salt	7 mL
2⅓ cups	white vinegar	575 mL
6 tbsp	all-purpose flour	90 mL
½ tsp	ground turmeric	2 mL
½ tsp	dry mustard	2 mL

In large heavy saucepan, combine cucumbers, onions, red pepper, celery, sugar, salt, and 1½ cups/375 mL of the vinegar. Bring to boil over medium-high heat and boil for 15 minutes.

Meanwhile, in small bowl, blend together flour, turmeric, mustard, and remaining vinegar until smooth; whisk into cucumber mixture. Boil for 15 minutes (reduce heat but maintain a boil), stirring and skimming off any foam. Be careful mixture doesn't burn.

Using sterilized utensils, ladle into sterilized jars, leaving ½-in/10-mm headspace. Seal with sterilized lids and bands. Process in boiling water canner for 15 minutes. See Canning Basics (page 210).

Makes about 8 cups/2 L.

*About 3½ large cucumbers. If cucumbers have large seeds, remove and discard before shredding.

Compare (per tbsp/15 mL)	mg sodium
This recipe	*31*
Sweet relish, store-bought	*71*
Sour relish, store-bought	*118*

Red Pepper Jelly

One year, I make this with red peppers; the next, I use green. It is extremely quick and easy to make, is delicious with roast pork or chicken, and is a nice hostess gift.

5 cups	granulated sugar	1.25 L
2 cups	finely chopped or puréed sweet red or green peppers (3 medium peppers)	500 mL
1½ cups	white vinegar	375 mL
2	pouches liquid pectin (170 mL total)	2

Use Cucumber Relish (page 207) and Red Pepper Jelly instead of gravy and rich sauces. Most store-bought condiments have a high salt content.

In large saucepan, combine sugar, red peppers, and vinegar; stir and bring to full boil. Boil over medium heat for 15 minutes, skimming off foam. Remove from heat; blend in pectin and stir for 2 minutes.

Pour into sterilized jars, leaving ¼ in/5 mm headspace. Seal with sterilized lids and bands. Process in boiling water canner for 5 minutes. See Canning Basics (page 210). Store in cool, dry place.

Makes about 6 cups/1.5 L.

Fresh Mint Sauce

3 tbsp	granulated sugar	45 mL
⅓ cup	cider vinegar	75 mL
¼ cup	water	50 mL
1½ tsp	cornstarch	7 mL
½ cup	firmly packed fresh mint leaves, finely chopped	125 mL

Serve with lamb chops or roast.

In small saucepan, combine sugar, vinegar, water, and cornstarch; bring to boil over medium heat, stirring constantly. Stir in mint; simmer for 3 minutes.

Transfer to sauce boat and let stand for 30 minutes to develop flavors. Refrigerate any leftovers (up to 2 months).

Makes about ½ cup/125 mL.

The New Lighthearted Cookbook

Homemade Ketchup

This tastes delicious, is a snap to make, and is much lower in sodium than commercial ketchup. Consider using it instead of barbecue sauce.

1	can (5½ oz/156 mL) tomato paste	1
¼ cup	packed brown sugar	50 mL
¼ cup	water	50 mL
2 tbsp	cider vinegar	25 mL
¼ tsp	dry mustard	1 mL
¼ tsp	cinnamon	1 mL
Pinch	each ground cloves and allspice	Pinch

Per 1-tbsp/15 mL Serving	
Calories	23
fat	trace
saturated fat	trace
cholesterol	0 mg
sodium	9 mg
carbohydrate	6 g
fiber	trace
protein	trace
3% Vitamin A • 8% Vitamin C	
1% Calcium • 3% Iron	

In jar or bowl, combine tomato paste, sugar, water, vinegar, mustard, cinnamon, cloves, and allspice; mix well. Cover and store in refrigerator for at least a day or up to 1 month.

Makes about 1 cup/250 mL.

Compare (per tbsp/15 mL)	mg sodium
This recipe	9
Commercial ketchup	202
Salsa	70

For marinades, see:

Lamb Tenderloins with Rosemary and Peppercorns (page 146)
Teriyaki Cod Fillets (page 128)
Italian Herb Marinade (page 137)
Ginger-Garlic Marinade (page 136)

For other sauce recipes, see:

Cucumber-Yogurt Sauce (page 127)
Tomato Salsa Sauce (page 129)
Watercress Sauce (page 130)
Cream Sauce (page 204)
Coriander Dipping Sauce (page 68)
Basic Chicken Stock (page 87)
Yogurt-Herb Dressing (page 96)
Vegetable Taco Sauce (page 189)
All-Purpose Quick Spaghetti Sauce (page 168)
Herbed Tomato-Tuna Sauce (page 160)
Pesto Sauce (page 164)
Quick Tzatziki Sauce (page 143)

Opposite:
Make this accompaniment to roast lamb in the summer when fresh mint is everywhere because it grows like a weed. Since I'm a lazy gardener, I just keep a pot of it near the back door.

Canning Basics

Use Mason-type home-canning jars that are free of cracks and nicks. It is not safe to use jars not designated as canning jars. Do not use other types of jars such as mayonnaise or jam jars. Assemble the number of jars required, plus one extra in case there is a little more preserve than expected.

Wash jars, metal tongs, a wide-mouthed metal funnel, and a metal measuring cup or ladle in hot soapy water, rinse, and air-dry. Jars processed in a boiling water canner for less than 10 minutes need to be sterilized.

To sterilize: About 30 minutes before the preserve is ready, placed washed equipment in boiling water canner, cover with hot water, letting jars fill with water, and bring to a boil; boil for 15 minutes; lift rack to drain jars.

Use new lid discs. Five minutes before filling jars, immerse discs in boiling water for 5 minutes to soften the sealing compound.

When filling jars, use sterilized metal measure for ladling and sterilized funnel to prevent rims from getting splashed with food. Remove any air bubbles in chunky preserves by sliding a clean spatula between glass and food. If rims do get sticky, wipe with damp paper towel.

Leave headspace recommended in each recipe. Place prepared disc on jar; screw on bands firmly without forcing.

Place jars in canner rack. Lower rack. Avoiding jars, pour in enough boiling water to come 1 inch/2.5 cm above tops of jars. Bring back to vigorous boil. Time processing from the return to full boil.

Use canning tongs to remove jars from boiling water canner. Let jars cool on racks for 24 hours, check seal; disc part of lid should be concave. (You may hear little popping noises as the jars cool and the discs bend.) Refrigerate any partially filled jars or unsealed jars (lids do not curve down after processing) and use within three weeks or time specified.

Wipe and label jars. Remove bands if desired. Keep preserves in a cool, dark, dry place.

The New Lighthearted Cookbook

BAKING

When I take the time to bake or make a dessert I want it to taste really delicious. Cookies may have to be a little higher in fat than I would like but there is no sense making low-fat cookies that nobody eats. You can make some adjustments to a recipe to make it more nutritious, such as using whole-wheat flour instead of all-purpose and keeping sugar to a minimum. Most home-made cookies, as long as you use a recommended margarine or oil, are probably going to be lower in saturated fat than commercial cookies.

Too many rich desserts can add a huge amount of saturated fat and calories to your diet. There are desserts, however, that taste wonderful and are also low in fat. Instead of trying to make a low-fat chocolate mousse, try a fresh strawberry mousse; instead of an apple pie, make an apple crisp. Imitation nondairy creams and toppings could be worse for you, as they usually contain saturated fats (palm and coconut oils). Fresh fruits in season are one of the best desserts for any type of meal.

Cranberry-Orange Muffins

These moist, high-fiber muffins are the best way I know to use up leftover cranberry sauce. It's even worth buying or making cranberry sauce just to use in these muffins.

³/₄ cup	wheat bran	175 mL
1 cup	whole-wheat flour	250 mL
¹/₂ cup	granulated sugar	125 mL
1¹/₂ tsp	cinnamon	7 mL
1 tsp	baking powder	5 mL
1 tsp	baking soda	5 mL
1 cup	whole-berry cranberry sauce	250 mL
1	egg	1
¹/₂ cup	buttermilk or low-fat plain yogurt	125 mL
¹/₂ cup	canola oil	50 mL
1 tsp	grated orange rind	5 mL

Apple-Raisin Muffins
Instead of cranberry, use 1 cup/250 mL applesauce plus ¹/₂ cup/125 mL raisins.

Banana-Date Muffins
Instead of cranberry, use 1 cup/250 mL mashed banana and ¹/₂ cup/125 mL chopped dates.

Zucchini Muffins
Instead of cranberry, use 1 cup/250 mL grated unpeeled zucchini and ¹/₂ cup/125 mL raisins.

In bowl, combine bran, flour, sugar, cinnamon, baking powder, and baking soda; mix well. Add cranberry sauce, egg, buttermilk, oil, and orange rind; stir just until combined.

Spoon batter into paper-lined or nonstick muffin tins. Bake in 400°F/200°C oven for 25 minutes or until firm to the touch.

Makes 12 muffins.

Oat Bran Banana-Raisin Muffins

Oat bran is available in the cereal section in most supermarkets. It is an excellent source of the kind of fiber that helps to lower blood cholesterol; wheat bran doesn't have the same cholesterol-lowering effect.

1	egg, lightly beaten	1
½ cup	milk	125 mL
¼ cup	canola oil	50 mL
½ cup	granulated sugar	125 mL
1 cup	mashed ripe bananas	250 mL
1 tsp	vanilla	5 mL
1 cup	whole-wheat flour	250 mL
1 tsp	baking soda	5 mL
1 tsp	baking powder	5 mL
1 cup	oat or wheat bran	250 mL
1 cup	raisins	250 mL

In bowl, combine egg, milk, oil, sugar, bananas, and vanilla; mix well. In another bowl, mix together flour, baking soda, baking powder, oat bran, and raisins, stir into egg mixture, mixing only until combined.

Spoon into 12 nonstick or paper-lined (or spray with vegetable oil) muffin tins, filling each about ⅔ full. Bake in 400°F/200°C oven for 20 to 25 minutes or until firm to the touch.

Makes 12 muffins.

Bananas

When you have very ripe bananas and no time to make muffins, freeze them without peeling. Thaw them when you want to make these muffins.

Freezing muffins

Wrap cooled muffins individually in plastic wrap and store in foil or freezer bags. Freeze up to 1 month. To thaw and serve, wrap one muffin in paper towel, and microwave on high (100%) power for 30 seconds.

Buttermilk, Bran, and Blueberry Muffins

Per Muffin	
Calories	159
fat	5 g
saturated fat	1 g
cholesterol	19 mg
sodium	133 mg
carbohydrate	28 g
fiber	6 g
protein	5 g
1% Vitamin A • 2% Vitamin C	
7% Calcium • 14% Iron	

These delicious and healthy low-fat high-fiber muffins are from Pastel restaurants on the West Coast.

3 cups	wheat bran	750 mL
2 cups	whole-wheat flour	500 mL
1/2 cup	granulated sugar	125 mL
1 tbsp	baking powder	15 mL
1 tsp	baking soda	5 mL
2	eggs, beaten	2
2 cups	buttermilk	500 mL
1/3 cup	canola oil	75 mL
1/2 cup	molasses	125 mL
1 cup	fresh or frozen blueberries	250 mL

When using frozen blueberries in this recipe, do not thaw them.

Instead of buttermilk, you can substitute 2 cups/500 mL milk plus 2 tbsp/25 mL white vinegar.

In large bowl, mix together bran, flour, sugar, baking powder, and baking soda. In another bowl, combine eggs, buttermilk, oil, and molasses; pour into bran mixture and stir just enough to moisten, being careful not to overmix. Fold in blueberries.

Spoon into nonstick or paper-lined (or spray with vegetable oil) large muffin tins, filling almost to top. Bake in 375°F/190°C oven for about 25 minutes or until firm to the touch. Remove from oven and let stand for 2 minutes before removing muffins from tin.

Makes about 20 muffins.

Oatmeal-Carrot Muffins

Grated orange or lemon rind flavors these tasty muffins.

1 cup	buttermilk	250 mL
1 cup	quick-cooking rolled oats	250 mL
1 cup	grated carrots	250 mL
¼ cup	packed brown sugar	50 mL
¼ cup	canola oil	50 mL
1	egg, slightly beaten	1
1 tsp	grated orange or lemon rind	5 mL
1 cup	all-purpose or whole-wheat flour	250 mL
¼ cup	granulated sugar	50 mL
2 tsp	baking powder	10 mL
1 tsp	salt	5 mL
½ tsp	baking soda	2 mL
¾ cup	raisins	175 mL

Per Muffin	
Calories	181
fat	6 g
saturated fat	1 g
cholesterol	16 mg
sodium	321 mg
carbohydrate	30 g
fiber	3 g
protein	4 g
22% Vitamin A • 2% Vitamin C	
6% Calcium • 9% Iron	

In large bowl, pour buttermilk over oats; stir to mix. Cover and let stand for 10 minutes.

Mix together carrots, brown sugar, oil, egg, and orange rind; stir into oat mixture. Stir together flour, granulated sugar, baking powder, salt, and baking soda; stir in raisins. Stir into batter just until moistened.

Spoon into nonstick or paper-lined (or spray cups with vegetable oil) large muffin pans, filling almost to top. Bake in 400°F/200°C oven for 20 to 25 minutes or until firm to the touch. Let stand for 2 minutes before removing from tins.

Makes 12 muffins.

Canola Oil

Any kind of vegetable oil can be used in these muffins. I use canola oil because it has a very mild taste and has the least amount of saturated fat of any of the oils.

Applesauce-Raisin Squares

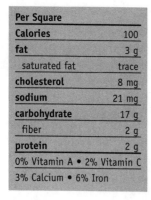
Cinnamon and lemon add extra flavor to these moist, muffin-like squares.

1	egg	1
¼ cup	canola oil	50 mL
½ cup	low-fat plain yogurt	125 mL
¾ cup	packed brown sugar	175 mL
1 cup	applesauce	250 mL
1 tsp	vanilla	5 mL
1 tsp	grated lemon rind	5 mL
½ cup	raisins	125 mL
1½ cups	whole-wheat flour	375 mL
½ cup	wheat bran	125 mL
1 tsp	baking powder	5 mL
2 tsp	cinnamon	10 mL
1 tsp	ground ginger	5 mL
¼ tsp	ground nutmeg	1 mL
⅓ cup	sliced almonds	75 mL

In large mixing bowl, beat egg; add oil, yogurt, brown sugar, applesauce, vanilla, and lemon rind; mix well.

In another bowl, stir together raisins, flour, bran, baking powder, cinnamon, ginger, and nutmeg; add to wet ingredients and mix only until combined.

Turn into lightly greased 9-in/2.5-L square cake pan. Lightly press almonds into top of batter. Bake in 375°F/190°C oven for 40 minutes or until tester inserted in center comes out clean. (Squares will be moist.) Let cool, then cut into squares.

Makes 25 1½-in/4-cm squares.

Microwave Oatmeal Squares

These are very easy and the fastest squares I know how to make. Add dried cranberries, raisins or even mini-chocolate chips. Use any crumbs left in the pan with yogurt as a topping over fruit.

½ cup	soft non-hydrogenated margarine	125 mL
½ tsp	almond or vanilla extract	2 mL
½ cup	packed brown sugar	125 mL
2 cups	rolled oats (not instant)	500 mL

Per Square	
Calories	74
fat	4 g
saturated fat	1 g
cholesterol	0 mg
sodium	51 mg
potassium	40 mg
carbohydrate	9 g
fiber	1 g
protein	1 g
5% Vitamin A • 0% Vitamin C	
1% Calcium • 3% Iron	
2% Thiamine • 1% Riboflavin	
1% Niacin • 1% Vitamin B-6	
1% Folate • 0% Vitamin B-12	
2% Zinc	

In 8-in/2-L square glass or microwave-safe dish, microwave margarine at high power for 40 to 60 seconds or until melted. Stir in extract and sugar; mix well. Stir in rolled oats; mix well.

Firmly press mixture into pan. Microwave at high power for 5 minutes. Let cool.

To Bake in Conventional Oven: Melt margarine, combine with extract and sugar, then add oats; mix well. Press into pan; bake in 350°F/180°C oven for 15 minutes or until bubbling and golden brown.

Makes about 25 squares.

Granola Energy Squares

Per Square	
Calories	104
fat	6 g
saturated fat	2 g
cholesterol	7 mg
sodium	32 mg
potassium	104 mg
carbohydrate	12 g
fiber	2 g
protein	2 g

3% Vitamin A • 0% Vitamin C
1% Calcium • 6% Iron
9% Thiamine • 2% Riboflavin
5% Niacin • 4% Vitamin B-6 6%
Folate • 0% Vitamin B-12
7% Zinc

These easy-to-make squares are great at lunch or for a snack and are a tasty alternative to commercial granola bars.

¹/₂ cup	butter, melted	125 mL
³/₄ cup	corn syrup	175 mL
2 cups	quick-cooking rolled oats	500 mL
1 cup	wheat bran	250 mL
1 cup	sunflower seeds	250 mL
1 cup	chopped dried apricots, dates, or raisins or a combination (about 6 oz/170 g)	250 mL
¹/₂ cup	chopped nuts (walnuts, almonds, pecans)	125 mL
¹/₄ cup	sesame seeds	50 mL

Friday-Night Dinner Party

Spinach Salad with Sesame
Seed Dressing (page 101)
Grilled Butterflied Leg of
Lamb with Lemon and
Garlic (page 145)
Bulgur Pilaf with Apricots
and Raisins (page 179)
Baked Parsnips and Carrots
(page 182)
Fresh Pineapple Slices with
Rum or fresh strawberries
(page 237)

In large bowl, combine butter and corn syrup; stir in rolled oats, bran, sunflower seeds, dried fruit, nuts, and sesame seeds.

Firmly press into lightly greased 9- x 13-in/2.5 L cake pan; bake in 350°F/180°C oven for 15 minutes or until golden. Let cool and cut into squares. Store in airtight container for up to 1 week or freeze for up to 2 months.

Makes about 40 squares.

Spiced Flax Cookies

Treat yourself to these good cookies spiked with flaxseed to add extra value in the nutrition line-up.

2/3 cup	packed brown sugar	150 mL
1/3 cup	butter, softened	75 mL
1	egg	1
1/3 cup	corn syrup	75 mL
1 tsp	pure vanilla	5 mL
2 tbsp	milk	25 mL
1 cup	all-purpose flour	250 mL
3/4 cup	ground flaxseed*	175 mL
1/2 tsp	baking soda	2 mL
1/2 tsp	baking powder	2 mL
1/2 tsp	each cinnamon, allspice, and nutmeg	2 mL
3/4 cup	each cranberries and raisins	175 mL
1/4 cup	whole flaxseed	50 mL

Per Serving	
Calories	101
fat	3 g
saturated fat	1 g
cholesterol	13 mg
sodium	32 mg
carbohydrate	17 g
fiber	2 g
protein	1 g
2% Vitamin A • 2% Vitamin C	
1% Calcium • 4% Iron	

In large bowl, using electric mixer, beat brown sugar with butter until mixed; beat in egg, corn syrup, vanilla, and milk until light and fluffy.

In separate bowl, combine flour, ground flaxseed, baking soda, baking powder, cinnamon, allspice, and nutmeg; stir in cranberries, raisins, and whole flaxseed. Stir into butter mixture, mixing well.

Drop by rounded tbsp/15 mL, about 2 in/5 cm apart, onto lightly greased baking sheets; flatten tops with back of spoon. Bake in 350°F/180°C oven for 8 to 10 minutes or until golden. Transfer to racks and let cool completely. Store in airtight container for up to 1 week or freeze up to 1 month.

Makes 30 cookies.

*Grind whole flaxseed in spice or coffee grinder. The seeds double in volume once ground.

About Flaxseed

Keep flaxseed in the refrigerator or freezer. Sprinkle ground flaxseed on cereals or yogurt, and add it to cookies, muffins, pancakes, and other baked goods.

Flaxseed is a good source of soluble fiber and Omega-3 fatty acids, both of which may reduce our risk of heart disease. Flaxseed also contains phytochemicals, naturally occurring plant chemicals that may also reduce our risk of cancer. The phytochemicals in flaxseed are called lignans, and they act as antioxidants.

You can also buy flaxseed oil for Omega-3 fatty acids, but the oil will not give you the fiber.

Oatmeal-Apricot Cookies

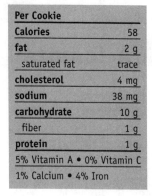
I test how good cookies are by how long they stay around my house. These passed with flying colors because they were all gone in a few hours. They are much lower in fat and higher in fiber than most cookies.

½ cup	soft non-hydrogenated margarine	75 mL
1 cup	packed brown sugar	250 mL
1	egg	1
½ cup	milk	125 mL
1 tsp	vanilla	5 mL
1 cup	whole-wheat flour	250 mL
1 tsp	baking powder	5 mL
½ tsp	baking soda	2 mL
2 tsp	cinnamon	10 mL
1¼ cups	rolled oats	300 mL
¼ cup	wheat germ	50 mL
1½ cups	chopped dried apricots (or dates, raisins, dried cranberries or a combination)	375 mL

Baking Sheets

Use rimless baking sheets because the absence of sides allows free movement of air over cookies and promotes even browning.

Choose sturdy, heavy aluminum or metal sheets that are light in color. Avoid using dark baking sheets because they absorb too much heat and can cause overbrowning.

Avoid insulated baking sheets when making crisp cookies—they will not crisp.

In large mixing bowl, combine margarine, sugar, and egg; beat well. Beat in milk and vanilla. Add flour, baking powder, baking soda, cinnamon, rolled oats, wheat germ, and apricots; mix well.

Drop batter a small spoonful at a time onto nonstick baking sheet. Bake in 350°F/180°C oven for 10 to 12 minutes or until golden.

Makes about 50 cookies.

Easy Cranberry-Chocolate Cookies

These easy-to-make, crisp cookies are a favorite in our house.

²/₃ cup	soft non-hydrogenated margarine	150 mL
1 cup	packed brown sugar	250 mL
1	egg, slightly beaten	1
1 tbsp	water	15 mL
1 cup	whole-wheat flour	250 mL
1 cup	oat bran	250 mL
¼ cup	wheat germ	50 mL
1 tsp	baking soda	5 mL
1 tsp	baking powder	5 mL
1 cup	chopped dried cranberries, raisins, or chopped dates	250 mL
½ cup	chocolate chips or chopped nuts	125 mL

Per Cookie	
Calories	97
fat	4 g
saturated fat	1 g
cholesterol	5 mg
sodium	90 mg
carbohydrate	14 g
fiber	1 g
protein	1 g
4% Vitamin A • 2% Vitamin C	
1% Calcium • 4% Iron	

In large bowl, cream margarine, brown sugar, egg, and water together thoroughly. Add flour, oat bran, wheat germ, baking soda, and baking powder; mix well. Stir in dried cranberries and chocolate chips.

Drop batter by spoonfuls onto lightly greased baking sheets; flatten slightly with floured fork. Bake in 350°F/180°C oven for 10–12 minutes or until light golden.

Makes about 3 dozen cookies.

Oat bran, an excellent source of soluble fiber, may help to reduce blood cholesterol.

Crisp or Chewy Cookies?

For a very crisp cookie, use butter; for slightly less crisp, use soft margarine. Using a reduced-fat spread will produce a soft, chewy cookie.

Streusel Plum Cake

¼ cup	butter	50 mL
¾ cup	granulated sugar	175 mL
2	eggs, separated	2
1¼ cups	all-purpose flour	300 mL
1 tsp	baking powder	5 mL
⅓ cup	milk	75 mL
3 cups	quartered fresh ripe plums or	750 mL
	2 cans (each 14 oz/398 mL)	
	drained and halved plums	

STREUSEL TOPPING

½ cup	packed brown sugar	125 mL
1 tbsp	butter	15 mL
1 tsp	cinnamon	5 mL

GLAZE (OPTIONAL)

¼ cup	icing sugar	50 mL
1 tsp	milk	5 mL
¼ tsp	vanilla	1 mL

Any variety of plum works well in this recipe.

Peach Streusel Cake
Instead of plums, use 2 fresh peaches sliced into wedges or 1 can (14 oz/398 mL) sliced peaches, thoroughly drained.

Apple Streusel Cake
Instead of plums, use 2 apples sliced into thin wedges. (If apples are unpeeled the fiber content is higher.)

Pear Streusel Cake
Instead of plums, use 2 pears sliced into wedges or 1 can (14 oz/398 mL) sliced pears, thoroughly drained.

Grease 9-in/2.5-L or 10-in/3-L square cake pan (for a thinner, quicker-cooking cake) or use greased springform pan.

In large bowl, cream together butter, sugar, and egg yolks until fluffy. Combine flour and baking powder; beat into egg mixture alternately with milk. Beat egg whites until stiff but not dry; fold into batter. Turn into prepared pan. Arrange plums on top.

Streusel topping: In small bowl, combine brown sugar, butter, and cinnamon; mix well and sprinkle over fruit.

Bake in 350°F/180°C oven for 35 to 45 minutes or until top is golden and toothpick inserted into cake comes out clean.

Glaze: Combine icing sugar, milk, and vanilla; mix well. Drizzle over cool cake.

Makes 10 servings.

Buttermilk Apple Cake

This coffeecake-type cake stays moist and is great for brunch, with fruit desserts or in packed lunches. I don't peel the apples because the skin adds fiber.

¼ cup	soft non-hydrogenated margarine	50 mL
⅔ cup	packed brown sugar	150 mL
1½ cups	buttermilk	375 mL
1 cup	all-purpose flour	250 mL
1 cup	whole-wheat flour	250 mL
1 tsp	baking powder	5 mL
1 tsp	baking soda	5 mL
1 tbsp	cinnamon	15 mL
½ tsp	salt	2 mL
2	medium apples, cored and finely chopped (about 2½ cups/625 mL)	2

TOPPING

¼ cup	packed brown sugar	50 mL
2 tsp	cinnamon	10 mL
2 tbsp	chopped nuts or ¼ cup/50 mL coconut (optional)	25 mL

Per Piece	
Calories	198
fat	4 g
saturated fat	1 g
cholesterol	1 mg
sodium	305 mg
carbohydrate	37 g
fiber	2 g
protein	4 g
5% Vitamin A • 2% Vitamin C	
7% Calcium • 11% Iron	

Lightly grease and flour 8- or 9-in/2 or 2.5 L square cake pan or Bundt pan.

In large bowl, beat together margarine and sugar until combined; beat in buttermilk. Add flours, baking powder, baking soda, cinnamon, salt, and apples; mix until combined. Spread batter evenly in pan.

Topping: Combine sugar, cinnamon, and nuts or coconut; sprinkle over batter. Bake in 350°F/180°C oven for 40 to 45 minutes or until toothpick inserted in center comes out clean. Let cool in pan.

Makes 12 servings.

Freezer Tips

Wrap cooled cake (whole or cut into pieces) with plastic wrap, then with foil. Freeze up to one month.

Whole-Wheat Oatmeal Bread

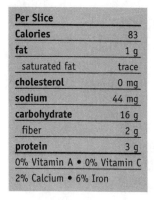

Whole-wheat bread has three times the fiber of white bread, more protein and much more flavor.

1 cup	milk	250 mL
⅓ cup	packed brown sugar	75 mL
2 tbsp	canola oil	25 mL
½ tsp	salt	2 mL
1 tsp	granulated sugar	5 mL
1 cup	warm water	250 mL
1	pkg active dry yeast (or 1 tbsp/15 mL)	1
4 cups	(approx.) whole-wheat flour	1 L
1 cup	rolled oats	250 mL
¼ cup	wheat germ or ground flaxseed (optional)	50 mL

TOPPING

1	egg white	1
1 tbsp	milk	15 mL
1 tsp	celery seeds	5 mL
2 tbsp	rolled oats	25 mL

Food Processor Method

Halve recipe, but use the same amount of yeast (1 pkg or 1 tbsp/15 mL). Dissolve granulated sugar and yeast as directed.

In food processor fitted with metal or dough blade, combine flour, rolled oats, and wheat germ (if using), brown sugar, and salt; process to combine. Stir oil into dissolved yeast mixture; add to flour mixture and process for 5 seconds.

With machine running, gradually add cold milk; process until dough forms ball, about 45 seconds. If dough is too dry, add more water 1 tbsp/15 mL at a time. If too sticky, add more flour a little at a time and process with off-on turns. Transfer dough to greased bowl and follow above recipe.

In saucepan (or large bowl in microwave), heat milk until hot; stir in brown sugar, oil, and salt until blended and sugar has dissolved. Let cool to lukewarm.

In small bowl, dissolve granulated sugar in warm water; sprinkle yeast over top and let stand for 10 minutes or until foamy.

In large bowl, combine milk mixture and yeast mixture. Using electric mixer or by hand, gradually beat in 3 cups/750 mL of the flour; beat for 2 to 3 minutes or until smooth.

Gradually mix in rolled oats and wheat germ (if using); add enough of the remaining flour to make medium-stiff dough. Turn out onto lightly floured surface and knead until smooth and elastic, about 10 minutes. (If dough is sticky, knead in more flour.)

Place dough in lightly greased bowl, turning to grease all sides. Cover bowl with greased plastic wrap. Let rise in warm place until doubled in bulk, about 1 hour.

Punch down dough and turn out onto lightly floured surface. Divide in half, forming each half into smooth ball. Cover and let rest for 10 minutes.

Shape each half into round or rectangular shape; place rectangular shapes in 2 greased 8- x 4-in/1.5 L loaf pans; place round shapes on baking sheet. Cover with plastic bag or greased waxed paper; let rise until doubled in bulk, about 1 hour.

Topping: In small bowl, mix egg white with milk; brush over top of dough. Combine celery seeds and rolled oats; sprinkle over dough.

Bake in 400°F/200°C oven for 15 minutes; reduce heat to 350°F/180°C and bake for 20 to 25 minutes longer or until crusts are brown and loaves sound hollow when tapped on bottom. Remove from pans and let cool on racks.

Makes 2 loaves, about 16 slices each.

Bread Machine Method (dough only)

Into pan of 1$\frac{1}{2}$ to 2 lb (750 g to 1 kg) bread machine, place (in order) milk, brown sugar, vegetable oil, salt, granulated sugar, warm water, 3$\frac{1}{2}$ cups/875 mL flour, oats, wheat germ (if using), and yeast. (Do not let yeast touch liquids.) Choose dough setting. When dough is made, remove from machine, punch down, shape, and bake in oven as directed in recipe.

Five-Grain Soda Bread

This is a quick and easy bread to make. It's particularly good served hot with brunch or with bean dishes, such as Beans with Tomatoes and Spinach (page 172). If you don't have all of these flours, use a combination of what you have to make a total of 3¼ cups/800 mL and add ¾ cup/175 mL rolled oats.

1 cup	all-purpose flour	250 mL
¾ cup	each whole-wheat flour, rye flour, graham flour and rolled oats *(½ cup red river cereal)*	175 mL
2 tbsp	granulated sugar	25 mL
1 tbsp	baking powder	15 mL
1 tsp	baking soda	5 mL
½ tsp	salt	2 mL
¾ cup	raisins (optional)	175 mL
3 tbsp	canola oil	45 mL
1¾ cups	buttermilk	425 mL

In bowl, combine all-purpose, whole-wheat, rye, and graham flours, rolled oats, sugar, baking powder, baking soda, and salt. Stir in raisins (if using). Whisk oil with buttermilk and stir into flour mixture to make soft dough.

Turn out onto lightly floured surface and knead about 10 times or until smooth. Place on greased baking sheet; flatten into circle about 2½ in/6 cm thick. Cut large "X" about ¼ in/5 mm deep on top.

Bake in 350°F/180°C oven for 1 hour or until toothpick inserted in center comes out clean.

Makes 1 loaf, about 16 slices.

Instead of buttermilk, you can substitute soured milk. To sour milk, place 1 tbsp/15 mL white vinegar in measuring cup, fill to 1¾ cup/425 mL with milk.

Sunday or Holiday Buffet Lunch

Tarragon Chicken Salad
  (page 90)
Curried Vermicelli Noodle
  Salad (page 157)
Spinach Salad with Sesame
  Seed Dressing (page 101)
Five-Grain Soda Bread
Strawberry Mousse Cake
  (page 242)

Whole-Wheat Zucchini Bread

This version of zucchini bread is lower in fat and cholesterol than most, yet it is moist and full of flavor.

1½ cups	all-purpose flour	375 mL
1½ cups	whole-wheat flour	375 mL
1 tbsp	cinnamon	15 mL
1 tsp	nutmeg	5 mL
1 tsp	baking soda	5 mL
1 tsp	baking powder	5 mL
½ tsp	salt	2 mL
¾ cup	raisins	175 mL
2	eggs	2
⅓ cup	canola oil	75 mL
¾ cup	low-fat plain yogurt	175 mL
¼ cup	milk	50 mL
1 cup	packed brown sugar	250 mL
2 tsp	vanilla	10 mL
2 cups	finely shredded unpeeled zucchini	500 mL

Per Slice	
Calories	134
fat	4 g
saturated fat	trace
cholesterol	15 mg
sodium	114 mg
carbohydrate	24 g
fiber	1 g
protein	3 g
1% Vitamin A • 2% Vitamin C	
4% Calcium • 7% Iron	

In bowl, combine all-purpose and whole-wheat flours, cinnamon, nutmeg, baking soda, baking powder, salt, and raisins.

In large bowl, beat eggs until foamy; beat in oil, yogurt, milk, sugar, and vanilla. Stir in zucchini. Add flour mixture and stir until combined.

Pour batter into 2 well-greased 8- x 4-in/1.5 L loaf pans. Bake in 350°F/180°C oven for 55 minutes or until toothpick inserted in center comes out clean. Remove from pan and let cool thoroughly before slicing.

Makes 2 loaves, about 13 slices each.

If you are on a low-cholesterol diet, you can reduce the cholesterol in Whole-Wheat Zucchini Bread to 0 by substituting 4 egg whites for 2 eggs.

Crisp Flatbread

You can buy strips of this crisp, thin, cracker-like bread; however, it is very easy to make and much less expensive. Arrange the flatbread in a wicker basket and serve with salads or soups, or break into small pieces and use instead of chips for dipping. (Recipe pictured opposite page 58.)

½ cup	sesame seeds	125 mL
½ cup	cracked wheat or bulgur	125 mL
1 cup	all-purpose flour	250 mL
1 cup	whole-wheat flour	250 mL
1 tbsp	granulated sugar	15 mL
½ tsp	salt	2 mL
½ tsp	baking soda	2 mL
⅓ cup	soft non-hydogenated margarine	75 mL
¾ cup	buttermilk	175 mL

TOPPING

1	egg white	1
1 tbsp	water	15 mL
2 tbsp	poppyseeds, sesame or caraway seeds	25 mL
	Coarse or regular salt (optional)	

In bowl, combine sesame seeds, cracked wheat, all-purpose, and whole-wheat flours, sugar, salt, and baking soda; cut in margarine. Add buttermilk; mix well.

Shape into 6 balls, each about the size of a lemon; roll out on lightly floured surface into circles less than ⅛ in/3 mm thick (as thin as you can). Using spatula, transfer to ungreased baking sheet.

Topping: Combine egg white and water; brush over top of circles. Sprinkle with poppyseeds and salt to taste (if using). Bake in 400°F/200°C oven for 8 to 10 minutes or until golden brown.

Let cool on wire rack until crisp. Break into smaller pieces and store in airtight container for up to 2 weeks.

Makes 24 servings, about 5 pieces each.

Recipe Modification for Baked Goods

When adjusting recipes to reduce the fat content, it is critical to understand the purpose of an ingredient before you change it.

- Flour forms the network of a baked product. In most recipes, to increase the fiber, you can substitute one-half the amount of all-purpose flour with a less refined flour, e.g., whole-wheat.
- Leavening agents are sodium-based (except yeast), but this ingredient can't be modified, or the baked goods won't rise.
- Shortening such as lard and other fats add tenderness, crispness, lightness, and volume. All sources of animal fat, plus coconut and palm oil and hydrogenated fats, should be avoided and replaced with less saturated products: canola or olive oil or a non-hydrogenated soft margarine.
- Sugar and other sweeteners add flavor, color, tenderness, and crispness and can sometimes be reduced without affecting the quality of a product. Flavors that give the illusion of sweetness (without adding calories) are cinnamon, nutmeg, and vanilla.
- Liquids act as solvents for other ingredients as well as activating chemical reactions. Low-fat liquids that can be substituted are water, fruit juice, skim milk, and buttermilk.
- Eggs add flavor, color, and moisture. To reduce cholesterol, you can often substitute two egg whites for one whole egg.
- Salt adds flavor and acts as a catalyst that controls chemical reactions. Salt is necessary to the yeast reaction in baking bread, but there is no need for excess salt in baked goods that call for margarine, as margarine already contains salt.

Multigrain Date Quickbread

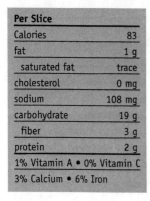
Serve this dark, flavorful bread for lunch with Tarragon Chicken Salad (page 90) or Pasta and Fresh Vegetable Salad (page 154) and sliced tomatoes.

1 cup	boiling water	250 mL
1 cup	chopped dates or raisins	250 mL
1 tsp	baking soda	5 mL
³/₄ cup	wheat bran	175 mL
1 cup	whole-wheat flour or graham flour	250 mL
1 cup	rolled oats	250 mL
¹/₃ cup	granulated sugar	75 mL
1 tsp	baking powder	5 mL
¹/₄ tsp	salt	1 mL
1 cup	milk	250 mL

Grease and flour 9- x 5-in/2-L loaf pan.

In large bowl, pour boiling water over dates or raisins; add soda and let stand for 5 minutes (do not drain).

Add bran, flour, rolled oats, sugar, baking powder, salt, and milk; mix until combined. Pour into pan. Bake in 350°F/180°C oven for 60 to 70 minutes or until toothpick inserted in center comes out clean.

Makes 1 loaf, about 20 slices.

DESSERTS

Apple and Raspberry Crisp

Rhubarb Stewed with Apple and Strawberries

Berries with Orange-Honey Yogurt

Winter Fruit Compote with Figs and Apricots

Oranges in Grand Marnier

Fresh Pineapple Slices with Rum

Basic Crêpes

Peach Crêpes with Easy Grand Marnier Sauce

Blueberry Cream Flan

Strawberry Meringue Tarts with Sauce

Strawberry Mousse

Iced Raspberry Mousse

Lemon Roll with Berries

Rhubarb-Strawberry Sorbet

Whole-Berry Blueberry Sorbet

Kiwi Sorbet

Pineapple-Orange Sorbet

Frozen Strawberry Yogurt

Hot Apricot Soufflé

Blueberry Wine Sauce

Too many rich desserts can add a huge amount of saturated fat and calories to your diet. There are desserts, however, which taste wonderful and are also low in fat. Instead of trying to make a low-fat chocolate mousse, try a fresh strawberry mousse; instead of an apple pie, make an apple crisp. Try the dessert sauces in this section instead of imitation nondairy creams and toppings that usually contain saturated fats (palm and coconut oils). Fresh fruits in season are one of the best desserts for any type of meal.

Done 1° time Oct. /07

Apple and Raspberry Crisp

Per Serving	
Calories	222
fat	7 g
saturated fat	1 g
cholesterol	0 mg
sodium	81 mg
carbohydrate	40 g
fiber	5 g
protein	2 g
8% Vitamin A • 15% Vitamin C	
3% Calcium • 9% Iron	

Combining two fruits such as apple and raspberry in a crisp adds more flavor and color to the crisp than if you use one fruit. Depending on the sweetness of the apples, you might want to add more sugar.

6 cups	sliced peeled apples	1.5 L
1	pkg (300 g) unsweetened frozen raspberries (1½ cups/375 mL fresh)	1
⅓ cup	granulated sugar	75 mL
2 tbsp	all-purpose flour	25 mL
2 tsp	cinnamon	10 mL

Apple-Cranberry Crisp

Prepare Apple and Raspberry Crisp, substituting 1 cup/250 mL fresh cranberries for raspberries and increasing granulated sugar to ⅔ cup/150 mL.

Apple, Pear, and Apricot Crisp

Prepare Apple and Raspberry Crisp using 4 cups/1 L sliced peeled apples, 2 cups/500 mL sliced peeled pears, and ½ cup/125 mL coarsely chopped dried apricots.

Maple-Yogurt Sauce for Fruit Crisps

Combine ½ cup/125 mL plain yogurt with 1 tbsp/15 mL maple syrup and mix well. Drizzle over individual servings of fruit crisp.

TOPPING

1 cup	quick-cooking rolled oats	250 mL
¼ cup	packed brown sugar	50 mL
1 tsp	cinnamon	5 mL
¼ cup	soft non-hydrogenated margarine	50 mL

In 8-cup/2-L baking dish, combine apples and raspberries (thawed or frozen). In small bowl, combine sugar, flour, and cinnamon; add to fruit and toss to mix.

Topping: Combine rolled oats, sugar, and cinnamon. With pastry blender or 2 knives, cut in margarine until crumbly. Sprinkle over top of fruit mixture.

Bake in 350°F/180°C oven for 55 minutes or microwave at high (100%) power for 15 minutes or until mixture is bubbling and fruit is barely tender. Serve warm or cold.

Makes 8 servings.

Rhubarb Stewed with Apple and Strawberries

Combine spring rhubarb with apple and orange, then add some dried fruit such as raisins or apricots during cooking. Or after cooking, add any other fresh fruit such as kiwi, grapes, banana, or strawberries.

1	orange	1
1 lb	fresh or frozen rhubarb	500 g
1	large apple	1
1 cup	water	250 mL
1/4 cup	(approx.) granulated sugar	50 mL
2 cups	fresh strawberries, halved (optional)	500 mL
1/2 cup	low-fat plain yogurt	125 mL
2 tbsp	packed brown sugar	25 mL

Per Serving	
Calories	91
fat	1 g
saturated fat	trace
cholesterol	1 mg
sodium	16 mg
carbohydrate	21 g
fiber	3 g
protein	2 g

1% Vitamin A • 43% Vitamin C
8% Calcium • 3% Iron

Grate rind and squeeze juice from orange. Cut rhubarb into 1-in/2.5-cm lengths. Peel, core, and thinly slice apple.

In saucepan, combine orange rind and juice, rhubarb, apple, water, and sugar; cover and bring to boil. Reduce heat and simmer for 10 minutes or until fruit is tender, stirring occasionally. Remove from heat and stir in strawberries. Add more sugar to taste. Serve warm or at room temperature. Top each serving with a spoonful of yogurt and sprinkle with brown sugar.

Makes 8 servings, 2/3 cup/150 mL each.

Apple and Raspberry Crisp, opposite, uses the minimum amount of fat—less than half of a standard crisp recipe—while extra flavor is gained through fruits and cinnamon. Oatmeal adds fiber and flavor. Fruit crisps have less fat than fruit pies. For example, see Sunday Family Dinner menu (page 194).

Berries with Orange-Honey Yogurt

Per Serving	
Calories	116
fat	1 g
saturated fat	1 g
cholesterol	4 mg
sodium	45 mg
carbohydrate	24 g
fiber	3 g
protein	4 g
1% Vitamin A • 142% Vitamin C	
12% Calcium • 5% Iron	

Any kind of fresh fruit is wonderful with this tasty, easy-to-make sauce. Choose the fruits depending on the season. This is attractive served in stemmed glasses.

ORANGE-HONEY YOGURT

1 cup	low-fat plain yogurt	250 mL
1 tsp	grated orange rind	5 mL
2 tbsp	liquid honey	25 mL
1/2 tsp	vanilla or almond extract	2 mL
4 cups	strawberries or combination of berries* (about 1 lb/500 g) Fresh mint leaves or 1 tbsp/15 mL toasted sliced or slivered almonds for garnish	1 L

Fruits to Combine with or Substitute for Berries

- Winter: sliced oranges, bananas, kiwi, pineapple, cantaloupe or honeydew melon
- Spring: strawberries, stewed rhubarb
- Summer: raspberries, blackberries, blueberries, melons
- Fall: peaches, plums, grapes

Granola Parfait

Layer low-fat granola, fruit, and Orange-Honey Yogurt in parfait or wine glasses for a quick dessert or snack.

Orange-Honey Yogurt: In bowl, combine yogurt, orange rind, honey, and vanilla; mix well.

Wash berries and hull; slice if large.

Either mix fruit with sauce, cover, and refrigerate for 1 hour or, alternatively, at serving time spoon fruit into individual bowls or stemmed glasses and pour sauce over. Garnish each serving with fresh mint leaves or almonds.

Makes 4 servings.

*Try: grapes and melon, melon and blueberries, blackberries and sliced peaches, raspberries and blueberries, strawberries and kiwi, bananas and kiwi or sliced oranges.

Winter Fruit Compote with Figs and Apricots

Figs, apricots, and prunes spiked with rum are a delicious base for an easy compote. Add the fresh fruits suggested here or any you have on hand such as pineapple or kiwi. You can substitute orange juice for the rum, if desired.

³/₄ cup	each dried figs, apricots, and prunes	175 mL
3	strips orange rind	3
1½ cups	orange juice	375 mL
2	sticks cinnamon, broken in half	2
½ cup	rum	125 mL
2 cups	seedless green grapes	500 mL
1 cup	purple or red grapes, halved and seeded	250 mL
1	can (10 oz/284 mL) mandarin oranges, undrained	1
1	grapefruit, peeled and sectioned	1

Per Serving	
Calories	165
fat	1 g
saturated fat	trace
cholesterol	0 mg
sodium	6 mg
carbohydrate	38 g
fiber	5 g
protein	2 g
11% Vitamin A • 60% Vitamin C	
4% Calcium • 9% Iron	

In saucepan, combine dried figs, apricots, prunes, orange rind, orange juice, and cinnamon sticks; cover and bring to boil. Simmer for 10 minutes; remove from heat and let stand for 20 minutes or until fruit is plump and tender. Add rum. Let cool.

In serving dish, combine fig mixture, green and purple grapes, mandarin oranges, and grapefruit. Cover and refrigerate up to 3 days. Serve at room temperature.

Makes 10 servings.

Use a vegetable peeler or paring knife to cut strips of rind from orange. Lemon or lime rind can be used instead of orange. Whole cloves or chopped, preserved, or candied ginger can also be added.

Oranges in Grand Marnier

Per Serving	
Calories	177
fat	1 g
saturated fat	trace
cholesterol	0 mg
sodium	18 mg
carbohydrate	41 g
fiber	3 g
protein	1 g
3% Vitamin A • 133% Vitamin C	
6% Calcium • 1% Iron	

This very elegant dessert is one of my favorites. It's a good choice in February and March, when navel oranges are so sweet and juicy. Serve with cake or wafer-thin cookies.

6	oranges	6
¼ cup	granulated sugar	50 mL
½ cup	water	125 mL
¼ cup	corn syrup	50 mL
¼ cup	(approx.) Grand Marnier or Triple Sec liqueur	50 mL

Using zester or vegetable peeler, peel thin strips of orange rind from 2 of the oranges, being careful not to include any white part. Cut into wispy thin strips and place in saucepan. Pour in enough cold water to cover and bring to boil (this removes bitter flavor); drain and set aside.

Using sharp knife, cut peel, including any white pith and membrane, from oranges. Cut oranges into round slices and place in glass bowl or in overlapping slices on platter.

In saucepan, combine sugar, water, and corn syrup; bring to boil, stirring only until sugar has dissolved. Add orange rind; boil gently, uncovered, for 15 minutes or until syrup is slightly thickened and reduced by half. Remove from heat. Let cool slightly; stir in liqueur, then pour over oranges. Let stand for 2 to 8 hours, turning oranges once or twice. Taste and add more liqueur if desired.

Makes 6 servings.

Fresh Pineapple Slices with Rum

Juicy and sweet, fresh pineapple spiked with a touch of rum is a quick and easy dessert. Serve with Easy Cranberry-Chocolate Cookies (page 221) or Spiced Flax Cookies (page 219)

1	pineapple	1
3 tbsp	packed brown sugar	45 mL
¼ cup	rum, preferably dark	50 mL
	Sliced kiwi fruit, orange segments, grapes or strawberries for garnish	

Per Serving	
Calories	86
fat	trace
saturated fat	trace
cholesterol	0 mg
sodium	4 mg
carbohydrate	16 g
fiber	1 g
protein	trace
0% Vitamin A • 20% Vitamin C	
1% Calcium • 3% Iron	

Cut top and bottom from pineapple. Cut down sides to remove peel and eyes. Cut pineapple into eighths. If core is tough or pithy, remove. Slice quarters into cubes.

In bowl, toss pineapple with brown sugar and rum.

Serve in frosted sherbet or wine glasses and garnish with fresh fruit.

Makes 6 servings.

Basic Crêpes

This all-purpose crêpe batter is low in cholesterol and fat. If you're on a low-cholesterol diet, use 2 whites instead of a whole egg. Prepare a batch of crêpes when you have time; freeze them, and you'll be able to make a main course such as Curried Chicken Crêpes (page 109) or a luscious dessert of Peach Crêpes with Easy Grand Marnier Sauce (opposite page) at a moment's notice.

Make Ahead

Crêpes can be made in advance; stack between waxed paper and refrigerate for 1 day or freeze up to 1 month.

Dessert Crêpes

For dessert crêpes, add 2 tsp/10 mL granulated sugar, ½ tsp/2 mL each grated orange and lemon rind to batter.

½ cup	all-purpose flour	125 mL
Pinch	salt	Pinch
2	egg whites, lightly beaten	2
⅓ cup	1% milk	75 mL
⅓ cup	water	75 mL
½ tsp	margarine or butter	2 mL

In bowl, combine flour and salt. Make a well in center and add egg whites. While whisking, gradually add milk and water, whisking until mixture is smooth.

Heat small nonstick skillet or crêpe pan (6 to 8 in/15 to 20 cm) over medium-high heat. Add margarine and brush over bottom of pan. Add 2 tbsp/25 mL of batter and swirl to cover bottom of pan. You should have just enough batter to lightly coat bottom of pan; pour off any excess. Shake pan and cook until edges begin to curl and crêpe no longer sticks to pan. Turn crêpe and cook for a few seconds or until golden. Remove from pan and set aside. Repeat with remaining batter. You shouldn't need to add any more margarine.

Makes eight 8-inch /20-cm crêpes.

Peach Crêpes with Easy Grand Marnier Sauce

Crêpes are a favorite any time of the year, but this version is particularly good in peach season. At other times, use 1¹/₂ cups/375 mL of fresh sliced strawberries. For a fancy dessert, it is surprisingly low in calories.

	Per Crêpe	
Calories		114
fat		2 g
saturated fat		1 g
cholesterol		4 mg
sodium		40 mg
carbohydrate		20 g
fiber		1 g
protein		3 g
3% Vitamin A • 13% Vitamin C		
4% Calcium • 4% Iron		

¹/₂ cup	low-fat plain yogurt	125 mL
1 tbsp	maple syrup or honey	15 mL
3	fresh peaches, peeled and sliced	3

EASY GRAND MARNIER SAUCE

³/₄ cup	orange juice	175 mL
1 tbsp	cornstarch	15 mL
3 tbsp	Grand Marnier, Drambuie, or other orange liqueur	45 mL
8	Dessert Crêpes (opposite page) Sliced peaches, blueberries or other fresh berries for garnish	8

In bowl, combine yogurt with syrup or honey; stir until smooth. Add peaches and mix lightly.

Grand Marnier Sauce: In saucepan, combine orange juice with cornstarch; whisk until smooth. Cook over medium heat, stirring constantly, until mixture thickens and comes to boil; simmer for 2 minutes. Remove from heat and stir in liqueur.

Wrap crepes in paper towels and heat in microwave at high (100%) power for 30 seconds. Or heat in 350°F/180°C oven for 5 to 10 minutes or until warm.

Spoon some peach mixture onto each crêpe; roll up and place on individual plates. Drizzle with warm sauce and garnish with fresh fruit.

Makes 8 crêpes, 4 large or 8 small servings.

Jiffy Peach Dessert

Sweeten yogurt with maple syrup and spoon over sliced peaches.

Peaches and Blueberries with Easy Grand Marnier Sauce

Spoon sauce over sliced peaches and blueberries.

Bananas and Kiwi with Easy Grand Marnier Sauce

Spoon sauce over sliced bananas and kiwi.

Blueberry Cream Flan

This is one of my most popular recipes. No one will ever guess that this cheesecake-type dessert is made with yogurt.

1 1/2 cups	all-purpose flour	375 mL
1/2 cup	granulated sugar	125 mL
1 1/2 tsp	baking powder	7 mL
1/3 cup	softened butter	75 mL
2	egg whites	2
1 tsp	vanilla	5 mL
3 cups	blueberries, fresh or frozen (not thawed)	750 mL

TOPPING

2 tbsp	all-purpose flour	25 mL
2 cups	low-fat plain yogurt	500 mL
1	egg, lightly beaten	1
2/3 cup	granulated sugar	150 mL
2 tsp	grated lemon or orange rind	10 mL
1 tsp	vanilla	5 mL

Easy August Dinner

Tossed Seasonal Greens
  (page 100)
Rotini with Fresh Tomato,
  Basil, and Parmesan
  (page 161)
Blueberry Cream Flan

In food processor or mixing bowl, combine flour, sugar, baking powder, butter, egg whites, and vanilla; mix well. Press into bottom of 10-in/3-L springform or flan pan or 10-in/3-L square cake pan*; sprinkle with blueberries.

Topping: In bowl, sprinkle flour over yogurt. Add egg, sugar, rind, and vanilla; mix until smooth. Pour over berries.

Bake in 350°F/180°C oven for 60 to 70 minutes or until golden. Serve warm or cold.

Makes 12 servings.

*To prepare cake pan, line bottom and sides with foil, ending 1 in/2.5 cm above the top of the pan, to use as handles to remove the cake.

Strawberry Meringue Tarts with Strawberry Sauce

Individual meringue shells filled with fresh fruit sherbet or frozen yogurt and covered with juicy berries or sliced fruit and a drizzling of fruit sauce make a delicious and glamorous dessert that is also light and refreshing. (Recipe pictured opposite page 186.)

MERINGUE SHELLS

3	egg whites, at room temperature	3
Pinch	cream of tartar	Pinch
²⁄₃ cup	granulated sugar	150 mL
½ tsp	vanilla	2 mL

FILLING

2 cups	Rhubarb-Strawberry Sorbet (page 246) or Frozen Strawberry Yogurt (page 248)	500 mL
2 cups	sliced fresh strawberries or other fruit	500 mL

STRAWBERRY SAUCE (OPTIONAL)

1	pkg (300 g) frozen unsweetened strawberries, partially thawed	1
1 tbsp	(approx.) honey or icing sugar	15 mL

Raspberry Sauce

Make Strawberry Sauce but substitute raspberries for strawberries. If sweetened, omit honey or sugar. Use fresh or frozen raspberries.

Strawberry Meringue Parfait

If you have extra meringue, make this wonderful, easy dessert. Break meringue into pieces and mix with Frozen Strawberry Yogurt (page 248). Spoon into parfait glasses and drizzle with Strawberry Sauce. Garnish with fresh berries if in season—strawberries, raspberries, blueberries, or blackberries.

Meringue Shells: In bowl, beat egg whites with cream of tartar until soft peaks form. Gradually add sugar a tbsp/15 mL at a time, beating until stiff peaks form. Beat in vanilla.

Spoon meringue onto parchment- or foil-lined baking sheet in six 4- to 5-in/10 to 12 cm rounds. Using spoon, shape into nests. Bake in 250°F/120°C oven for 2 hours or until meringues are crisp but not browned and can be removed from parchment. If parchment sticks, continue baking. Cool, then store in airtight container up to 2 weeks.

Strawberry Sauce: In food processor, blender or food mill, purée strawberries. Stir in honey or sugar, adding more to taste. Cover and refrigerate for up to 2 days.

Spoon sherbet into meringue shells; spoon fresh fruit over. Pass sauce separately. **Makes 6 servings.**

Strawberry Mousse

This is a wonderful dinner-party dessert. It's light yet full of flavor, can be prepared in advance, and is easy to make. Even better, this recipe can easily be doubled.

1	envelope unflavored gelatin	1
¼ cup	orange juice	50 mL
3 cups	fresh strawberries	750 mL
½ cup	whipping cream	125 mL
⅓ cup	icing sugar	75 mL
	Fresh strawberries, hulled, for garnish	

Strawberry Mousse Cake

Prepare Strawberry Mousse. Cut a sponge cake or a small angel food cake into 2 layers.

Place one layer on serving platter. Spread one-third of strawberry mousse over cake. (If mousse is too firm to spread, let stand at room temperature to soften slightly.) Cover with second cake layer. Spread remaining mousse over top and sides of cake. Refrigerate for up to 8 hours.

Just before serving, arrange fresh strawberries around or over top of cake. **Makes 8 servings.**

Strawberry Mousse in Chocolate Cups

Serve in individual chocolate cups that you can make yourself or buy. Top with a fresh strawberry.

In small microwave-safe dish or saucepan, sprinkle gelatin over orange juice; let stand for 5 minutes to soften. Microwave at medium (50%) power for 30 seconds or warm over low heat until gelatin has dissolved.

Meanwhile, hull strawberries and place in food processor or blender; process just until puréed (you should have about 1½ cups/375 mL). Transfer to mixing bowl and stir in gelatin mixture. Refrigerate until mixture is consistency of raw egg whites.

In large bowl, beat cream until it thickens and mounds; gradually add icing sugar, beating until stiff peaks form. Whisk about ¼ of the cream into strawberry mixture.

Fold strawberry mixture into remaining whipped cream. Pour into 6-cup/1.5-L glass serving bowl or individual sherbet or stemmed glasses; refrigerate for at least 4 hours or up to 2 days. Garnish with fresh strawberries.

Makes 5 servings, ½ cup/125 mL each.

Iced Raspberry Mousse

This make-ahead dessert looks very pretty served in small ramekins or a soufflé dish. You can also chill it in a mold, unmold, and surround it with fresh fruit, then garnish with mint leaves and flowers.

2	envelopes unflavored gelatin	2
½ cup	water	125 mL
1	pkg (425 g) frozen raspberries in light syrup or 2 cups/500 mL puréed raspberries	1
¾ cup	low-fat plain yogurt	175 mL
½ tsp	grated orange rind	2 mL
½ cup	whipping cream	125 mL
½ cup	granulated sugar	125 mL
	Fresh raspberries, mint leaves, flowers for garnish	

Per Serving	
Calories	229
fat	8 g
saturated fat	5 g
cholesterol	27 mg
sodium	35 mg
carbohydrate	38 g
fiber	3 g
protein	5 g
9% Vitamin A • 20% Vitamin C	
7% Calcium • 4% Iron	

In saucepan or microwave-safe dish, sprinkle gelatin over water; let stand for 5 minutes to soften. Heat over low heat or microwave at medium (50%) power for 50 seconds or until gelatin has dissolved.

In food processor or blender, purée raspberries; strain to remove seeds (if using unsweetened, add about ¼ cup/50 mL sugar). Transfer to bowl and stir in gelatin mixture, yogurt, and orange rind. Refrigerate until mixture begins to set or is consistency of raw egg whites.

In bowl, beat cream until it thickens and mounds. Gradually add sugar, beating until stiff peaks form. Whisk about ¼ of cream into raspberry mixture; fold in remaining cream.

Divide among individual dishes. Cover and refrigerate for at least 1 hour before serving. Garnish with raspberries, fresh mint, and flowers.

Makes 6 servings, ½ cup/125 mL each.

To Serve as a Soufflé

Cut 5 pieces of waxed paper 4 in/10 cm wide and slightly longer than circumference of ½-cup/125 mL ramekins or soufflé dishes, demitasse or espresso coffee cups. (Or cut 1 strip for 4-cup/1-L soufflé dish.) Fold in half lengthwise. Using string, tie each strip around outside of dish so that 1 in/2.5 cm extends above rim. Divide raspberry mousse mixture among prepared dishes and refrigerate for at least 1 hour before serving.

To Increase Fiber in Your Diet

Don't strain raspberry purée mixtures. Raspberries, including the seeds, are an excellent source of fiber.

Lemon Roll with Berries

Portable Picnic Dessert

Take to picnic a container of sliced strawberries sprinkled with a small amount of sugar, a container of plain yogurt, and a small jar of brown sugar. Also pack some clear plastic glasses and spoons. Spoon strawberries into glasses, top with yogurt and sprinkle with brown sugar.

For maximum flavor, be sure to serve fruit, including berries, at room temperature, not straight from the refrigerator.

Serve this light lemon-filled cake roll with whatever fruit is in season—orange and kiwi slices are nice in winter, strawberries in spring, blueberries in summer, peaches or grapes in the fall.

LEMON FILLING

3 tbsp	cornstarch	45 mL
1/3 cup	granulated sugar	75 mL
1 tsp	grated lemon rind	5 mL
1/3 cup	lemon juice	75 mL
3/4 cup	water	175 mL
1	egg yolk	1
1 tbsp	butter	15 mL

CAKE

5	egg whites	5
1/8 tsp	salt	0.5 mL
1/8 tsp	cream of tartar	0.5 mL
1/2 cup	granulated sugar	125 mL
1/2 cup	sifted cake-and-pastry flour	125 mL
2 tsp	lemon juice	10 mL
1/2 tsp	vanilla	2 mL
1/4 tsp	almond extract	1 mL
3 tbsp	icing sugar	45 mL

GARNISH

4 cups	strawberries or blueberries	1 L
	Strawberry or Raspberry Sauce (page 241), optional	

Lemon Filling: In small saucepan, combine cornstarch with sugar: whisk in lemon rind, juice, and water. Bring to boil over medium heat, stirring constantly, and cook for 2 minutes or until thickened and smooth. Blend a little of the hot mixture into egg yolk; stir yolk mixture into saucepan. Cook over low heat, stirring constantly, for 2 minutes. Remove from heat and stir in butter. Let cool, stirring frequently to prevent skin from forming on top.

Cake: Line 15- x 10-in/2 L jelly-roll pan or baking sheet with parchment paper or foil (thoroughly grease and flour foil).

In large bowl, beat egg whites, salt, and cream of tartar just until mixture mounds on spoon (not quite to soft peak stage). Using spatula, fold in granulated sugar, a large spoonful at a time. Sift half of the flour over egg-white mixture and fold in gently; repeat with remaining flour. Fold in lemon juice, vanilla, and almond extract.

Spread in prepared pan; bake in 300°F/150°C oven for 25 minutes or until firm to the touch. (Cake will be light in color.)

Sift half of icing sugar over cake; cover with tea towel then inverted baking sheet. Turn cake over and carefully remove jelly-roll pan and foil. Trim any crusty edges. While cake is hot, roll up in towel, starting at long side, jelly-roll fashion; let cool. (Cake and filling can be prepared to this point, covered and refrigerated for up to 1 day.)

Unroll cake and spread evenly with lemon filling. Roll up cake, using towel to help roll. Sift remaining icing sugar over top. Place seam-side-down on serving platter. Just before serving, arrange fresh berries around lemon roll. Cut into slices and serve with Strawberry or Raspberry Sauce or frozen yogurt, if desired.

Makes 8 servings.

Sherbets, Sorbets, Ices

Whether you call them sherbets, sorbets or ices, a light refreshing frozen mixture of fresh fruit is the dessert I order most often in restaurants. They taste so much better than bought and are extremely easy to make, especially if you have an ice-cream maker. For a special dinner, serve a combination of these delicious sherbets with fresh berries. Here is a selection to make year-round.

Per Serving	
Calories	113
fat	trace
saturated fat	trace
cholesterol	0 mg
sodium	3 mg
carbohydrate	29 g
fiber	1 g
protein	trace
0% Vitamin A • 40% Vitamin C	
2% Calcium • 1% Iron	

RHUBARB-STRAWBERRY SORBET

1½ cups	sliced fresh rhubarb	375 mL
1 cup	granulated sugar	250 mL
1½ cups	water	375 mL
2 cups	strawberries	500 mL
1 tbsp	lemon juice	15 mL
1 tsp	grated orange rind or 2 tbsp/25 mL orange liqueur	5 mL

Raspberry Sorbet

In food processor, purée 1 package (9 oz/225 g) frozen sweetened raspberries, thawed. Add ½ cup/125 mL water and 1½ tsp/7 mL lemon juice. Freeze according to instructions on opposite page.
Makes 4 servings.

In saucepan, combine rhubarb, sugar, and half of the water; simmer, covered, until rhubarb is very tender. Purée in food processor; transfer to bowl.

In food processor, purée strawberries; stir into rhubarb mixture. Add lemon juice, orange rind, and remaining water.

Freeze according to instructions on opposite page.

Makes 8 servings, ½ cup/125 mL each.

Per Serving	
Calories	110
fat	trace
saturated fat	0 g
cholesterol	0 mg
sodium	4 mg
carbohydrate	28 g
fiber	1 g
protein	1 g
1% Vitamin A • 27% Vitamin C	
1% Calcium • 1% Iron	

WHOLE-BERRY BLUEBERRY SORBET

2 cups	blueberries (fresh or frozen)	500 mL
½ cup	granulated sugar	125 mL
½ cup	water	125 mL
1 cup	orange juice	250 mL
1 tbsp	lemon juice	15 mL

In saucepan, combine blueberries, sugar, water, orange, and lemon juices; simmer for 10 minutes. Chill then freeze according to instructions on opposite page.

Makes 6 servings, ½ cup/125 mL each.

The New Lighthearted Cookbook

KIWI SORBET

12	kiwi fruit	12
1 cup	granulated sugar	250 mL
1 cup	water	250 mL
1 tbsp	lemon juice	15 mL

Per Serving	
Calories	133
fat	trace
saturated fat	0 g
cholesterol	0 mg
sodium	5 mg
carbohydrate	33 g
fiber	3 g
protein	1 g
1% Vitamin A • 82% Vitamin C	
2% Calcium • 3% Iron	

Using sharp knife, peel kiwi; purée in food processor or pass through food mill and place in bowl.

In saucepan, bring sugar, water, and lemon juice to boil, stirring occasionally, until sugar has dissolved. Add to kiwi and mix well.

Freeze according to instructions at lower right.

Makes 10 servings, 1/2 cup/125 mL each.

PINEAPPLE-ORANGE SORBET

1/2 cup	water	125 mL
1/2 cup	granulated sugar	125 mL
1	pineapple or 1 can (19 oz/540 mL) crushed pineapple	1
2 cups	orange juice	500 mL
2 tsp	grated orange rind	10 mL
1 tbsp	lemon or lime juice	15 mL

Per Serving	
Calories	84
fat	trace
saturated fat	trace
cholesterol	0 mg
sodium	1 mg
carbohydrate	21 g
fiber	1 g
protein	1 g
1% Vitamin A • 45% Vitamin C	
1% Calcium • 1% Iron	

In saucepan, combine water and sugar; simmer until sugar dissolves. Peel pineapple and cut into quarters; purée quarters or undrained pineapple in food processor.

In bowl, combine sugar syrup, orange juice, pineapple, orange rind, and lemon juice. Freeze according to instructions at right.

To Serve: Remove from freezer 15 to 30 minutes before serving or until mixture is soft enough to scoop. Serve on dessert plates surrounded with fresh berries or in sherbet glasses, each garnished with its own fruit or fresh mint leaf.

Makes 10 servings, 1/2 cup/125 mL.

Freezing and Serving Instructions for Sorbets

Freeze in ice-cream maker following manufacturer's instructions. Alternatively, transfer to metal pan or bowl and freeze until barely firm. Then either process in food processor or beat with electric mixer until smooth. Transfer to freezer container and freeze until firm.

Frozen Strawberry Yogurt

Creamy and full of flavor, this frozen dessert is a refreshing finale to any meal and a favorite of my daughter Susie. In strawberry season, serve with fresh berries and a crisp cookie.

2 cups	strawberries or 1 pkg (10 oz/300 g) frozen, thawed	500 mL
1 cup	low-fat plain yogurt	250 mL
1/3 cup	icing sugar	75 mL
1 tbsp	lemon juice	15 mL

In food processor or blender, purée strawberries; you should have about 1⅓ cups/325 mL. Add yogurt, sugar, and lemon juice; process for 1 second or until mixed.

Pour into pan or ice-cream machine and freeze according to instructions on page 247.

Makes 5 servings, ½ cup/125 mL each.

Sorbet, Fresh Fruit, and Fruit-Sauce Combinations

There are countless variations of sorbets (sherbets), fresh fruit, and sauces you can use. Consider:

Kiwi Sorbet (page 247): fresh sliced kiwi and peaches, Raspberry Sauce (page 241)

Whole-Berry Blueberry Sorbet (page 246): fresh blueberries and Blueberry Wine Sauce (page 250)

Pineapple-Orange Sorbet (page 247): sliced oranges, Blueberry Wine Sauce (page 250) or Strawberry Sauce (page 241)

Rhubarb-Strawberry Sorbet (page 246): blackberries or blueberries (or any other berry), Raspberry Sauce (page 241)

Hot Apricot Soufflé

This light dessert is surprisingly easy to make—and no one will guess that it's low in calories and fat. Try to buy apricots canned in a light or low-sugar syrup.

1	can (14 oz/398 mL) apricot halves	1
½ tsp	grated lemon rind	2 mL
1 tsp	lemon juice	5 mL
4	egg whites	4
¼ tsp	cream of tartar	1 mL
2 tbsp	granulated sugar	25 mL
1 tsp	cornstarch	5 mL

Per Serving	
Calories	79
fat	0 g
saturated fat	0 g
cholesterol	0 mg
sodium	55 mg
carbohydrate	17 g
fiber	1 g
protein	4 g
13% Vitamin A • 8% Vitamin C	
1% Calcium • 1% Iron	

Drain apricots; place between paper towels and pat dry. In food processor, blender or food mill, purée apricots, lemon rind, and lemon juice.

In large bowl, beat egg whites and cream of tartar until soft peaks form; gradually add sugar and beat until stiff; sift cornstarch over whites and fold in. Add about ¼ of the beaten whites to apricot mixture and mix just until combined. Add apricot mixture to remaining beaten whites and fold together.

Pour into ungreased 8-cup/2-L soufflé dish. Bake in 350°F/180°C oven for 30 to 35 minutes or until puffed and golden brown. Serve immediately.

Makes 4 servings.

Serve with Raspberry Sauce (page 241). Drizzle sauce on plate and spoon soufflé over top.

Blueberry Wine Sauce

Rich with blueberries, this easy-to-make sauce is delicious over ice cream, sherbets or angel-food cake.

½ cup	granulated sugar	125 mL
1 tbsp	cornstarch	15 mL
1 cup	dry white wine	250 mL
1 tbsp	lemon juice	15 mL
1½ cups	blueberries (fresh or frozen)	375 mL

In small saucepan, stir together sugar and cornstarch; stir in wine and lemon juice. Cook, stirring constantly, over medium heat until mixture thickens, clears, and comes to boil.

Stir in blueberries and simmer, stirring, for 2 minutes or until some of the berries burst. Let cool and refrigerate.

Makes 2 cups/500 mL, about 6 servings.

Appendix A

Canadian Diabetes Association Food Choice System

People with diabetes should consult a qualified dietitian-nutritionist to find out how to balance the kind and amount of food they eat with their activity and/or medication, by using an individualized eating plan based on the Food Choice System of the Canadian Diabetes Association. The following Food Choice values have been assigned to the recipes in this book in accordance with the *Good Health Eating Guide*.

For more information on diabetes and the complete *Good Health Eating Guide*, contact: Canadian Diabetes Association, 15 Toronto St., Suite 800, Toronto, Ontario M5C 2E3 or www.diabetes.ca or 1-800-Banting (226-8464).

Page	Recipe (Portion Size)	Starch ■	Fruits & Vegetables ◗	Milk ◆	Sugars ✳	Protein Foods ◐	Fats & Oils ▲	Extras ++
62	Salmon Spread with Capers (2 tbsp)					¹/₂		
63	Spinach-Onion Dip (2 tbsp)			¹/₂ (2%)				
64	Broccoli and Mushroom Dip (4 tbsp)					¹/₂		1
65	Black Bean and Corn Salsa (¹/₄ c)	¹/₂					¹/₂	
66	Italian Tomato Bruschetta (2 slices)	1					¹/₂	
67	Mussels on the Half Shell (¹/₆)					1	¹/₂	1
68	Spiced Meatballs with Coriander Dipping Sauce (3)		¹/₂			1	¹/₂	
69	Seafood Lettuce Rolls (3)			¹/₂ (2%)		1¹/₂		
70	Marinated Mushrooms (¹/₁₀)		¹/₂				¹/₂	
71	Marinated Spiced Carrots (¹/₁₀)		¹/₂		¹/₂			
72	Curried Chicken Croustades (2)	¹/₂				¹/₂	¹/₂	
72	Low-Salt Bagel Thins (4)	¹/₂					¹/₂	
74	Asparagus and Potato Bisque (¹/₆)	¹/₂		¹/₂ (1%)				1
75	Mushroom Bisque with Tarragon (¹/₄)		¹/₂	¹/₂ (1%)		1		
76	Creamy Corn Chowder with Dill (¹/₆)	1	1	¹/₂ (2%)			¹/₂	
77	Cream of Parsnip Soup with Ginger (¹/₅)		1¹/₂			¹/₂	¹/₂	
78	Chilled Cucumber-Chive Soup (¹/₆)			¹/₂ (2%)		¹/₂		1
79	Carrot and Coriander Soup (¹/₆)		¹/₂			¹/₂		
80	Harvest Pumpkin and Zucchini Soup (¹/₈)	¹/₂	¹/₂				¹/₂	
81	Zucchini and Watercress Vichyssoise (¹/₈)	¹/₂		¹/₂ (1%)				
82	Fresh Beet Soup with Yogurt (¹/₈)		1			¹/₂		
83	Fresh Tomato Soup Provençal (¹/₆)		¹/₂			¹/₂		1
84	Chunky Vegetable-Bean Soup (¹/₈)	¹/₂	¹/₂			1		
85	Split Pea, Bean, and Barley Soup (¹/₇)	1¹/₂				¹/₂		1
87	Basic Chicken Stock (1 c)					¹/₂		
88	Turkey Noodle Soup (¹/₈)		¹/₂			1¹/₂		
90	Tarragon Chicken Salad (¹/₆)		¹/₂			3		

Page	Recipe (Portion Size)	Starch ■	Fruits & Vegetables ◗	Milk ◆	Sugars ✳	Protein Foods ◉	Fats & Oils ▲	Extras ➕
91	Classic Tuna Salad with Fresh Dill (¼)					1		1
92	Warm Vegetable Salad with Tomato-Shallot Dressing (⅛)		½				1½	
93	Roasted Red Pepper, Chèvre, and Arugula Salad (⅛)					½	1	1
94	White Bean, Radish, and Red Onion Salad (⅛)	½				½	½	
95	Snow Pea and Red Pepper Buffet Salad (⅛)		½				1	
96	Carrot and Bulgur Salad with Yogurt-Herb Dressing (¼)	1		1 (2%)				
97	Italian Rice and Mozzarella Salad with Vegetables (1/8)	1½					1	1
98	Danish Potato Salad with Dill (⅙)	1½		½ (2%)			½	
99	Sliced Cucumbers with Chives, Yogurt, and Basil (⅙)		½					
100	Tossed Seasonal Greens (⅛)		½				½	
101	Spinach Salad with Sesame Seed Dressing (1/10)		½				1½	
102	Red and Green Cabbage Slaw (⅙)		½				½	
104	Mustard-Garlic Vinaigrette (1 tbsp)						1	
104	Fresh Tomato-Chive Dressing (2 tbsp)						½	
105	Yogurt-Orange Dressing (2 tbsp)				½			
105	Creamy Herb Dressing (2 tbsp)							1
106	Ranch-Style Buttermilk Dressing (1 tbsp)						½	
108	Grilled Tandoori Chicken (⅙)					3		
109	Curried Chicken Crêpes (2 crêpes)	1				3	½	
110	Curried Chicken and Tomato (1/10)		½	½ (2%)		3		
111	Tarragon-Roasted Chicken (⅙)					3	½	
112	Mushroom-Onion Stuffing (⅛)	½						1
113	Chicken and Shrimp Creole (⅛)	2½	½			3½		
114	Szechwan Orange-Ginger Chicken (¼)		1			3½		
115	Stir-Fried Chicken with Broccoli (⅛)		½			3		
116	Make-Ahead Paella (1/10)	1½	½			4	½	
117	Barbecued Lemon Chicken (¼)					3		
118	Chicken with Preserved Lemons, Olives, and Coriander (⅙)					4		1
120	Herb-Breaded Chicken (¼)					2½		1
121	Stir-Fry for One (1)	½	½			4	½	1
122	Grilled Turkey Scallopini with Herbs and Garlic (¼)					3½		
124	Fresh Fillets with Herbed Crumbs (¼)					2½		
125	Fresh Fillets with Basil and Lemon (¼)					2½		
126	Sole with Tomatoes (1)		½			3		
127	Dilled Trout Fillets with Cucumber-Yogurt Sauce (¼)					3½		1
128	Teriyaki Cod Fillets (¼)				½	2		
129	Grilled Halibut Steaks with Tomato Salsa Sauce (¼)					3½		
130	Quick and Easy Salmon Steaks with Watercess Sauce (¼)			½ (2%)		4		
131	Barbecued Skewered Salmon with Red Peppers and Snow Peas (¼)		½			2½	1	
132	Mussel, Clam, and Fish Stew (⅙)	½	1			2		

The New Lighthearted Cookbook

Page	Recipe (Portion Size)	Starch ■	Fruits & Vegetables ◢	Milk ◆	Sugars ✳	Protein Foods ◉	Fats & Oils ▲	Extras ++
133	Swordfish Steaks with Lime and Coriander (¼)					3		
134	Coconut Shrimp Curry (light) (¼)		1			2½		1
136	Ginger-Garlic Marinated Flank Steak (¼)					4		
137	Italian Herb Marinated Flank Steak (¼)					4		
138	Beef and Tomato Stir-Fry (¼)		1			3	½	
140	Family Favorite Shepherd's Pie (⅕)	1½	½			2½	½	1
141	Easy Oven Beef and Vegetable Stew (⅛)	1	1			2½		
142	Frozen Hamburger Patties (1)					2½		
143	Middle-Eastern Burgers (¼)	2		½ (2%)		2½	½	
144	Mexican Beef Tacos or Tostadas (⅙)	1½	½			2½	1	
145	Grilled Butterflied Leg of Lamb with Lemon and Garlic (⅛)					4		
146	Lamb Tenderloins with Rosemary and Peppercorns (¼)					3		
147	Pork Chops with Rosemary and Orange (¼)		½			3		
148	Brochette of Pork with Lemon and Herb Marinade (¼)		1			3		
149	Cauliflower and Ham Gratin (¼)	½		½ (skim)		1½	1	
152	Tortellini with Tuna Salad (⅛)	1½				1	1	1
153	Shell Pasta with Salmon and Green Beans (⅛)	1½				1½	½	
154	Pasta and Fresh Vegetable Salad (⅒)	1	½				1½	
155	Tomato, Broccoli, and Pasta Salad (⅙)	1	½			1	2	
156	Penne and Mussel Salad (⅛)	1½	½			½	1½	
157	Curried Vermicelli Noodle Salad (⅒)	1	1				2	
158	Beef and Pasta Casserole for a Crowd (1/14)	1½	1			4		
159	Last-Minute Pasta Casserole (¼)	2	½			1½		
160	Penne with Herbed Tomato-Tuna Sauce (¼)	2½	1			2		
161	Rotini with Fresh Tomatoes, Basil, and Parmesan (¼)	3				1	2	
162	Tuscan-Style Capellini with Clams and Garlic (¼)	3				1	1	
163	Fettuccine with Mussels, Leeks, and Tomatoes (¼)	3	1			2	½	
164	Fettuccine with Pesto Sauce (⅙)	3 ½				1	1	1
165	Fettuccine with Basil and Parsley (¼)	1½					1	
166	Linguine with Salmon and Chives (¼)	3		½ (skim)		1 ½	1	
167	Vegetable Lasagna (⅛)	1½	1			3 ½		
168	All-Purpose Quick Spaghetti Sauce (⅙)		1			2 ½		1
169	Tofu Alfredo (¼)	3				½	1	
172	Beans with Tomatoes and Spinach (¼)	1½	1			1½		
173	Barley, Green Pepper, and Tomato Casserole (⅙)	1 ½	1			1½	1	
176	Mexican Rice and Bean Casserole (⅙)	1½	1			1	1	
177	Quick Lentils with Coriander and Mint (⅕)	1				1		
178	Barley and Mushroom Pilaf (⅛)	1½					½	
179	Bulgur Pilaf with Apricots and Raisins (¼)	1½	1½			½	½	
180	Cabbage and Potato Pie (¼)	2	½	½ (skim)		1	1½	
181	New Potatoes with Herbs (¼)	1						
181	Oven-Baked French Fries (¼)	2					½	
182	Baked Parsnips and Carrots (¼)		1½				1	
183	Rutabaga and Apple Pureé (⅙)		1				1	
184	Stir-Fry Ratatouille (⅙)		½				1	

Page	Recipe (Portion Size)	Starch ■	Fruits & Vegetables 🖊	Milk ◆	Sugars ✳	Protein Foods ⊘	Fats & Oils ▲	Extras ++
185	Middle-Eastern Eggplant Baked with Yogurt and Fresh Mint (¹⁄₆)		¹⁄₂	¹⁄₂ (2%)			1¹⁄₂	
186	Spaghetti Squash with Parsley and Garlic (¹⁄₈)		1				¹⁄₂	
187	Gratin of Fall Vegetables (¹⁄₈)		1			1		
188	Mushroom, Broccoli, and Onion Pizza (¹⁄₄)	3	1			3	1	1
189	Vegetable Taco Sauce (¹⁄₆)	1¹⁄₂	¹⁄₂			¹⁄₂	1¹⁄₂	
190	Broccoli with Ginger and Lemon (¹⁄₆)						¹⁄₂	1
191	Broccoli and Red Pepper Casserole (¹⁄₈)		1	¹⁄₂ (1%)		¹⁄₂	1¹⁄₂	
192	Steamed Fresh Vegetables (¹⁄₄)		1¹⁄₂				1	
193	Carrots and Leeks with Parsley (¹⁄₆)		1				¹⁄₂	
194	Green Beans with Sautéed Mushrooms (¹⁄₄)		¹⁄₂				¹⁄₂	1
195	Skillet Zucchini with Chopped Tomatoes (¹⁄₄)		1					
196	Peas with Green Onions (¹⁄₆)		1				1	
197	Asian-Style Vegetables (¹⁄₈)		¹⁄₂			¹⁄₂		
198	Cherry Tomatoes and Mushroom Sauté (¹⁄₆)						¹⁄₂	1
199	Tomatoes Broiled with Goat Cheese and Basil (¹⁄₆)					¹⁄₂	¹⁄₂	
200	Brussels Sprouts with Peppers and Potatoes (¹⁄₈)		1				¹⁄₂	
201	Mushroom-Stuffed Zucchini Cups (¹⁄₄)		¹⁄₂				¹⁄₂	
202	Skillet Greens with Ginger and Celery (¹⁄₅)		1				¹⁄₂	
204	Cheese Sauce (¹⁄₄ c)			¹⁄₂ (skim)		1		
205	Yogurt Bérnaise Sauce (2 tbsp)			¹⁄₂ (2%)				
206	Old-Fashioned Pickled Beets (¹⁄₄ c)		¹⁄₂					
207	Fresh-Tasting Cucumber Relish (1 tbsp)				¹⁄₂			
208	Red Pepper Jelly (1 tbsp)				¹⁄₂			
208	Fresh Mint Sauce (1 tbsp)				¹⁄₂			
209	Homemade Ketchup (1 tbsp)				¹⁄₂			
212	Cranberry-Orange Muffins (1)	¹⁄₂			1¹⁄₂		1	1
213	Oat Bran Banana-Raisin Muffins (1)	¹⁄₂	1¹⁄₂		1		1	
214	Buttermilk, Bran, and Blueberry Muffins (1)	1			1		1	
215	Oatmeal-Carrot Muffins (1)	¹⁄₂	1		1		1	
216	Applesauce-Raisin Squares (1)	¹⁄₂			¹⁄₂		¹⁄₂	1
217	Microwave Oatmeal Squares (1)				¹⁄₂		1	1
218	Granola Energy Squares (1)	¹⁄₂			¹⁄₂		1	
219	Spiced Flax Cookies (1)		¹⁄₂		1		¹⁄₂	1
220	Oatmeal-Apricot Cookies (1)		¹⁄₂		¹⁄₂		¹⁄₂	
221	Easy Cranberry-Chocolate Cookies (1)	¹⁄₂			¹⁄₂		1	
222	Streusel Plum Cake (¹⁄₁₀)	1	1		2		1¹⁄₂	
223	Buttermilk Apple Cake (¹⁄₁₂)	1	¹⁄₂		1¹⁄₂		1	
224	Whole-Wheat Oatmeal Bread (1 slice)	1					¹⁄₂	
226	Five-Grain Soda Bread (1 slice)	1¹⁄₂					¹⁄₂	
227	Whole-Wheat Zucchini Bread (1 slice)	¹⁄₂	¹⁄₂		1		1	
228	Crisp Flatbread (¹⁄₂₄)	¹⁄₂					1	1
230	Multigrain Date Quickbread (1 slice)	¹⁄₂	¹⁄₂		¹⁄₂			
232	Apple and Raspberry Crisp (¹⁄₈)	¹⁄₂	1		1 ¹⁄₂		1 ¹⁄₂	1
233	Rhubarb Stewed with Apple and Strawberries (¹⁄₈)		1		1			
234	Berries with Orange-Honey Yogurt (¹⁄₄)		¹⁄₂	1 (2%)	1			
235	Winter Fruit Compote with Figs and Apricots (¹⁄₁₀)		3 ¹⁄₂				¹⁄₂	
236	Oranges in Grand Marnier (¹⁄₆)		2		2		¹⁄₂	
237	Fresh Pineapple Slices with Rum (¹⁄₆)		1		¹⁄₂		¹⁄₂	

The New Lighthearted Cookbook

Page	Recipe (Portion Size)	Starch ■	Fruits & Vegetables 🌿	Milk ◆	Sugars ✳	Protein Foods ⊘	Fats & Oils ▲	Extras ++
238	Basic Crêpes (1 crêpe)	½						
239	Peach Crêpes with Easy Grand Marnier Sauce (1)	1	½				½	
240	Blueberry Cream Flan (¹⁄₁₂)	1		½ (2%)	2		1	1
241	Strawberry Meringue Tart (no sauce) (¹⁄₆)		½		4			
242	Strawberry Mousse (¹⁄₅)		½		1		1½	
243	Iced Raspberry Mousse (¹⁄₆)		1½	½ (2%)	1 ½		1½	
244	Lemon Roll with Berries or Fresh Fruit (¹⁄₈)	½	1		2		½	
246	Rhubarb-Strawberry Sorbet (¹⁄₈)		½		2			1
246	Whole-Berry Blueberry Sorbet (¹⁄₆)		1		1½			
247	Kiwi Sorbet (¹⁄₁₀)		1		2			
247	Pineapple-Orange Sorbet (¹⁄₁₀)		1		1			
248	Frozen Strawberry Yogurt (¹⁄₅)		½	½ (2%)	½			
249	Hot Apricot Soufflé (¼)		1		½	½		
250	Blueberry Wine Sauce (¹⁄₆)		1		1		½	

Appendix B

About the Nutrient Analysis

Nutrient analysis of the recipes was performed by Info Access (1988) Inc., Toronto, Ontario, using the Nutritional Accounting component of the CBORD Menu Management System. The nutrient database was the 2001 Canadian Nutrient File supplemented when necessary with documented data from reliable sources.

The analysis was based on:

- Imperial measures and weights (except for foods typically packaged and used in metric quantity),
- Smaller ingredient quantity when there was a range
- The first ingredient listed when there was a choice.

Unless otherwise stated, recipes were analyzed using canola oil, 1% milk, canned chicken broth, and non-hydrogenated margarine.

Optional ingredients and ingredients in unspecified amounts (including salt to taste) were not included in the analysis.

Nutrient values for calories, fat, saturated fat, cholesterol, sodium, carbohydrate, dietary fiber, and protein were rounded to whole numbers with non-zero values of .49 and less appearing as "trace." Information for vitamins and minerals was presented as the percent Daily Value established for labelling purposes.

Appendix C

Nutrient Content Claims

In addition to the new food label format (see pages 29–31), food manufacturers are also applying stricter common definitions of the terms used when making claims about the nutrient content of their products. Now consumers know exactly what a nutrient claim means and that those claims are comparable among products and brands.

A nutrient content claim describes the amount of nutrient in a food. The nutrient content claims listed below are based on specific reference amounts of foods as well as servings of a stated size. A small serving of food will also be based on a density criterion.

Nutrient Content Claim: of stated size):	Means (per reference amount and serving
For Calories:	
Calorie-free	Less than 5 Calories
Low in Calories	40 Calories or less
Reduced or lower in Calories	At least 25% less energy (compared to the original product)
Source of Calories	At least 100 Calories
For Fat:	
Fat-free	Less then 0.5 g fat
Low in fat	3 g or less fat
Reduced or lower in fat	At least 25% less fat (compared to the original product)
100% fat-free	Less than 0.5 g fat per 100 g; no added fat and free of fat
For Saturated Fatty Acids:	
Saturated fatty acid-free	Less then 0.2 g saturated fatty acids and less than 0.2 g trans fatty acids
Low in saturated fatty acids	2 g or less saturated fatty acids and trans fatty acids combined and 15% or less energy from saturated fatty acids plus trans fatty acids
Reduced or lower in saturated fatty acids	At least 25% less saturated fatty acids and trans fatty acids not increased (compared to the original product).
For Trans Fatty Acids:	
Free of trans fatty acids	Less than 0.2 g trans fatty acids and "low in saturated fatty acids"
Reduced or lower in trans fatty acids	At least 25% less trans fatty acids and saturated fatty acids not increased. (as compared to the original product)

The New Lighthearted Cookbook

For Cholesterol:

Cholesterol-free	Less than 2 mg cholesterol and "low in saturated fatty acids"
Low in cholesterol	20 mg or less cholesterol and "low in saturated fatty acids"
Reduced or lower in cholesterol	25% less cholesterol and "low in saturated fatty acids"

For Sodium:

Sodium-free or salt-free	Less than 5 mg sodium
Low in sodium or salt	140 mg or less sodium
Reduced or lower in sodium or salt	At least 25% less sodium (compared to the original product)
No added sodium or salt	No salt or other sodium salts added during processing
Lightly salted	At least 50% less added sodium or salt (compared to the original product)

For Sugars:

Sugar-free	Less than 0.5 g sugars and (except chewing gum) "free of calories"
Reduced or lower in sugar	At least 25% less sugars (than the original product)
No added sugar	No sugars added in processed or packaging

For Fibre:

Source of fibre	2 g or more fibre
High source of fibre	4 g or more fibre
Very high source of fibre	6 g or more fibre

For the term "Light":

Light	"Reduced in calories" or "reduced in fat" (by at least 25% compared to the original product)

Index

The New Lighthearted Cookbook